O9-ABF-589

africa

africa

JOHN READER

PHOTOGRAPHS BY MICHAEL S. LEWIS

NATIONAL GEOGRAPHIC

WASHINGTON, D.C.

Contents

AFRICA

- • Major city
- ⊛ Capital

Western Sahara, formerly Spanish Sahara, was divided by Morocco and Mauritania in 1976. Morocco has administered the territory since Mauritania's withdrawal in August 1979. The United Nations does not recognize this annexation, and Western Sahara remains in dispute.

MEDITERRANEAN SEA

20°E

Ilhas Selvagens (Salvage Is.) (Portugal)

Canary Islands (Spain)

ATLAS MOUNTAINS

Casablanca • Rabat

Alger (Algiers) ⊛

Tunis ⊛

TUNISIA

Tarābulus (Tripoli) ⊛

El Iskandarîya (Alexandria) •
Shubra el Kheima •
El Gîza • El Qâhira (Cairo) ⊛

WESTERN SAHARA (MOROCCO)

MOROCCO

ALGERIA

LIBYA

EGYPT

Nile

Boundary claimed by Egypt

Lake Nasser

RED SEA

MAURITANIA

S   A   H   A   R   A

Nouakchott ⊛

MALI

NIGER

CHAD

SUDAN

Khartoum ⊛

ERITREA
Asmara ⊛

Lake Assal ~512 ft (–156 m) Lowest point in Africa

Dakar ⊛

S A H E L

Blue Nile

DJIBOUTI ⊛ Djibouti

Banjul ⊛
GAMBIA

SENEGAL

Bamako ⊛

Niamey ⊛

Niger

Lake Chad

N'Djamena •

White Nile

Tana Häyk'

Adīs Ābeba (Addis Ababa) ⊛

Bissau ⊛ GUINEA-BISSAU

Ouagadougou ⊛

BURKINA FASO

Abuja ⊛

ETHIOPIA

Conakry ⊛

GUINEA

BENIN

NIGERIA

Benue

Boundary undemarcated and in dispute

Freetown ⊛ SIERRA LEONE

CÔTE D'IVOIRE

GHANA

TOGO

Ogbomosho •
Ibadan •
Lagos •

SOMALIA

Monrovia ⊛

LIBERIA

Yamoussoukro ⊛

Lake Volta

Accra ⊛
Lomé ⊛
Porto-Novo ⊛

Niger

CENTRAL AFRICAN REPUBLIC

Bomu

Muqdisho (Mogadishu) ⊛

Abidjan •

CAMEROON

Douala •
Yaoundé ⊛

Bangui ⊛

Ubangi

UGANDA
Kampala ⊛

KENYA

EQUATOR

0°

Malabo ⊛
EQUATORIAL GUINEA →

Congo

0°

SAO TOME & PRINCIPE →

São Tomé ⊛
Libreville ⊛

Annobón (Eq. Guinea)

GABON

CONGO

DEMOCRATIC REPUBLIC

Lake Victoria

Nairobi •

CAPE VERDE

16°N

0   mi   100
0   km   100

24°W

Kwa

RWANDA
Kigali ⊛

Serengeti Plain

Kilimanjaro + 19,340 ft (5,895 m) Highest point in Africa

Victoria ⊛

SEYCHELLES

Brazzaville ⊛
Kinshasa (Léopoldville) ⊛

OF THE CONGO

Bujumbura ⊛ ⊛ BURUNDI

CABINDA (Angola)

Congo

Kasai

TANZANIA

Dar es Salaam •

INDIAN OCEAN

Luanda ⊛

Lake Tanganyika

Agalega Is. (Mauritius)

ATLANTIC

OCEAN

Lubumbashi •

ANGOLA

Lake Malawi (Nyasa)

Moroni ⊛ COMOROS

Îles Glorieuses (France)

Mayotte (France)

Tromelin I. (France)

ZAMBIA

MALAWI

Lilongwe ⊛

Lusaka ⊛

MOZAMBIQUE

Zambezi

Harare ⊛

Antananarivo ⊛

MADAGASCAR

Port Lou

MAURITIUS

AFRICA

- • Major city
- ⊛ Capital

ZIMBABWE

Bassas da India (France)

Réunion (France)

NAMIBIA

BOTSWANA

Windhoek ⊛

Île Europa (France)

KALAHARI DESERT

0   miles   800
0   kilometers   800

Gaborone ⊛

Pretoria ⊛
Johannesburg •

Maputo ⊛
Mbabane ⊛
SWAZILAND

SOUTH AFRICA

Maseru ⊛ LESOTHO
Durban •

Cape Town ⊛

20°E

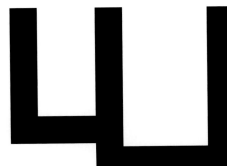

E ALL BELONG to Africa. It is the birthplace of humanity, the nursery where we learned to walk, to talk, to play, to love. Our everyday life is founded upon a talent for innovation that was first used to make stone tools in East Africa nearly three million years ago. From those beginnings we have colonized the globe, built modern civilizations, and traveled to the moon. The thread that joins us to our African ancestors stretches across thousands of generations, but still tugs at the heartstrings as we marvel at Africa's landscapes, wildlife, and people.

Africa is huge—much larger than most people think. All of the continental United States would fit comfortably within the Sahara alone, leaving room in the rest of the continent for China, India, New Zealand, Argentina, and Europe. But size is not everything. Africa is also the oldest and most stable of the continents. Its basic form is nearly as old as Earth itself. Its ancient rocks have been less disturbed by volcanoes or earthquakes than any other large landmass. It holds a treasure house of gold, diamonds, and other jewels, as well as vast quantities of minerals such as iron, copper, chromium, and coal.

Once the center of the mighty supercontinent, Pangaea, Africa remained almost stationary as the other continents drifted to their present positions. The Equator has always spanned some part of the continent during the past several hundred million years, bestowing a belt of tropical warmth that helped to make Africa a hothouse of evolution. Africa has witnessed every major stage in the evolution of life. Fossil algae in the 3.6-billion-year-old rocks of the Barberton Mountain Land in southern Africa are among the earliest known examples of life on Earth, while the same living algae today feed millions of flamingos on the Rift Valley lakes. Crocodiles throughout the continent are the living relatives of the extinct reptilian dinosaurs whose fossil bones have been found in Niger, Tanzania, Zambia, and Lesotho.

The variety of landscapes in Africa is breathtaking. Lofty mountains rise from sun-bleached savannas to snowcapped peaks. The waters of the Nile and the Niger rivers lay green braids of vegetation through barren desert. The Rift Valley stands alone as a unique geological phenomenon. The Great Lakes of central Africa are some of the largest and deepest in the world. The majestic forests of the Congo Basin are the home and last refuge of gorillas and chimpanzees—our closest relatives. The grasslands of the Sahel are unequaled in their expanse. The isolation of Ethiopia's spectacular high mountains has fostered the evolution of unique plants and animals. Coral reefs fringe the tropical coasts, and kelp forests grow tall in cooler waters.

With such a variety of environments, it is not surprising that Africa is home to the greatest numbers of animals in the world. Even today, when wildlife everywhere is threatened, there are healthy populations of elephant, hippopotamus, giraffe, and rhinoceros in Africa. Vast herds of buffalo, wildebeest and zebra roam the savanna, and predators—lion, leopard, cheetah, wild dog, and hyena—stalk and hunt and scavenge as they have done since time immemorial.

Africa's landscapes and wildlife are fascinating, but our closest affinity is with her people, and it is sad that history conspired to keep Africans and non-Africans apart for so long. Even as late as the 19th century, maps of Africa showed vast areas of the continent as blank spaces, labeled "parts unknown." The coastline had been surveyed, and some inland parts had been explored, but the interior remained another world, whose inhabitants were assumed to be primitive natives awaiting the benefits of civilization. As a result of these ideas, Africa has been persistently misunderstood and misused by the rest of the world. Even today, many people are unaware of humanity's debt to Africa.

AFRICA HAS BECOME widely known as the "Dark Continent"—a phrase loaded with double meaning. The term does not refer simply to the darkness of Africa's forests, to the blackness of African skin, or even to widespread ignorance concerning the continent. Above all, the label refers to the darkness of humanity. The dark continent is where people do terrible things, because Africa is said to be more barbaric than the rest of the world.

That people have behaved barbarically in Africa is undeniable. But this is not an exclusively African characteristic. The capacity for evil lies just beneath the surface of all peaceful societies. As history has shown time and again, the stress of collapsing economies and social unrest can tear the social fabric apart, sweeping away the individual's obligations to society, and burying hopes for the future under the problems of day-to-day existence.

Africa has given us some chilling examples of what people are capable of doing to one another when economies collapse and societies fragment. There have been equally chilling examples from other parts of the world, but those in Africa should be of particular concern, for the roots of everything human are anchored in the continent. Africa's tragedies diminish us all.

The human line originated in Africa more than four million years ago. The shape of our bodies, the way we stand and walk, our bare skin, and the scope of our minds are all evolutionary adaptations to the African environment. Our species—modern humans—existed nowhere else until about 100,000 years ago, when some left the continent via the isthmus of Suez. Though the migrants were few in number, their descendants eventually colonized every inhabitable niche on the planet. But while the spirit of humanity was exploring the globe, its soul remained bound to Africa.

The drive for prosperity that dominates world history—with its succession of kings, empires, and wars—has little relevance in Africa. Kingdoms and empires rise from agricultural societies that have grown large enough to provide a reliable supply of artisans, soldiers, and administrators—as well as farmers. This rarely happened in Africa. In humanity's cradleland, the main theme of history has been a succession of struggles against a hostile environment. Poor soils, fickle climates, insect pests, parasites, and disease unique to Africa worked against rapid population growth. While civilizations rose and fell around the world, most African communities stayed just large enough to tend the crops and manage the livestock they needed to feed themselves—with little left over. Some regions were densely populated at times, it is true, and a few kingdoms and empires did develop, but they were exceptions. Even today, when it is often said that Africa's population growth is out of control, the continent supports less than one-quarter the number living on equivalent acreage outside Africa. Compared with other parts of the world, Africa is underpopulated.

The influence of environment on African history can also be seen in the continent's conservative social and political systems. The communities that endured in Africa were those which directed their energies toward minimizing the risk of failure, rather than maximizing returns. This created societies that were reluctant to experiment and take the risks that development often requires. Knowledge of the past was all-important, and thus gerontocracy (rule by the elderly) became Africa's defining political system. The oldest members of the community held the greatest authority.

DEMOGRAPHERS HAVE ESTIMATED that by the end of the 15th century, about 47 million people were living in Africa. The population was growing very slowly, but should have reached 100 million by 1850. In fact, it was half that—about 50 million. What happened? The other 50 million were lost to foreign exploitation. Beginning in the 15th century, descendants of the migrants who had left Africa many thousands of years before returned to the continent and took whatever they could get.

While Berbers and Arabs traded across the Sahara, the Portuguese sailed down the Atlantic coast, soon followed by adventurers from Europe's other seafaring nations. Gold was the commodity the invaders sought initially, but before long they were taking slaves as well. Eighteen million slaves left Africa between 1500 and 1850. But the cost to Africa was far greater. Researchers estimate that for every 9 slaves that crossed the Atlantic Ocean another 12 died. These were people Africa could not afford to lose. Their absence denied the continent both labor and children. Who knows what Africa might have become without these losses? The slave trade transformed the demographic, economic, and political foundations of the continent.

The slave trade was abolished in the early 1800s, but by the end of the century colonial imperialism had replaced it as the main influence on African affairs. Africa was already the world's servant; now it became the world's treasure trove as well. The European powers carved up the continent among themselves as they scrambled for Africa's valuable raw materials and mineral resources. Colonial governments assumed control of Africa's destiny. African development came at the whim of foreigners—with paternalistic overtones. It was as though the so-called civilized world had discovered a continent of children who must be schooled and nurtured to adulthood. Even the most far-sighted observers believed that many years would pass before Africans were capable of managing their own affairs.

Then, as independence brought Africa a measure of meaningful status on the world stage, the continent became a popular venue for tourists, travel writers, and documentary filmmakers. Animals and exotic tribes following traditional ways of life were prominent among the images they brought back. On safari, in the forests, along the coasts, and on the plains, they portrayed Africa as a surviving remnant of the world at the dawn of humanity. Many believed it should be preserved in that state. "Dark Continent" imagery still lingered. But the 21st century brings heartening signs of enlightenment.

The African Renaissance movement has stirred the pride and self-confidence of Africa's post-independence generation. They are determined to set the continent firmly on its own feet. Abroad, a growing awareness of humanity's obligations to Africa is evident. There is more to Africa than wildlife and exotic tribal ceremony. Visitors cannot fully appreciate the spectacle of Serengeti migrations unless they understand the role that people have played on the savanna. The flamboyant ceremonies of the Dogon are meaningless without knowledge of their function in Dogon society. Culture seems to set us apart—the Fulani from the Dogon, the farmer from the fisherman, the herder from the company manager, the African from the American—but different cultures are no more than different expressions of a talent we all share: the talent to adapt, innovate, and create. Born in Africa millions of years ago, that shared heritage endows us with a universal sense of humanity. We all belong to Africa.

Savanna

On Africa's golden plains, a miracle of creation sets the stage for the greatest show on Earth. Sunlight, stored as energy in the plants of the savanna, feeds a million wildebeest and zebra, thousands of buffalo, elephant, antelope, and gazelle. Lions lurk in the tall grass, awaiting their chance, and a cheetah races toward its unsuspecting prey like a flash of ancient sunlight.

The scene is timeless. The show has been running for several million years—but never unchanging. Where a giraffe nibbles daintily on acacia treetops in the riverside woodland of a national park, the skyscrapers of Nairobi loom in the background. Here on the plains of Africa, the icons of modern human endeavor rise from the savanna—the place that engineered us.

We learned to be human on the African plains and have taken the talents that Africa gave us to every corner of the world. How this happened—and how we made our debut here—is the great saga of the savanna.

Wildebeest gather at sunset in the Masai Mara Reserve, Kenya.

Savanna

The mist has cleared from the valley, drifting downriver on a breeze that the warming sunrise has coaxed from the plains. The landscape assumes a more substantial form. Trees that minutes ago had been mere shadows amid the shifting skeins of mist become solid forms, touched now by the first rays of sunlight. Acacias predominate, each rooted a respectful distance from the other, as though making room. A giraffe appears, moving unhurriedly among the trees, browsing daintily from the uppermost branches. The giraffe and the flat-topped acacia trees seem made for each other, and indeed they are.

Just as the giraffe's elongated physique enables it to exploit a food resource that other animals cannot reach, so in turn the leaves on the uppermost branches of the acacia provide a diet that is rich in just those minerals, such as calcium, that the giraffe needs for the maintenance of its large bone mass, its powerful heart (which has to pump blood nine feet up to the brain), and its arterial system. But this is not a passive relationship.

Watch, and we see that the giraffe takes very little from each tree—just a few nibbles before moving on. A fussy eater, we might say, but in fact the giraffe moves on because the acacia responds to its browsing

by pumping distasteful tannins into its leaves, and this can rapidly build up to lethal proportions. As soon as the giraffe finds its breakfast turning sour, it goes off in search of more palatable fare. But it may have to go some distance. In addition to increased tannin production, browsing also provokes the acacia to emit an ethylene gas that wafts downwind to "warn" neighboring trees of an approaching predator. Within five to ten minutes, acacias up to 160 feet away have also stepped up their tannin production. We find that giraffes browse on only about one tree in ten, and tend to avoid trees that are downwind.

Moving elegantly through the woodland in the early

PREVIOUS PAGES: **Numbering about 350,000, the seminomadic Masai herd cattle across the savannas of Kenya and Tanzania. ABOVE: The reticulated giraffe is distinguished from its southern cousin, the Masai giraffe, by bolder and less broken markings — an evolutionary result of separation.**

morning light, the giraffe is an archetypal image of Africa's pristine wilderness. There is an air of peace and stately order in its progress. The giraffe threatens nothing. Antelope and gazelle hardly bother to move aside, zebra merely toss their heads—and the lion keeps its distance from hooves that could crack open its skull. Paradoxically, the only living things that take exception are the trees without which the giraffe would not be there in the first place, and which cannot move out of its way. As always in Africa, there is much more to the scene than meets the eye.

N THE FAMILIAR rectangular map of the world, Africa appears small in comparison with regions farther from the Equator. But this is a distortion of Mercator's projection. In fact, Africa comprises a full 20 percent of the Earth's land surface. Africa is also very old. Ninety-seven percent of the continent has been in place for more than 300 million years, most of it for more than

550 million years, and some of it for as long as 3,600 million years. The shape of the continent has not changed a great deal during all that time. While the squeezing together of the Earth's crustal plates has raised the great mountain chains of the world on other continents—the Rockies and the Andes, the Himalaya and the Alps—Africa has remained untouched by such tectonic forces for 300 million years. The only significant mountains since then are the Atlas and Cape Fold Mountains at the northern and southern extremities of the continent, respectively.

Until 140 million years ago, all the continents were clustered together in the form of a huge supercontinent called Gondwana, of which Africa was a core element. Then, as tectonic forces split Gondwana apart, the Americas, Asia, and Australasia drifted to their present positions. Africa, remaining in isolation for most of the time, has hardly moved at all since then. The continent has occupied virtually the same regions of longitude throughout, moving only latitudinally toward the South Pole and then north again, but never so much that the Equator and tropics have not always straddled the continent at some point along its length.

Africa's isolation from the other continents and its limited movement have been crucial factors in the evolution of life on the continent. Indeed, the special characteristics of Africa's development—its age, geology, stability, isolation, and position on the face of the Earth in relation to the sun—have combined with variations in climate to make the continent a unique showcase for the evolution of life itself. It would be an exaggeration to say that the most significant developments in evolutionary history occurred first or only in Africa, but Africa has been the cradle of many life-forms that have profoundly influenced the history of life on Earth. And Africa retains the evidence still—from the earliest single-cell organisms preserved as fossils in the 3.6-billion-year-old rocks of southern Africa, to the earliest forms of vegetation and the dinosaurs that fed on it, to the early flowering plants, the first mammals, the first primates, and, most significant of all, the earliest ancestors of our own kind.

MORE THAN ON any other continent, Africa's geological evolution has been dominated by extension rather than compression. While the Americas, Asia, and Europe have been squeezed by tectonic forces, Africa has been stretched. Nowhere is this more true than along the length of the East Africa Rift Valley, which extends more than 2,800 miles from Djibouti on the Red Sea to southern Mozambique. The Rift Valley is currently widening at a rate of up to 0.23 inches per year at its northern end, a process that has been going on for 30 to 40 million years and will eventually split the continent into two parts. The process is driven by huge plumes of molten rock rising from the mantle deep beneath the continent. In other parts of the world these hot spots tend to penetrate the crust and dissipate their energy in volcanoes. But Africa is a very old, geologically inactive continental mass—colder, denser, and therefore more difficult to penetrate. Volcanic activity has been relatively limited, and the plume heads have instead spread horizontally beneath the continent, raising the entire mass.

Geologists call this phenomenon the African "superswell." Measured from the height of the shelf break (the true edge of a continent, where the shelf drops abruptly to the oceanic depths) relative to sea level, Africa overall stands about 1,300 feet higher than the other continents. Around 30 million years ago, plumes of molten rock rising beneath the eastern side of the continent created a dome, stretching and thinning sections of the crust to the point at which splits developed along parallel lines of weakness. Like the brittle crust of a pie crudely pulled apart from the sides, enormous segments of the surface dropped into the gaps to create the East Africa Rift Valley—thousands of feet deep, tens of miles wide.

Volcanic lava spewed up along the edges. In some places it built classic volcanoes like Mount Kenya and Kilimanjaro. Elsewhere the landscape was smothered with lava, which has ultimately broken down to leave those regions endowed with more fertile soils than other parts of Africa. In Ethiopia, for instance, the volume of volcanic rocks extruded is estimated at 84,000 cubic miles, which is enough to cover the entire land surface of North America to a depth of 42 feet. Farther south, 48,000 cubic miles was deposited through the heartlands of Kenya and Tanzania. On the western arm of the Rift, volcanic activity built up the fertile highlands of Rwanda and Burundi and western Uganda.

The formation of the East Africa Rift Valley and its associated mountainous highlands broke up the belts of equatorial and subtropical forests that had previously covered the continent, creating an opportunity for the evolution of a distinctive montane forest vegetation. Farther afield, Antarctica drifted south to its present position at the pole,

The style and pattern of traditional Masai beadwork identifies the age and status of its wearer.

and the growth of ice sheets over the southern continent and at the North Pole led to a drastic drop in global sea levels; meanwhile, the Benguela Current began drawing icy waters from the Southern Ocean and carrying them northward along the southwest coast of Africa. Cold waters do not generate rain clouds. Southwest Africa became parched, creating the Kalahari and Namib Deserts. At the height of the arid period, the sands of the Kalahari extended all the way to the Congo Basin.

The stage was now set for the greatest show on Earth. Together, the movements of the continents, the lowering of the oceans, the changes in global climate, and the formation of the East Africa Rift

Valley combined to create conditions under which plants and animals evolved, multiplied, and diversified to a greater extent than anywhere else on Earth. As the trend to cooler and drier climatic conditions reduced the area of rain forest in Africa, the savanna grasslands spread. This development prompted an increase in the numbers and kinds of herbivores feeding on the rich new pastures. Inevitably, the numbers and diversity of predators feeding on the grazers increased too. And so on. Twenty-nine new families and 79 new genera made their appearance during this period of dramatic upheaval, with a further 18 families making their entrance later. The world has seen nothing else like it. The growth of the savanna virtually eliminated the temperate rain forest flora from the continent, but the teeming life that the savanna provided in such abundance is an impressive replacement.

The Serengeti ecosystem alone supports a million wildebeest, 600,000 zebra, 700,000 Thompson's gazelle, tens of thousands of impala, Grant's gazelle, kongoni, topi, eland, dik-dik, bushbuck, waterbuck, giraffe, elephant, rhinoceros, buffalo, hippopotamus. Among the carnivores are lion, cheetah, leopard, hyena, wild dog, caracal, serval, and jackal. Though no one can ever see more than a fraction of this wildlife bonanza at any one time, even a glimpse is the sight of a lifetime. Africa's savannas support up to 200 times more animal life than its forests, which are so often cited as the environment to be most valued.

FOLLOWING PAGES: **Lake Natron lies in a closed basin on the floor of the Great Rift Valley, Tanzania. Fed by streams draining volcanic highlands rich in sodium salts, the lake is highly alkaline; circles of soda form in the shallows during periods of intense evaporation.**

E MIGHT THINK that it is simply warmth and sufficient rain that are responsible for the abundance and diversity on Africa's tropical savannas, but in fact the absence of long cold periods—winter, in other words—has played no less an important role in the region's history. In the high latitudes, much evolutionary adaptation has been applied solely to the problems of staying alive through the winter. But on tropical savannas, where temperatures do not fall much below 50° F at any time of year, plant and animal life did not have to evolve ways of surviving months of cold.

It is of course the sun that keeps things nice and warm, and it is the shape of the Earth's orbit around our friendly star that gives the tropics such a useful share of its bounty all year-round. The sun creates its energy by a thermonuclear process that converts about 650 million tons of hydrogen to helium every second. Only a very small fraction of the sun's energy output reaches the Earth, but it is more than enough to fuel all natural processes, and so reliable that it varies by only a few tenths of one percent every 30 years.

No animal can live on raw sunlight. But plants can. While we marvel at the spectacle of the wildebeest migrating across the plains, or gaze in awe at the arrogant majesty of the lion, we tend to regard the vegetation—the grasses, the trees, and all the pretty flowers—as mere scene setting and decoration. But green plants sustain us all—directly or indirectly. Even the fossil fuels that take us by plane and car to witness the wonders of the world owe their origin to green plants many millions of years ago. The process by which plants capture the sun's energy is of course photosynthesis, literally "making with light"—a miracle linking heaven and Earth.

Wildebeest cross the Mara River, Kenya. As the seasonal rains move northward from the Serengeti to the Masai Mara, over one million wildebeest follow in their unceasing quest for fresh grazing. The migration is a round-trip of more than 500 miles.

The simple equation of photosynthesis—carbon dioxide plus water plus sunlight produces oxygen and sugars—is a metaphor for a complex biochemical process, which goes on so long as there is light and life. Cells divide, plants grow, and there is always a residue of sugars in their tissue—the first table setting of edible energy and materials in the food chain, capable of sustaining the entire animal kingdom.

Since grass (and all other vegetation) is concerned only with being grass, most of the energy it absorbs from the sun is devoted to keeping itself alive. Only about one-tenth is left to nourish the gazelle that eats the grass, and only about one-tenth of the energy it gets from the grass is available to the lion that eats the gazelle. And so the lion gets only a one-hundredth part of the sun's energy that was originally trapped by the grass. Thus, energy inevitably diminishes as it moves up through the food chain. This explains why there could never be more gazelle meat than grass tissue, and never more lions than gazelles. There is not enough energy to maintain them.

The production of the savanna grasslands is immense. During the rains, for example, every square yard of grass on the Serengeti Plain can produce almost two pounds of edible material every month—some 2,850 tons to the square mile. Furthermore, about half of all savanna vegetation can be eaten by some animal or other (compared with less than one-twentieth in a rain forest). So it is not surprising that the Serengeti ecosystem is so densely populated with so many different species of animals. But although the savanna has evolved over millions of years, the scenes of milling herds on freshly watered pasture, and predators lurking in the tall grass that we witness today have not been constant throughout. The relationships between the different elements of an ecosystem are always changing—especially when people are taking a share of the system's resources.

Let's take an example from 100 years ago. For centuries the Serengeti Plain was inhabited by the Masai, nomadic pastoralists whose cattle grazed through-

While other antelope and herbivores eat one main food source all year-round, the impala changes its diet with the seasons.

out the region. The grasslands were heavily grazed, and with people cutting wood for their huts and their fires, and cattle inhibiting the regeneration of trees, the landscape was more open than it is today. Plains game abounded—wildebeest, zebra, gazelle, and antelope. Though there is a romantic notion that herders have always coexisted with wildlife in a harmonious relationship, the truth is that wildlife eat grass the Masai would prefer to see their cattle eating. If they had been able to eliminate the competition, they would have done so, but the wildlife were too many and the Masai too few. Then, in the 1890s, the rinderpest epidemic struck.

Rinderpest is a viral cattle disease unknown in Africa until it was introduced into Ethiopia with cattle that the Italian army brought in to feed its invasion force. From Ethiopia the disease swept through the continent, causing devastating losses among both domestic and wild grazers. With no natural or acquired immunity, 90 percent of the continent's cattle died. Losses among the wild ruminants most closely related to cattle (such as buffalo and wildebeest) are likely to have been equally devastating.

The Masai were virtually eliminated as cattle herders. Their open pastures in the wetter regions of the Serengeti rapidly reverted to woodland, which in turn provided a perfect habitat for the tsetse fly. The tsetse fly effectively prevented the return of the Masai, since it carries trypanosomiasis—sleeping sickness—which is lethal to people and cattle. With the people gone and wildlife numbers building up, the colonial government declared that the Serengeti, Ngorongoro, and the Mara should be set aside as wildlife reserves. Not until the 1960s, when elephants invaded the park, were the Serengeti woodlands once again opened up for grazing animals. By that time a vaccination campaign had finally eliminated rinderpest from cattle populations around the park. That in turn protected

wildlife in the park from reinfection and prompted a massive increase in their numbers.

Between 1961 and 1977 the wildebeest population multiplied sixfold, leaping from 250,000 to 1.5 million. Subsequently the population leveled off and has remained at approximately 1.3 million animals ever since. Meanwhile, in just three decades what had been a relatively insignificant presence in the Serengeti ecosystem became an annual migration of huge proportions.

The sixfold increase in wildebeest numbers over a period of just 16 years is an eloquent demonstration of the bounty of the Serengeti. With the constraint of disease lifted, the wildebeest flourished. As grazers, they were adapted to exploit an environmental niche that

neither the semi-migratory zebra nor the sedentary antelope and gazelle had been able to fill. In the natural world, reproduction is the first imperative of life, and that reproductive potential is awesome.

On the Serengeti, every adult female herbivore is likely to produce an offspring each year. Thus the populations are probably capable of doubling in less than three years. Even the offspring of a single pair of elephants (the slowest of mammalian breeders, with a gestation period of 22 months) would fill Africa shoulder to shoulder in 500 years in the absence of some controlling factors. But of course they don't. Just as the explosion of the wildebeest population demonstrates their reproductive potential, so does the restriction of their numbers since then demonstrate natural controls. Not all offspring survive to maturity. Predators take their toll. Death winnows out the weakest before they reproduce.

Death is fundamental to every living system. Energy and the minerals essential to life could not be recycled without it. If we assume that an individual wildebeest or zebra has an average lifespan of ten years, then it follows that in a population of two million animals, 200,000 will die of old age each year. And that is just two of the medium-size animals in the Serengeti. Add the death of the region's numerous other species, and we can see that death in the Serengeti creates a very large resource. They are eaten by the carnivores, scavengers, and decomposers that are such essential parts of the recycling process.

Mention scavengers on the African savanna, and probably the hyena comes first to mind. But the noble lion will not hesitate to dine on the carcass of an animal that died naturally or was killed by other predators—if it can manage to chase them away. Lions, leopards, cheetahs, wild dogs—virtually all predators will scavenge if they have the chance, though they are not very good at it. In fact, it is estimated that the Serengeti's 7,000 killers miss over 60 percent of the animals that die from natural causes. The most efficient scavengers in the Serengeti ecosystem are the vultures, which consume more meat than all the mammalian carnivores combined.

The vultures' advantage, of course, is the ability to spot carcasses from the air. Having soared aloft on the columns of warm air that rise from the plain as the day heats up, vultures can glide for hours over great distances with a minimum of effort. They can spot an animal lying dead on the ground from three miles away, and dive down to it at about 40 miles an hour. Their disadvantage is that a diving vulture attracts attention. Most vultures find their food by watching the activities of other vultures—which is not so bad, because each individual vulture can consume only a small portion of what is available. But both lions and hyenas also watch for vultures

descending and will run toward the birds' target area, even if the carcass is out of sight.

In a situation where mammalian and avian scavengers are equally abundant, it might be assumed that the vultures would be chased away when the lions or the hyenas arrive. But this is not what happens in practice. A researcher who watched 64 carcasses found that in 84 percent of the cases, not one mammalian carnivore turned up—no lion, no hyena—though the vultures usually fed for several hours and were joined throughout by others of their kind.

We may not find the idea of being directed by vultures to a meal of recently dead meat particularly attractive, but this rich and underexploited niche was tailor-made for a distinctive animal that made its appearance on the savannas of East Africa nearly four million years ago—and these were our ancestors.

bers of stone tools have been found at the butchery sites that are a relatively common feature of the archaeological digs in East Africa. Cut marks on fossil bones show where meat was sliced from the carcass. A profusion of shattered long bones indicates a prediliction for the fatty marrow they had contained. This is particularly revealing, for game meat is notoriously lean, and fat is an essential item of the high-quality diet that the human animal must have to sustain its unique physical form and behavior.

It was of course the bipedal gait and the cognitive brain that enabled humans to exploit the resources that other animals had missed. Standing erect on two legs, with the capacity to think about the present and plan for the future on the basis of past experience, humans were unique. Small, not especially robust, few in number—fragile figures sharing an ancient landscape with the greatest number and diversity of animals on Earth—they were poised on the first step of a trajectory that would carry their descendants to the stars.

Reconstructions of that ancient landscape indicate that environmental conditions then were not very different from recent times. With over 60 percent of carcasses being the result of natural death, not predation, we may assume that, as was observed in the 1960s, there would have been at least one carcass within three miles of any point on the migration route—every day. Enterprising scientists tested this hypothesis by hiking across the Serengeti Plain for several days. They found plenty of meat and had no serious conflict with predators and scavengers. Vultures located the carcass for them and, when necessary, the men with knives did them the favor of breaching the skin (which vultures cannot easily do) and butchering the carcass.

In the early days of our evolutionary history, our ancestors brought stone tools to the job. Large num-

T A PLACE called Laetoli, on the southeastern edge of the Serengeti Plain, archaeologist Mary Leakey and her team were carefully sweeping back a shallow portion of the African landscape to reveal a poignant moment in the human story. We walked in stocking feet over what had been a mud pan 3.5 million years ago. In wonder we gazed at a trail of footprints that had been preserved in the delicate fossilized surface. Though so old, the prints were as human as those we leave on wet sandy beaches each summer. Three individuals had crossed the mud pan,

The flat-topped acacia, *Acacia tortilis*, is perfectly adapted to Africa's heat and sporadic rains. The crowning layer of tiny leaves balances the tree's need for sunlight with the dangers of drying out.

FOLLOWING PAGES: **Surprise attacks from the cover of tall grass are more than just play for 14-month-old cheetah cubs. Such behavior teaches young cheetahs the skills of survival on the plains.**

one walking in the footsteps of another and a third walking to one side.

As I stood at the head of the trail, with the Serengeti spread below, my mind's eye could see the group walking away from the woodlands that an erupting volcano was dusting with ash. The even depth of each print indicated that their pace had been unhurried. They knew where they were going; this was their homeland. Noting that the prints and stride of one trail were larger than the others, Mary Leakey set aside the rigor of science for a moment and wistfully suggested that the prints had been made by a family—a man and a woman walking together with their teenage child following behind. The woman's prints were deeper than might be expected for her size, particularly those of the left foot, suggesting that she was carrying an uneven load—perhaps a baby on her left hip. At one point in the trail the woman appeared to have stopped, paused, and turned to glance back over her shoulder at some

threat or irregularity. It was an intensely human reaction that transcended time, Mary said. Millions of years ago, a remote ancestor had experienced a moment of doubt—just as we might today.

Sadiman, the volcano whose ash created the Laetoli fossil beds, is no longer active, but the Laetoli landscape is otherwise not very different from that which existed over three million years ago. The foothills of the highlands are covered in acacia bush, and the upper slopes are swathed in grasses that turn from green to golden as the dry season advances. Westward, the plain extends to a distant horizon, the broad, undulating expanse broken here and there by steep-sided outcrops of granite and gneiss that rise from the grassland like islands. In shallow valleys, strands of woodland mark the watercourses. Elephants come down from the highlands, giraffes browse on the acacia tops, lions lie concealed in the dun-colored grass, herds of zebra and antelope mingle nervously. Laetoli preserves a sense of Africa in its pristine state, when

From maned lions on the Tanzania savanna to bongo antelope in the Cameroon rain forest, Africa's hunting concessions claim to offer the best sport of its kind. But at a price. A three-week safari can cost $40,000—plus additional trophy charges.

humanity had but recently learned to walk and was advancing on to the savanna.

Africa was the cradle of all humanity, and there is little doubt that the colonization of the savanna was the initial and most decisive step of our entire evolutionary history. All our distinctive characteristics—our ability to walk on two legs for long distances; our hands, with an opposable forefinger and thumb able to perform delicate tasks; our bare skin; sweating; and our brain—were all adaptations that evolved in response to the demands of the savanna environment. Of these, the brain has turned out to be the most crucial. While other animals have evolved specialized physical attributes to enhance their chances of survival—the giraffe's long neck and the elephant's trunk are classic examples—evolution endowed our ancestors with a highly specialized capacity for thinking. Initially it may have grown to control the demands of eye-hand coordination (without which it would be impossible to make a stone tool), but it was destined to become our main survival tool.

Our brain could not have evolved its distinctive characteristics without the physical changes that an upright stance imposed upon the basic primate skeleton. Standing up and walking away from our primate cousins changed everything.

Humans are so closely related to the apes that more than 99 percent of our DNA is identical to that of the chimpanzee. This means that chimpanzees and humans diverged from their common ancestor only in the recent past. The common ancestor lived between seven and five million years ago in the luxuriant forests to the west of the Rift Valley. Exactly how and why one branch of its descendants evolved to become human, while the other retained the ancestral form and became the modern apes—the gorillas and chimpanzees—is a matter of speculation. Fossil hunters have yet to discover the crucial evidence. Meanwhile, it is as though a magician had drawn a veil over the scene, then ushered forth the bipedal ancestor of humanity. The transformation certainly had magical qualities, for standing and walking call for some extensive adaptation of the primate form.

The human bipedal gait is unique, probably because it is such an inefficient way of getting around. In terms of the energy required to move our bodies, humans are only a little more efficient than penguins. Mice, squirrels, ponies, and gazelles are much more efficient—dogs even more so. Among our closest cousins, gorillas use relatively more energy than humans when moving about on the ground on all fours, but chimpanzees use 25 percent less. Furthermore, chimps are also faster and more agile.

The fact that 60 percent of the apes' body weight is carried on their hind legs implies that the ancestral form could support bipedalism. But even so, the physical adjustments required for walking around entirely on two legs were considerable. The main problem was transferring the weight of the upper body to the hind limbs, and then arranging for it to be balanced on alternate legs as each stride was taken. To achieve this, several things had to happen. The head shifted so that it balanced on the top of the backbone (and was no longer held in place by powerful neck muscles, as in the apes). The backbone developed curves in the neck and lower back regions, giving it the function of a spring. The pelvis broadened, the arms shortened, the legs lengthened, and the thighs angled inward so that the knees could take the weight of the body. Finally, the foot lost its capacity to grasp like a hand and turned into a stiff lever of propulsion. All of these skeletal adaptations were accompanied by equally demanding muscular adaptations.

The transition from shuffling ape to striding human ancestor must have been completed over a relatively brief period of time. The process could not have been gradual, simply because no animal can make regular

Introduced to Kenya during the colonial period, tea flourishes in the highlands and is picked every 14 days all year-round. Kenya is the largest producer in Africa and the world's foremost exporter.

use of *both* quadrupedal and bipedal gaits. One or the other had to predominate from an early stage.

A rapid transition implies that the external forces provoking the adaptation were intense. And indeed, Africa was becoming cooler and drier at the time, which meant the forests were shrinking. It is probable that competition for dwindling resources drove the ancestral humans from their primeval home and onto the savanna, where access to a new, more widely dispersed food supply led to the evolution of bipedalism.

But while the edible resources of the savanna are over 20 times more plentiful than those of the forest, the savanna imposed new constraints on the human ancestor. Resources were scattered over a wide area, and gathering them called for hours of walking about in the heat of the sun—which in turn posed the question of water and where to find enough of it.

People can live for weeks without food, but without water they die within days. In temperate climates we need about 2.6 quarts per day, but anyone walking about on the savanna may need three or four times as much. This is because we sweat to keep cool. The human ancestors who crossed the Laetoli mud pan were about the size of a modern eight-year-old. Their water requirements were less than ours, but even they could not have traveled more than seven miles from water as they foraged for food.

On the face of it, sweating seems a perverse way of keeping cool in a tropical environment where water is not always nearby. After all, grazing animals spend their days exposed to the full impact of the tropical sun. Some, such as the oryx and the Thompson's gazelle, can survive on the moisture they derive from the vegetation alone. But then antelopes do not have large brains and, paradoxical though it may seem, the large brain and sweating to keep cool are inextricably linked.

All mammalian brains are extremely sensitive to temperature. Variations of more than a few degrees can be lethal. The body temperatures of the animals out on the plain may rise well above danger levels, but they survive because they have evolved elaborate ways of keeping their brain cool while their body heats up. Their long muzzle is the key. In its length, the evaporation of water from the moist nasal lining removes heat from the blood flowing beneath the membranes. This cooled blood then collects momentarily in an expanded section of the jugular vein, called a sinus, at the base of the skull. Meanwhile, blood flowing to the brain along the carotid artery is conducted through a network of fine blood vessels, called the carotid rete, which passes through the sinus, where excess heat from the arterial blood is transferred to the pool of cooled venous blood and the brain receives blood at the critical temperature.

With a "radiator" in the nose and a "heat exchanger" in the skull, the savanna mammals can keep their brain cool even when their body is very hot indeed. Humans (and most primates), with their foreshortened face, possess neither radiator nor heat exchanger. Furthermore, primates (including humans) do not have a carotid rete. These factors are confirmation of our ancestry in a forested environment, where our closest cousins are still found. They stayed behind and are very poorly equipped to deal with heat stress. We moved out and evolved the most effective body-cooling system of any living mammal.

The main factors are standing erect, naked skin, and highly developed sweat glands. While animals on four legs have 20 percent of their body exposed to the sun during the day, humans standing erect in the tropics have only 7 percent exposed to the sun at noon, when

Grown by a half million Kenyan farmers, coffee is the country's second largest export earner after tea.

it is vertically overhead. Overall, humans avoid 60 percent of the direct solar radiation to which quadrupeds are exposed. Plus, hair protects their head and shoulders when the sun is most intense. Furthermore, standing erect exposes a greater area of skin surface to the movement of air. This advantage is enhanced by a naked skin that leaves sweat pores fully exposed, and highly developed sweat glands whose output rapidly transfers body heat directly into the surrounding air.

Our whole-body cooling system is a far more efficient means of protecting the brain from heat stress than the radiator and heat exchanger of other mammals. It evolved as we moved onto the savanna, enabling our ancestors to forage longer. The brain was still relatively small at that stage, but the whole-body cooling system helped the brain evolve into the large survival tool we possess today. This is not to say that the whole-body cooling system *caused* the evolution of the large brain, only that it removed certain physiological constraints and rendered enlargement possible. But there was a downside.

Brain is expensive tissue—the Rolls-Royce of cognitive equipment, costly to run. The modern human brain is six times larger than most mammals' its size, and although on average it represents only 2 percent of body weight in modern humans, it consumes over 16 percent of the body's energy budget. By comparison, skeletal muscle, where energy is most obviously expended, consumes less than 15 percent of the body's budget, even though it constitutes over 40 percent of average body weight.

Furthermore, the human brain burns up energy nine times faster than the rest of the body, and since it has no means of storing energy for future use, it must be continuously supplied with fuel. As the human brain evolved, keeping it running soon became no less demanding than keeping it cool. Accordingly, food intake should have increased as the large brain evolved. By now the stomach and digestive tract should be correspondingly large relative to body size. But the human gut is half the size that would be predicted. Not for us the large bellies through which the other primates process huge quantities of leaves and grass, with only an occasional taste of something more nutritious. We learned to seek out high-quality foods of which relatively small quantities will keep us going. Our small gut runs exclusively on high-quality food, principally the nutrient-rich reproductive material of other organisms—seeds, nuts, tubers, and eggs—topped off with significant quantities of protein in the form of meat.

Thus, satisfying the demands of the large brain has called for a good deal of cognitive effort on the part of the brain itself. The success of this interactive relationship is self-evident, for it is the foundation of all human behavior and achievement: technology, language, and culture. All of it is a consequence of adaptations to the demands of life on the tropical African savanna.

NE **SUNDAY AFTERNOON,** some weeks after I had moved to Nairobi in early 1969, I took the car and drove out of the city, down the Mombasa road. Where the ribbon of tarmac crossed the Athi Plains—an expanse of savanna grassland then still dotted with zebra, giraffe, gazelle, and antelope—I turned onto a dirt track. The track petered out after half a mile or so and I continued on foot, not heading anywhere in particular, just wanting to get into the country and be alone for a while. I followed a succession of game trails winding through the low, scrubby vegetation and shoulder-high stands of whistling thorn. It was the dry season. The sward had been heavily grazed. In some places the earth was completely bare, and at one point, where the downpours of a previous wet season had converted the trail into a shallow watercourse, some fragments of stone caught my eye. I knelt and found I had stumbled upon a small cache of stone tools that had eroded from the banks of the watercourse. At first I thought they were crude arrowheads, but in fact they were small blades that you might hold between thumb and forefinger to cut through skin perhaps or to slice meat from the bone. Certainly the flintlike stone was hard and glassy enough to have produced a flake with a very sharp edge when it was first chipped from a large block.

That I should have found stone tools during a Sunday afternoon stroll on the Athi Plains did not seem remarkable at the time. After all, not long before, I had been at Koobi Fora in northern Kenya. There the fossil remains of all manner of creatures were being excavated—including early man. I was learning that Africa frequently reveals unexpected connections with our ancient past. Nonetheless, kneeling there on the Athi Plains, alone with a scattering of stone flakes, was an evocative moment. The flakes could have been made more than a hundred thousand years ago, when stone tools were the cutting edge of human survival. Tools like these enabled people to make fuller and more effective use of the savanna. They were a crucial step in the evolutionary process. The flakes I had found may have been used to slice meat into strips for drying, or to sharpen a stick for digging up nutritious roots. Perhaps they had lain untouched ever since. And now here I was, with the modern city of Nairobi shimmering in the heat haze to the north.

We have been alone in the world since the last Neandertals became extinct about 25,000 years ago, free to colonize the globe and exploit the Earth's resources without competition from other hominids. No other mammals have ever been so widespread and so alone. But it was not always like this. Although the belief that human evolution has proceeded along a single line from one species to the next has always been popular, recent fossil discoveries and the reassessment of exist-

The Kenya coast, with silver sands and coral reefs, is a popular venue for tourists. By day Kenya's young Masai patrol the beaches with handicrafts for sale; in the evenings they gather at the hotels to entertain the tourists with traditional dancing.

ing collections make it clear that the evolution of the human line is no different from that of other successful animal families. Our evolutionary history is not a linear progression that led directly from the earliest australopithecines to *Homo habilis*, to *Homo erectus*, and thence to *Homo sapiens*. On the contrary, it is a typical story of evolutionary tinkering and experiment. Over the past 4.4 million years, new hominid species have emerged, competed, coexisted, and succeeded—or failed. Some authorities believe that at least 20 species of hominid have come and gone since our ancestors stepped from the forest onto the savanna four to five million years ago. A host of fossils from the shores of what is now Lake Turkana in the Rift Valley, for instance, proves conclusively that at least four of them lived there together around 1.8 million years ago.

The first exodus of hominids from Africa must have occurred around that time. Fossils of a related species dating from 1.8 million years ago have been found in China and Java. Europe appears to have been colonized somewhat later. The fossil evidence indicates that hominids were present in Spain about 800,000 years ago. From this branch of the hominid line the Neandertals evolved, who remained relatively common throughout the continent until they became extinct.

Meanwhile, branches of the ancestral tree were growing in Africa too, culminating with the appearance of a very distinctive hominid between 150,000 to 200,000 years ago. The fossil evidence indicates that the newcomers were tall and slender, their chins were pointed and jutted forward, their faces were short and tucked in under the skull, they had a high forehead but no heavy brow ridges, and their brains were as large as ours. The connection is unmistakable. These were the first representatives of our species, *Homo sapiens*—wise man.

All the other representatives of the hominid family disappeared from Africa not long after this, for reasons we may never fully know. Perhaps they were trapped in deteriorating environmental conditions. Perhaps they depended too much on scarce foods that disappeared with a change in the climate. Or perhaps they lost out to the newcomers in competition for available resources. Whatever the case, Africa filled up with people like ourselves. Before long they spilled out of the continent via the isthmus of Suez and colonized the rest of the world. Within the span of 4,000 generations they reoccupied the regions in which the ancestral lines descending from the earlier exodus had become extinct. Then they went on to colonize lands that people had never occupied before. In short, they took over the world.

Geneticists have estimated that the numbers involved in the second exodus were very small—

mean that she was the only woman alive at the time (Eve, as creationists might like to believe), simply that her mtDNA steadily became dominant as some maternal lineages disappeared (not every mother produces a daughter to whom her mtDNA is passed on). The geneticists referred to this ancestor as "our common mother," but she soon became more popularly known as the "African Eve."

OL DOINYO LENGAI rises at the southern end of Lake Natron, near the eastern tip of the Serengeti Plain, a steep, deeply scoured cone of gray ash that wears a mantle of green when the rains have been good. It is the last active remnant of the volcanic chain associated with the formation of the Rift Valley, whose eruptions created the fertile Plain so many years ago, when humanity was in its infancy. Ol Doinyo Lengai last dusted the Serengeti with ash in 1967—a gentle reminder of the beneficence bestowed in the past. Lengai means "god" in the Masai language, and it is also the word they use for "rain."

Farther north, the majestic snowcapped peaks of Mount Kenya are similarly revered by the Kikuyu as the home of their god, known as Ngai—a Kikuyu rendition of the Masai name. A Kikuyu legend describes the origin of the Masai, the Kikuyu, and the Dorobo people who, it was believed, were the first inhabitants of East Africa. The legend goes like this: An old man (some say a god) was dying, and he sent each of his sons out into the world with a gift that would set them up for life. The first received an arrow and went off to make a living by hunting—these were the Dorobo. The second was given a hoe and learned how to till the land and grow crops—the Kikuyu. The third received a stick and began herding cattle—the Masai.

The legend of the arrow, the hoe, and the stick broadly summarizes the means by which people have exploited the terrestrial resources of Africa. Hunters, farmers, and herders. The divisions are so old and

possibly as few as 50 individuals, with six females breeding at any one time over a period of 70 years, or no more than 500 individuals over 200 years. A bottleneck so narrow means that the descendants of the migrants all are very closely related. In fact, a New Yorker and an Australian Aborigine are likely to be genetically more similar than two people from the same town in Africa. This is because the Africans have inherited the genetic diversity of a large population, about one million at the time of the exodus. But the migrants still have lots in common with the African population, simply because all—African and non-African—are the descendants of a species that had evolved in the relatively recent past.

Just how recent has been confirmed by genetic studies. Every human being today carries the mitochondrial DNA (mtDNA) of an African woman who lived about 10,000 generations ago. This does not

The jagged peaks of Africa's second highest mountain, Mount Kenya, are the fractured core of an ancient volcano. The god of the Kikuyu people, Ngai, is said to reside in a cave high on the mountain.

deeply established that they seem culturally inspired—upheld by distinguishing features of appearance, custom, belief, and, in some instances, mutual antagonism. But at root the distinctions are ecological, related to the environmental zones each group occupies. They define the activities by which people can make best use of the available resources. Intriguingly, the distinctions are also linguistic. The languages spoken by various groups of hunters throughout Africa belong to a different linguistic family from those spoken by the farmers, and both differ from the herders'.

The ability to speak and thus share information, news, and ideas with others is a defining characteristic of humanity. Perhaps it is *the* defining characteristic, for it is hard to imagine that people would remain human for very long if they could not speak to one another. The talent evolved in Africa, almost certainly with the emergence of the large-brained modern humans, 150,000 to 200,000 years ago. Ultimately, the capacity for language became innate, so deeply engrained that "people know how to talk in more or less the sense that spiders know how to spin webs."

Language is as old as humanity; the original mother tongue has long since been changed and modified, but evidence of Africa's ancient linguistic history survives to this day. Archaeologists have discovered the first fossils in Africa, and linguists have shown that the most ancient languages are found there.

On the basis of shared words and structure, the world's several thousand languages have been grouped into 20 or so linguistic families. Of these, four bear only the most distant relationship with all the rest. All four are African, and three of those are spoken predominantly by the people of the arrow (the Khoisan languages), the hoe (Niger-Congo), and the stick (Nilo-Saharan). Even more remarkable, these languages are still heard today, spoken by the Hadza

hunters and gatherers, the Sukuma farmers, and the Masai herders in a corner of East Africa that is just a day or two's walk from the savannas where our ancestors first stepped out of the forest.

The Hadza and the Sukuma are tied to their land, ringed around by other groups, but the Masai range along the full length of the East Africa Rift Valley. No longer do they cross the plains of the Serengeti, but they still herd their cattle on savanna environments elsewhere. To the north of the Serengeti and east of the Mara in Kenya, where the savannas rise gently to the Loita Hills, the Mau escarpment, the Nyandarua Range (known in colonial times as the Aberdares), and the foothills of snowcapped Mount Kenya, the cool uplands provided grazing to which the Masai and their cattle could retreat in the dry season, when the savanna was parched. On the rising gradient above this dry-season pasture, where the grass glades merge into woodland and forest, Kikuyu farmers cleared the land, built houses and fences, and planted crops that flourished at that altitude. Higher still, where the forest grows on steep slopes from which the topsoil would be washed away in a season if cleared, and on the heights where grain crops would not flourish, the Dorobo took charge, exploiting the resources of the forest. They collected honey and wild fruits, trapped wild animals, and were conversant with the medicinal properties of little-known forest plants.

In good times the Dorobo gathered more forest produce than they needed for themselves. They traded the excess with the farmers, seeking in particular the carbohydrates (grain and root crops) that are scarce in the forest. In turn, the farmers were grateful for a supply of game meat, for that meant not having to slaughter their own animals. Likewise, the Kikuyu farmers traded with the Masai herders, exchanging grain for dairy produce, leather, and young animals. These relationships were always prone to the shortcomings of human nature—distrust, dishonesty, dislike—but were sustained because they were mutually advantageous. Making

A baker delivers bread by bicycle in Nyeri, near Mount Kenya. The bread is baked locally, but the bicycle is imported; so too are the raw materials of the plastic crates and the machinery that made them. As in much of Africa, Kenya's industrial development lags far behind the country's needs.

the most of the arrow, the hoe, and the stick called for specialized talents; each group always produced a surplus that could be traded for the essentials they needed from a neighboring ecological niche.

This is of course an idealized account. Climate, lack of sufficient numbers, antagonism, and—most important of all—the events of history have often conspired against such a Garden of Eden scenario. For one thing, the Dorobo were not always confined to the forests they have occupied in recent times. These Khoisan-speaking peoples, together with the Hadza of Tanzania and the !Kung San of the Kalahari, once hunted and gathered throughout the continent's entire range of ecological zones. They were the earliest inhabitants of Africa and retreated to their refuges in the forests and the deserts only as other groups moved in and took over the most productive lands they had occupied.

There is evidence that people with cattle had moved onto the high savanna of southern Kenya by 2,600 years ago. The people of the arrow may not have been totally averse to their arrival: Domestic stock are easier to kill than wild game, and cattle bones have been found where archaeologists have excavated ancient hunter-gatherer campsites. But the more overwhelming incursions came centuries later, with the arrival of farmers from the west, speaking Niger-Congo languages.

HERE CENTURIES AGO Kikuyu farmers used tools of iron to clear the forest north of Nairobi for their farms and homesteads, golfers today might use a number 4 iron to drive down the fairways and onto the greens of the Limuru golf club. The players are probably unaware that the course follows the beliefs of the Kikuyu farmers. The massive trees in the rough, with

tangled branches waiting to trap the badly hit ball, are African wild fig trees, which the Kikuyu people will never chop down. For them, the fig tree is sacred.

By the time British colonial settlers began planting coffee and tea in the Kenya highlands in the early 20th century, the Kikuyu had already felled vast swathes of forest. But fig trees remained standing everywhere. They were useful markers for the location of a village or spring, but they were protected more because of the power of the myths and legends attached to them. At their father's knee, children were told how God himself had sent the Kikuyu to the land where the fig tree grew. As the Kikuyu flourished, the fig trees became venues for ritual, for village and clan gatherings. Each year harvest thanksgiving ceremonies were held in their shade. Like the cathedrals of Europe, the greatest

and oldest trees became the revered focus of social and cultural identity—the physical manifestations of a people's unity and shared belief.

The Kikuyu are but one of many groups descended from the farmers who were steadily advancing westward from the Great Lakes region of central Africa during the 11th century A.D. The migrants' advance was eased by their iron tools. With these they felled trees (for charcoal with which to smelt iron, as well as to clear the land), built villages, and planted crops, but their momentum was that of expansion rather than conquest. As they came around the southern shore of Lake Victoria onto the highlands of northern Tanzania, via Kilimanjaro and along the rim of the Rift Valley toward the beckoning bulk of Mount Kenya, farmers settled along the way, and when the communities they had established grew

too large for their land, some families moved on. The advance split and diverged as the migrants moved eastward, like the branches of a slow but strongly growing tree, creating numerous closely related populations throughout East Africa. They shared common ancestries and followed similar lifestyles, but each soon developed a quite different identity.

No written account of the Kikuyu existed until Jomo Kenyatta published his famous *Facing Mount Kenya* in 1938, but the stories told by the elders and passed on from generation to generation have enabled later historians to trace Kikuyu roots back to the early 1500s. The record of those earliest times is shadowy, known only by the names of the age sets—or generations—to which the senior elders of the day belonged: Tene, "long ago"; Agu, "ancestors"; and "Manjiri," creation. These ancestors of the Kikuyu settled first on the eastern and southern slopes of Mount Kenya, where they found good soils, moderate temperatures, and adequate rainfall. Furthermore, the region was free of the tsetse fly and the malarial mosquito, which restricted human habitation in other parts.

The Dorobo hunters and gatherers who had previously occupied the region were steadily absorbed into the Kikuyu population (by marriage or by simply joining) or displaced as waves of the Kikuyu pioneers moved onto the mountain and pushed back the forest on all fronts. A British administrator described the process in 1910: "The Aikuyu pushed on and on. Their progress was like that of the locusts—the ranks at the rear, finding food supply exhausted, taking wing over the backs of the main body to drop to the ground in the forefront. And as locusts clear a sturdy crop, so have the Aikuyu cleared the forest." But this account reflects colonial attitudes and is not at all how the

Children walk to their school in Karatina—many barefoot and from homes without running water or electricity. An educated child is the promise of relief from poverty. But there is no free education in Kenya; poor families struggle to find school fees.

Kikuyu themselves viewed the process. The pioneers were generally young men, historians report, who formed an *mbari,* a pioneer band, which would occupy a ridge on the high, forested slopes of Mount Kenya and then, having worked together to clear the forest, divided the land among themselves. It was extremely hard work. Merely to clear the 2.5 acres each family needed for its basic sustenance is said to have taken up to 150 days of labor.

By the beginning of the 17th century the Kikuyu had colonized virtually the entire southeastern shoulder of Mount Kenya. They established a main center at the confluence of the Thika and Thagana Rivers, about 50 miles northeast of present-day Nairobi. The mbari pushed on, upstream along the course of the Thagana River and west into the valleys of the many tributaries that flow from the Nyandarua Range. This is beautiful high country, rising from around 3,900 feet in the valley to a summit plateau at over 8,200 feet and to the peaks of Satima and Kinangop at nearly 13,000 feet—high enough to receive an occasional dusting of snow. Facing east, the Nyandaruas catch the moisture-laden monsoon winds blowing in from the Indian Ocean and are well watered.

Much of the vegetation that the pioneers were obliged to clear was useful. A belt of sturdy bamboo that flanks the Nyandaruas and Mount Kenya provided fencing as well as a means of channeling water to places where it was needed. The timber of the pencil cedar splits cleanly and is resistent to termites, making it ideal for housing. The camphor tree was the source of a soothing medicinal rub as well as timber. Furniture was made from the forest's bounty of mahogany, iroko, African olive and yellowwood. But one tree, above all others, was revered by the first pioneers—the wild fig, *Ficus natalensis.*

The mature wild fig is a massive tree, wide in girth, with branches so close together and leaves so densely packed that even a bird or a leopard might get lost in its canopy. The wild fig demands respect. It was never felled—perhaps because of its daunting appearance, perhaps because its sap is sticky and can cause rashes, perhaps because its timber is soft and useful neither for building nor burning—or perhaps because its location usually signifies the presence of a spring in the vicinity. Whatever the case, the wild fig is revered by the Kikuyu to this day. They are the people of the *mukuyu,* which is their name for the fig. A huge specimen stands on the slopes of the Nyandaruas, facing Mount Kenya, at Mukurue wa Gathanga. According to Kikuyu tradition, this is the Garden of Eden—their birthplace—though historians tell us that the Kikuyu came here during the 17th century.

The slopes of the Nyandaruas were fertile and highly suited to intensive agriculture. Of the pioneers who still hunted and gathered part of the year, the majority converted to full-time farming. The population increased rapidly, spreading yet more waves of settlers south to present-day Nairobi. During this period of expansion the Kikuyu developed their symbiotic relationship with the Masai of the savanna. Goods were exchanged, words borrowed, and customs adopted. A good deal of intermarriage took place as well. More than half the Kikuyu in some districts are believed to have Masai blood in their veins.

The Kikuyu reached the limits of their expansion during the latter part of the 18th century. At that time they began to identify themselves as a single group—the Kikuyu. This happened little more than 200 years ago, as clans and families that previously would have split and moved on became more and more inclined to stay put. Mukurue wa Gathanga and the giant fig tree became precious symbols of Kikuyu identity, instilling a fervent belief that the Kikuyu possessed a God-given right to live there—on the land facing Mount Kenya—forever.

lice Wangui is a single mother expecting her second child. A thoroughly modern and successful woman who runs her own hairdressing salon in Nairobi, Alice has access to the best of the city's medical attention, but has decided to have the baby in the village where she herself was born. Her first child, seven-year-old Scott, was born there and his sister (if the baby is the hoped-for girl) must be born there too, she says, in the land of the family's Kikuyu forefathers. Like most Kikuyu, Alice feels a strong attachment to the land of her birth—even though she lives and works so far away.

The Kikuyu are the largest of Kenya's ethnic groups, an eastern outpost of the farming communities that were spreading steadily south and east from the Great Lakes region of central Africa one thousand years ago. By the early 1600s the Kikuyu had settled throughout the highlands of what is now Kenya, with their spiritual homeland firmly established in the beautiful high country of the Nyandarua Range, facing Mount Kenya, where monsoon winds from the Indian Ocean brought ample rains to fertile soils.

Alice's village nestles in the foothills of the Nyandaruas, close to the small market town of Nyeri, but still over 90 miles from Nairobi. The bus journey will be long and uncomfortable—and risky for a woman in the last month of pregnancy. The doctor urges Alice not to make the journey at this late stage, but Alice is determined to go. A baby born in Nairobi comes from nowhere, she says.

Rested after a bumpy, spine-jolting ride from Nairobi, Alice Wangui walks with her son, Scott, down lanes where she had played as a child. Though she lives in the city, this is the place Alice calls home. Generations of her family have treasured this precious corner of the Kikuyu homeland. Both she and Scott were born here, as were her father and grandfather.

"That is a must," Alice says. "You're supposed to give birth where you were born. It's very important. You are supposed to go back to your home."

With her mother, Charity Wacuka, to look after her, Alice (left) can relax.
"The importance of me going to Nyeri is that I want my children to
follow the culture and to know where they come from," she explains,
"I want them to follow Nyeri ways—not to be a Nairobi dweller—
I want her to be a real Kikuyu."

Proudly, Alice holds the framed photograph of her parents that has hung in the living room for as long as she can remember.

The birth will be soon. Wanjiku, a neighbor, teases Alice for being so traditional, but like everyone else in the village is pleased that she came home to have the baby. But the birth will not be entirely traditional. Alice will check in at the village clinic, where a doctor and midwife will be in attendance.

Scott will wait for news at his grandmother's house, hoping

the baby will be a girl. "He really wants a sister," Alice says.

esert

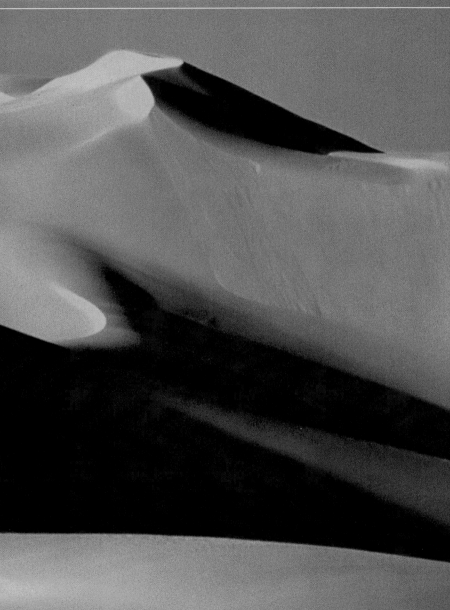

The Sahara is the largest desert on Earth. A wasteland of terrifying beauty, with golden dunes winding sinuously to distant horizons. An environment of contrasts, where the burning sand destroys life and the shady oasis sustains it, where the sun saps moisture from the body by day, and where the cold of deep space freezes the desert at night.

The Sahara is also the Earth's most compelling record of climate change. Fifteen thousand years ago the desert was even drier than it is today. Nine thousand years ago it was a paradise of savanna, lakes, rivers, and woodlands in which Africans first began to plant crops and herd livestock. When the desert dried out again, the pioneers took their new-found talents into the Nile Valley and the distant reaches of Africa.

But evidence of the desert's former generosity remains—in the huge volumes of water that lie under the sands, feeding desert wells and green oases, and in the salt of dried-out lakes that Tuareg camel caravans transport from the desert to the towns.

Dunes of the Sahara rise to heights of nearly 1,000 feet.

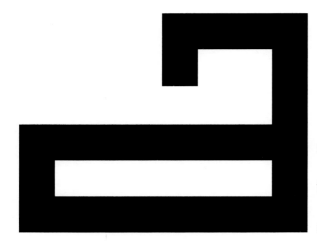s a young city boy sent to spend the war years in the countryside of Wales, I was fascinated by the bird life. Sparrows and starlings were the most I could expect my crumbs to attract to our London home. Yet the garden in Llantwit Vadre thronged with tits and finches, blackbirds, thrushes, and the occasional wagtail. By the time I was eight, I knew all the common birds and quite a few of the rarer ones, but for all my searching I never did see the cuckoo, the herald of spring that we would listen for as April advanced into May. The swallows and

swifts soon followed, nesting under the gables and in the sheds on the farm. In autumn I would watch them gathering in rows on the telephone wires, ready to migrate south. The idea that these small creatures could fly all the way to Africa was almost beyond belief, but I admired their ability to escape the European winter.

I thought of the birds flying away as our birds. But now I know that although they hatched in Europe, many of them actually spend most of the year in Africa and should perhaps be thought of as Africa's birds that have chosen to grace the European summer and are now flying home. Europe's bird life would be much impoverished without them. Of the more than 700 species listed in a popular handbook of British and European birds, 187 are migrants from Africa.

The distances they travel are prodigious—even within Europe. The bluethroat (*Luscinia svecica*), for instance, flies to the North Cape of Scandinavia—well inside the Arctic Circle—having already crossed the Mediterranean and the Sahara. The trans–Sahara crossing is the most demanding part of the trip. It amounts to 930 miles on the most direct route and rises to over 1,200 miles on the diagonal trajectory that the birds often follow. Flight times range from 40 to 60 hours and the crossing is made without a stop in most cases, for oases are few and far between.

PREVIOUS PAGES: **Men have farmed the banks of the Nile for thousands of years, reaping the benefit of both the water and the silt brought down from central Africa.** ABOVE: **Water cascading from the mountains behind Timia, in central Niger, provides a swimming pool for the Tuareg village children.**

Storks, hawks, swallows, and starlings; larks, pipits, and doves; sparrows, wagtails, thrushes, and robins: Millions upon millions of birds fatten up on the savannas on the southern fringes of the desert before heading north across the empty wastelands. The total number involved in the annual migration has been estimated at 2.5 billion birds. Few are seen from the ground, but radar observations have confirmed the passage of thousands flying at altitudes of 9,800 feet and above, where airliners cruise. As with the jets, the thin air at those altitudes offers less resistance, the birds gain a 20 percent improvement in air speed, and their energy reserves last longer. The majority are songbirds flying somewhat lower and weighing little more than the 0.36-ounce airmail letters we send winging around the world. Small birds in particular must take on a heavy load of fuel before setting off on the trans–Sahara flight. A sedge warbler feeding on the savanna fringes of Lake Chad, for instance, will put on more than half again its weight in fat before taking off. Thus the beneficence of the Earth's most

prolific pastures fuels Africa's winged messengers to Europe across the forbidding wastes of the Sahara.

I F PLANTS AND animals have maximized their potential on the savanna, the desert has severely tested their ability simply to survive. Water—life's solvent—is the reason why. Nowhere on Earth is the living world's dependence on water so clearly demonstrated. A round of seasons without rain means that the seeds of annual plants in the soil do not germinate. Several years without rain will persuade even the hardiest of perennial shrubs and trees to shut down their life processes. In the desert, seed and root-stock must remain in a state of viable dormancy for years—even decades—ready to spring back to life with the first shower of rain.

Only those plants that have evolved special adaptations can survive the blistering heat through long periods of unbroken drought. The succulents have bulbous leaves that store moisture and tough skins that inhibit transpiration. The tap-rooted desert shrubs survive on the residues of past rainfall that has accumulated on hard pans that lie 30 or even 60 feet under the sands. And though it may never rain, atmospheric moisture is sometimes present and will condense during the cold desert nights to dress exposed surfaces with beads of dew. Dew refreshes the plants and supplements the water supply of animals.

Though few places are more inhospitable, deserts fascinate us. Perhaps we intuitively recognize that they are an example of what an abused world could become. Deserts are one of the world's most widespread environments, covering between one-quarter and one-third of the land surface. In Africa alone, 40 percent of the land's surface is dry and hot enough to qualify as desert: the Kalahari, the Namib, and the

Swathed in his *tagelmust*, Algabit looks into the rising sun as his camels begin the nine-day journey across the desert from Timia to Bilma. The tagelmust protects against cold, heat, and sandstorms.

Karoo in southern Africa; the Danakil, Ogaden, and Chalbi in East Africa; and of course the Sahara.

The Sahara is the largest and most awe-inspiring desert on the planet. It covers about 3,500,000 square miles, which is about 6 percent of the Earth's entire land surface—an area roughly the size of the United States. From the savannas of northern Mali, Niger, Chad, and Sudan, the Sahara stretches 1,200 miles north to the Atlas Mountains and the Libyan coast of the Mediterranean, where its sands blow across the ruins of 2,000-year-old Roman cities. From the Red Sea in the east, the desert spans the continent to the Atlantic Ocean—3,000 miles away. Nor does its influence stop at the coast. Windblown Sahara sands lie in the seabed deposits of the mid-Atlantic, and Sahara dust is carried all the way to the Caribbean and eastern South America. The Sahara alone accounts for 60 percent of all the sands and dust that are blown into the atmosphere each year—approximately 300 million tons in total, enough to build a small mountain. In the Sahara itself, airborne dust is responsible for many health problems. In Mali, for instance, where the average concentration of dust in the air is ten times greater than international health standards recommend, respiratory disease is common.

Most of the world's deserts straddle the northern and southern tropics. This is because the global pattern of air pressure and wind systems produces atmospheric conditions that trap ridges of high pressure with accompanying dry winds at those latitudes and so inhibits the formation of cloud and rain. The Sahara is larger and drier than the rest of the world's deserts because Africa is widest at the Tropic of Cancer, which puts most of the Sahara well beyond the influence of the oceans that greatly modify the temperature and humidity of air masses elsewhere. The Sahara consequently has less "weather," as the term is understood in temperate climes, than virtually any other place on Earth. The weather hardly changes from day to day. High clouds or scattered cumulus are sometimes seen, and on rare occasions they may

Beginning at Cairo, the delta disperses the Nile's water into the Mediterranean Sea through a network of shallow channels. Silts deposited by the Nile have made the delta a fertile haven as big as Vermont.

build up to produce light rain or even a heavy downpour. Predominantly, though, this is a climate of sunny days and clear nights. The Sahara receives an average of over ten hours of sunshine every day throughout the year, which means that it gets very hot indeed. Average maximum temperatures rise well above 104° F in the southern part of the desert and exceed 95° F over wide areas. The world's highest ever temperature was recorded in the Libyan desert: 136.4° F in the shade. Of course, shade is not a common feature of the desert, and the temperatures actually experienced are much higher, and the ground temperature is higher still.

As the Earth revolves around the sun between the December and June solstices, the ridge of high pressure that sits obstinately over the Sahara weakens along its northern and southern edges, respectively. Moist winds from the Mediterranean bring some rain to the northern fringes of the desert around the end of the year and from the Atlantic to the western and southern Sahara in the middle of the year. These invasions of brief seasonal rains produce the belts of scant vegetation that define the limits of the desert. Still, rain is a rare phenomenon. Monthly or even annual averages are meaningless. At In Salah in the central Algerian desert, for instance, a significant shower may occur once every ten years; it is not uncommon for one place to receive more than its annual average in a single day while another, just a few miles away, remains bone-dry. At the Kharga Oasis in Egypt children have lived to the age of seven before ever experiencing a fall of rain.

Though rain is the prime factor, it is of course vegetation that defines the limits of the desert. The location of the desert edge is not easily drawn, but it has become an important issue since the 1980s, when a succession of droughts produced anecdotal evidence of the Sahara advancing southward at an alarming rate. A study

commissioned to investigate the issue compared the southern boundary of desert vegetation in Sudan in 1958 with its location in 1975. It concluded that the desert had indeed moved between 55 and 62 miles south during that 17-year period. This caused the news media to report that the sands of the Sahara were advancing southward at a rate of 3.4 miles per year. The cumbersome term "desertification" entered the environmentalists' lexicon and quickly became a point of reference for concerns about climate change, global warming, and environmental degradation.

Meanwhile, efforts were being made to establish the facts of the matter. If the desert were indeed advancing so rapidly, its progress should be monitored and attempts made to discover what was responsible. Was it caused by short-term climate change, global warming, overgrazing by Sahelian herders, or a combination of several factors?

A 1984 field study conducted in the same part of Sudan found no evidence whatsoever of the desert's encroachment. Although this relieved concern in some quarters, at root the findings merely drew attention to inadequacies of method. If two studies produce exactly opposite results from the same body of evidence, then neither conclusion could be relied upon. The trouble is of course that such investigations are too subjective. The vegetation is sparse at the best of times on the desert fringes, and eyeball assessments of total amounts over a wide area can vary considerably. A more rigorous measuring tool was required, and soon satellite imagery was used.

Green living plants emit radiation that is recorded in the red and near-infrared spectrum measurements made by satellites. The density of red correlates to the density of living vegetation, plus the amount of rainfall. The savannas degrade into desert when the rainfall drawn in around the edges of the Sahara's high-pressure ridge falls below 7.8 inches per year. With this index established, scientists have been able to determine the location of the desert fringes and monitor their movements year by year since 1980.

Results published in 1999 show that although the size of the desert has varied significantly between 1980 and 1997 (varying by over a half a million square miles between 1984 and 1994), there has been no overall increase in size during that time. Contrary to popular belief, the Sahara has not been advancing remorselessly southward since 1980, and there is no reason to suppose that it is today.

PEERING FROM THE window as we fly at 30,000 feet over the Sahara, I am surprised to see large circles of vivid green, laid out below like counters on a grubby beige tablecloth. What miracle is this? But it is merely the benefit of water pumped from below the desert to foster the growth of cereals and alfalfa.

The desert can bloom, and nowhere more spectacularly than in the Namib or the Karoo (a semidesert, properly speaking), where seasonal rain will produce a dense carpet of flowers within days. They grow so close together that you cannot avoid crushing them underfoot. Even the most barren desert possesses the seeds and nutrients required to produce a flush of vegetation. It lacks only water, and the sun withholds life's solvent from the desert sands.

The sun beats down on the Sahara with such force that it could evaporate water to the depth of an eight-story building in the course of a year. A small lake (should it exist) would disappear within weeks, a man would be dead and desiccated within days, and a thoroughly wet towel dries within minutes. The heat is remorseless. Evaporation rapidly draws every drop of moisture into the dry air.

Although rainfall in the Sahara is rare, the fact that it usually comes in a downpour produces more vegetation than would otherwise be the case. A brief shower penetrates only the surface soils and evaporates very quickly when the sun comes out again. The rain from a heavy downpour sinks deeper, especially in sandy soils, to levels at which it is cut off from evaporation by the dry layer of sand at the surface. Four inches of rain falling over a short period will produce far more vegetation than the same amount falling in equal portions every week throughout the year.

So despite too much sunlight and too little rain, the Sahara supports a surprisingly large number of plant species. Its estimated 1,200 compares favorably with the total of 1,492 species found in the more congenial climes of the British Isles. Eighty of them are not found anywhere else in the world. As might be expected, the plants of the Sahara are distinguished by their adaptations to the harsh environment.

Plants breathe through the pores in their leaves, exhaling oxygen and inhaling the carbon dioxide they need for photosynthesis. But they can also lose up to 95 percent of available water through their leaves. They could close their pores to conserve water, but this would also cut off the supply of carbon dioxide. Desert plants must find a way of balancing one danger against the other. The lichens and algae that are found clinging to desert rocks shut down their life processes almost completely whenever water is not available, and rapidly become dry as air. The trick of their survival is the capacity to reactivate the processes when it does rain, which means they grow very slowly indeed.

Annual flowering plants, on the other hand, grow very fast. They produce the swaths of colorful flowers that are so well-known from the Namib Desert and the Karoo but less so from the Sahara. They effectively escape drought by not even attempting to live except when it rains, and then only briefly. Great banks of their seeds may lay dormant in the sand for years, even decades. A study of the Karoo flora found 34,200 viable seeds per square yard in the top three inches of the sandy soil. Their trick is to germinate with the first rain, grab available nutrients (actually more plentiful in dry sands than in humid soils, where nutrients are tied up in organic matter), mature, and set seed as quickly as possible. The process cannot be stalled or reversed. The plants have no built-in reserves. If the rains fail after the seed has germinated, the young plant will wither and die before it has flowered and set seed.

Perennial plants take no such chances. They have adopted a more selfish strategy and are more concerned with keeping themselves alive than with producing the seed of future generations. They build up reserves whenever times are good, then hunker down to keep life ticking during the bad times that inevitably follow. Among the perennials, some have developed thick, fleshy leaves (the succulents), which serve a dual purpose of both storing moisture and reducing the amount of surface with pores. Others restrict water loss by shedding first their leaves and then even whole branches until only a single small branch with a few dormant buds remains alive. The rest of the plant is dead, but life will burst forth again from those dormant buds when it rains again.

While the aboveground portion of the perennial does its best to reduce water loss, the portion below ground tries to absorb as much water as it can. In temperate zones the roots of a plant usually spread no more widely than its canopy, but in the Sahara the spread can be many times greater. Extensive root systems are common, and some plants carry the strategy to excess. For example, a small bush, *Leptadenia pyrotechnica*, stands only about 60 inches high but typically has roots that delve 38 feet underground and extend up to 33 feet all around the plant. Such a root system exploits about 30,014 cubic feet of soil (the volume of a four-bedroom two-story house)—all for a bush that would not overcrowd a suburban patio—gathering enough water to keep it going for at least four years without rain.

THE SAHARA HAS a hidden history. At its heart stand the Tassili-n-Ajjer Mountains, a sandstone massif scoured by the wind into a labyrinth of winding chasms and grotesque sandstone pillars. In this moonscape the days are scorching hot, the nights freezing cold. The wind frays the nerves and the thread of life itself never seemed so fragile. Yet in a narrow gorge a naturalist visiting the region in the early 1980s came upon a group of living cypress trees. The delicate green of their needles formed a welcome contrast to the unremitting sunburned landscape. The trees crowned a jumble of rock and wind-polished boulders, and their exposed roots twisted through crevices and beneath tilting boulders as they probed for water. The cypresses produced cones with viable seeds, but none germinated. The ground was too dry.

Tree ring analysis has established that the cypresses are between 2,000 and 3,000 years old. When they were saplings, gurgling streams ran through the Tassili-n-Ajjer Mountains. The Sahara was a well-watered savanna that supported a tremendous diversity of plants and wildlife. There were lakes teeming with fish and wildfowl. A scattering of people hunted and fished and kept herds of cattle with elegant curved horns. They harvested sorghum, and from time to time they sheltered in the shallow caves of the Tassili-n-Ajjer, where they decorated the smooth sandstone walls with paintings that tell the story of their everyday lives. They drew wildlife such as giraffe, gazelle, rhinoceros, hippopotamus, sable antelope, and elephant. They depicted scenes of hunters carrying bows and arrows, herders with cattle, and people sitting beside their huts—the arrow and the stick are present, and the hoe is in the wings.

The Tassili-n-Ajjer caves contain more than 4,000 paintings and many more rock engravings. Experts regard it as one of the world's greatest collections of prehistoric art. The Tassili artists made their paints by grinding ochers to a powder that they mixed with a liquid (not necessarily water) and applied with feathers or animal-hair brushes. They worked in vivid yellows, reds, and browns, flamboyantly and confidently, in a style that would have made Picasso proud. The oldest of the paintings are thought to date back to 6000 B.C. and the most recent date from before 100 B.C. Those 6,000 years span a progression of human activities and interests that is most evocatively recorded in the paintings.

The early paintings show hunters and wild animals—including a giant but now extinct buffalo—and masked figures whose sinuous bodies exactly convey the movements of a dance. One enigmatic masked figure from the early period evokes a sense of ritual or ceremony. It stands alone, about five feet, abstract though clearly human, sprouting plants from its arms and thighs. Herders entered the gallery around 5000 B.C., covering the walls (and some earlier paintings) with their bold pictures of piebald cattle with sweeping horns and swishing tails. Their depictions of people and their activities are more realistic than in the earlier paintings. Two men are chasing a runaway steer, another is tethering a docile, flop-eared cow that perhaps is about to be milked, while other men appear to be engaged in animated conversation, and a woman lounges provocatively beside them.

From 1200 B.C. paintings of horses and chariots appear in the Tassili galleries, documenting the time when people from the Mediterranean were in contact with the inhabitants of these central Saharan regions. A horse-drawn chariot carries two men, one holding the reins and the other what looks like a spear in his left hand. A woman in a long skirt watches as the chariot passes, and a loping dog chases after it. The urgent activity of these scenes suggests an invasion by outsiders. Indeed, the people were being threatened—but not by coastal invaders. The environment itself had turned against them. The remorseless influence of a changing global climate sucked the moisture from the land, burned off the vegetation, and created the barren desert wastes.

Rock art in the depths of the Sahara depicting giraffe and other savanna animals dates from between 8,000 and 3,000 years ago—when much of the Sahara was a lush savanna.

FOLLOWING PAGES: **Cairo, seen here across the Nile and the Sixth of October Bridge, is home to ten million people and growing fast. Housing is a serious problem since people want to build on Egypt's already scarce agricultural land.**

The old fort at Fachi, Niger, where caravans halt briefly to water their camels, was fortified during colonial times when Tuareg opposition to French rule often erupted into violence.

Like folk memories lingering on from better times, the very name Tassili-n-Ajjer means "plateau of the rivers." The paintings are like snapshots of an Elysian paradise decorating the walls of what is now a Hadean furnace. No other place on Earth offers such a compelling image of climate change. In a twinkling of geological time a garden became a desert. The sun, which in more congenial times had nurtured life, evicted all but those with the capacity to adapt to a completely different way of life. The cypresses hang on in their original form, but soon they too will be gone forever.

But it would be a mistake to think that the drying up of the Sahara was a unique event. On the contrary, it had happened before. This was merely the latest in a series of climate swings to afflict the region. And of course, with global climate as the agent of change, it was not only the Sahara that was affected—the whole world was involved. The Sahara is but a local record, but its isolation and lack of extensive disturbance by people make it an invaluable source of information on the Earth's climatic history. And the evidence reveals a pattern of dramatic variation.

Seven thousand years ago the Sahara was the landscape of savannas, lakes, and rivers that inspired the earliest Tassili artists. Yet 15,000 years ago it was even drier than it is today. Twenty-five thousand years ago it was wetter than even in the time of the Tassili artists. The oscillations from wet to dry and back again, each spanning thousands of years, have been going on for millions of years. Globally they are caused by the geometry of the Earth's orbit around the sun, which gives rise to variations in the amount of solar radiation striking the Earth, measured on a scale of tens and hundreds of thousands of years. Forty million years ago, for instance, the Sahara was dominated by a network of great rivers flowing from east to west across the continent from the mountains then standing along what is now the Egyptian coast of the Red Sea.

This trans–African drainage system (or TADS, as it is known) was twice the size of the Congo Basin, three times the size of the Nile. Its major channels were hundreds of feet deep. Its broadest valleys were up to 20 miles across—as wide as the English Channel. Its existence was barely guessed at (though the vast reservoirs of water known to lie under the Sahara were a clue) until the 1980s, when satellite imagery revealed the network of ancient watercourses. Ground surveys subsequently confirmed their age, size, and extent. TADS flowed for at least 20 million years until about 15 million years ago, when it was disrupted by geological uplift in the region of the Red Sea. The waterways dried up and gradually filled with windblown sands—hiding a drainage system that was as great as any the world has known.

in the development of agriculture and settled human society in Africa. The Sahara acted as a pump, drawing people from surrounding regions during good times, and driving them out again as conditions deteriorated. The Nile Valley, for its part, was a refuge for people retreating from the desert, and then a reservoir from which the desert was repopulated as conditions improved. In the process, the Sahara's inhabitants applied the human talent for adaptation and innovation to greater effect than elsewhere on the continent. Paradoxically, many of the developments that subsequently became the foundation blocks of human society in Africa occurred first in what is now arid desert. The first pots known to be made in Africa were fashioned from Saharan clays over 9,000 years ago. The continent's first cereal crops—sorghum, which is indigenous to Africa—were planted in the Sahara 8,000 years ago. Africa's earliest known domesticated cattle were herded across the savannas of the Sahara more than 6,000 years ago.

Until 10,000 years ago, everyone in Africa lived by hunting and gathering. The Sahara of lakes, streams, and ample grasslands spawned new variations. For the first time in Africa, distinct groups began to follow different ways of life. The paintings of the Tassili-n-Ajjer confirm the presence of herders and their cattle. Harpoons and arrowheads show that people were fishing and hunting. Grindstones are found everywhere, suggesting if not always the cultivation of crops, then at least the gathering and preparation of wild grains for cooking. Pottery is equally common, and the invention of pottery was an especially important development. The pots not only facilitated the collection of water and storage of food but also gave women a means of boiling up a gruel that could be used as a substitute for a mother's milk. Reducing the breast-feeding period shortened the spacing between births, which led to an appreciable increase in the population.

All in all, the Sahara appears to have been a veritable Garden of Eden at this time, with abundant wild resources, cultivated cereals, and cows, which enabled

THOUGH THE SAHARA today is not the sort of place that would appeal to a farmer, it has played a crucial role in the development of agriculture in Africa. We might think that the Nile was the birthplace of farming in Africa, but the Sahara was far more important. Ancient Egyptian civilizations did develop the practice of extensive agriculture, but the crops they grew—wheat, barley, peas, and lentils—all had been domesticated first in the Fertile Crescent of the Near East and were a fairly recent introduction to the Nile Valley. They arrived long after the cultivation of indigenous African food crops had begun in what is now the empty and waterless Sahara.

The verdant green croplands of the Nile Valley are the very antithesis of the bleached Saharan sands through which the river flows, but these two contrasting features together constituted a primary force

Caravans with thousands of camels once plied the route to Bilma across the Sahara, carrying salt from the desert to the Sahel and forest regions of West Africa. Modern caravans usually number 100 or so.

people to fill their pots with milk as well as honey. Such affluence is probably an exaggeration, but a mixed agricultural economy was emerging, accompanied by cultural diversity. Climatic and ecological reconstructions of conditions at the time show that the region could have supported nearly 21 million cattle, which in turn could have supported millions of people. These figures are hypothetical, but they give an idea of how many people moved into the rest of Africa as the Sahara dried out again. The cultures of the stick and the hoe would spread throughout the continent. Not until the arrival of the camel in Africa sparked trans–Saharan trade between the second and fifth centuries A.D. did people venture once again into the Sahara.

Like many people, I was brought up with the idea that Timbuktu is the most faraway place imaginable. So it was an agreeable surprise to discover that I could fly there from Mopti, in Mali, where I had been reporting on some archaeological work. Since the flights operated only twice a week, most visitors made only a day trip. I stayed over, though, and as the only visitor in town I soon made the acquaintance of Mohamed Ali, who would leap from the shade of the palms whenever I ventured from the hotel, insisting that I should climb aboard one of his camels standing nearby and ride out into the desert. Mohamed was a Tuareg, and his family ran a camel train bringing gravestone-size slabs of salt to Timbuktu from the Sahara mines at Taoudenni, nearly 400 miles away. I declined the offer of a ride, but drank mint tea with him and his family at their house and talked about our different ways of life. On hearing that I had a 15-year-old daughter, Mohamed immediately offered 200 camels for her hand, assuring me that she would be happy and well cared for. He even wrote her a letter, offering to send camels for the journey to Timbuktu if I refused to buy her a plane ticket.

Red tape probably would have hindered Mohamed's camels more than anything else if Alice had accepted his invitation, for the camel is probably the toughest creature on Earth. It can drink as much as 40 gallons in a single session, then go without water for up to nine days. This means it can forage up to four and a half days from the nearest water, giving it a food-gathering range of over 250 miles (the elephant has a range of less than 30 miles). Camels cope so well because they tolerate a high degree of heat without perspiring. Instead, their body temperature rises and falls with the temperature, while their "radiator and heat exchanger" maintains an equable brain temperature. Furthermore, the camel's kidneys do not need large quantities of water to flush out wastes from the system. When nearly out of stored water, a camel's urine is more sludge than liquid, and its dung is dry enough to be used on a fire almost as soon as it is produced.

As with water, so with food. Camels eat a lot when they can, and survive for a long time when they cannot. A highly specialized enzyme system enables them to adjust rapidly to fluctuating conditions of want and plenty. Only the pig matches the rate at which a camel converts surplus food to fat, and when it comes to utilizing fat reserves, the camel is in a class by itself. Other ruminants lose muscle tissue when starving, but the camel's enzyme system enables it to live off its fat reserve until it is exhausted.

The origins of the camel lie not in Africa, nor in Arabia, as might be supposed, but in North America, where the fossil remains of a rabbit-size creature that lived 50 million years ago have been identified as the progenitor of the camel family. By about two million years ago the descendants of these diminutive ancestors had grown and spread via the Bering Strait throughout the semiarid regions of Asia and the Middle East. Another branch of the family spread south to become the llama and alpaca of South America. Of the two species of camel today, the Bactrian with its thick coat and two humps is ideally suited to the deserts of its central Asian habitat, which can be extremely cold in winter.

The single-humped dromedary is equally well adapted to the extreme heat of deserts.

The dromedary was domesticated 4,000 years ago in southern Arabia, and it rapidly superseded the ox-drawn cart as the preferred means of long-distance transport throughout the Middle East. With only two toes on each foot, joined by a web of skin, the camel's foot splays out as it walks and does not sink into even the softest sand. This enables it to carry twice as much as an ox at double the speed across terrain impassable to any wheeled vehicle. In due course the camel was shipped across the Red Sea, becoming established first in the Horn of Africa. It spread across the continent via the belt of the Sahel, west to the Atlantic, and north to the Nile Valley, where it appears to have arrived around 600 to 800 B.C.

In East Africa and along the fringes of the Sahara from Somalia to Senegal, camels enabled nomadic pastoralists to exploit the arid regions where cattle could not survive, adding another dimension to the existing network of interactions that were beginning to characterize society in Africa. In the Sahara itself, camels began to carry goods and people between oases and across the entire breadth of the desert. The trans–Saharan trade routes had existed for centuries—zigzagging between oases and refuges such as the Tassili-n-Ajjer Mountains—but their capacity was severely restricted by the forage and water requirements of pack animals. The introduction of camels—the "ships of the desert"—extended both the trade routes and the volume of goods that could be carried. Probably the forebears of the present-day Tuareg first used camels on the trans–Saharan trade routes.

The name Tuareg comes from an Arabic term meaning "God forsaken," which is presumably a comment on their resistance to the advance of Islam into the central Sahara during the 11th century A.D. The Tuareg's vigorous opposition was primarily commercial and only secondarily motivated by religious concerns. The interest of the Arab traders was keenly focused on the considerable quantities of gold believed to lie for the taking in the ancient rocks to the south of the Sahara, in what is now Mali and Ghana. An encyclopedia of the Muslim world compiled circa A.D. 900 reported: "It is said that beyond the source of the Nile is darkness and beyond the darkness are waters that make the gold grow.... gold grows in the sand as carrots do, and is plucked at sunrise."

Gold had embellished the cultures of ancient Egypt, Greece, and Rome, but it was never a feature of indigenous African culture; the greater part of Africa's extensive gold deposits was untouched until foreign demand stimulated exploitation. But the trade did not get under way until the introduction of the camel made trans–Saharan journeys practical. Gold coins struck in Carthage between A.D. 296 and 311 are probably the first indication of a trans–Saharan gold trade. The amount of coinage was small to begin with, but the increasing volume of gold circulating in Roman North Africa from the fourth century A.D. indicates a substantial trans–Saharan trade in the metal—no other source could have sufficed.

Coins and a bill of sale witness the slave trade: "My slave called Luis from the land of Angola...for the price of four hundred fifty pesos."

With the Arab conquest of all North Africa by 711 A.D., the demand for West African gold intensified, and the trans–Saharan trade was boosted still further when Europe began minting gold coins for the first time since the fall of the western Roman Empire: at Florence in 1252, in France from 1254, and in England from 1257. Between the 11th and the 17th centuries, West Africa was the leading supplier of gold to the international economy, and in the late Middle Ages it accounted for almost two-thirds of world production. But the trans–Saharan share dwindled to a trickle toward the end of the 15th century, when the Portuguese finally achieved their ambition of outflanking the trade with

a sea route to the West African coast. Their caravels landed on the shores of what is now Ghana in 1472. The trading center they established soon became known as El Mina (the mine), the seaboard as the Gold Coast (the name it bears still), and for decades the Portuguese were shipping tons of gold to Europe.

Though the gold was plentiful, the Portuguese had difficulty paying for it. Horses did not live long in the equatorial climate and there was a limit to the amount of cloth and sundry goods that the Akan people who controlled the Gold Coast trade would accept. Firearms were requested, but banned as an item of trade by the Pope, who feared they might reach the hostile forces of Islam. However, the Portuguese discovered an African commodity that the Akan would readily accept in exchange for their gold, one that was abundantly available a short distance along the coast: slaves.

When the Portuguese arrived on the Gold Coast, a branch of the Akan now known as the Asante were expanding throughout the forested regions of the hinterland where the gold was mined. They needed more labor for forest clearance, farming, and mining than their own numbers could supply. They were already acquiring slaves from the north in exchange for gold, and now they began to get slaves from the south as well. The Portuguese acquired them at anchorages along the Bight of Benin and the Niger Delta, where Benin and Igbo leaders readily handed over people they had captured in exchange for trade goods. Thus the seaboard adjacent to the Gold Coast acquired the sobriquet by which it is still identified in some reputable atlases—the Slave Coast—and the Portuguese became middlemen in a network of indigenous exchange. Between 1500

and 1535 they shipped 10,000 to 12,000 slaves across the Bight of Benin from the Slave Coast to the Gold Coast.

Meanwhile, they were also shipping significant numbers back to Portugal. The first human cargo arrived at Lagos on August 8, 1444, and an account of the event written by the royal librarian survives:

Very early in the morning, by reason of the heat, the seamen began to make ready their boats, and to take out those captives, and carry them on shore.... But what heart could be so hard as not to be pierced with piteous feeling to see that company? For some kept their heads low and their faces bathed in tears, looking upon one another; others stood groaning very dolorously, looking up to the heavens,

Salt evaporation ponds at Fachi, Niger, attest to the transformation of the Sahara from well-watered savanna to desert. Ten thousand years ago this region was a vast lake. Salts leached from the surrounding landscape accumulated in the lake; the lake's evaporation created a salt pan.

fixing their eyes upon it, crying out loudly, as if asking help of the Father of Nature; others struck their faces with the palms of their hands, throwing themselves at full length upon the ground; others made lamentations in the manner of a dirge, after the custom of their country. And though we could not understand a word of their language, the sound of it right well accorded with the measure of their sadness.

But sentiment did not deter the traders. African slaves were brought to Portugal in such numbers that by the 1550s they made up nearly 10 percent of the Lisbon population and were a large part of the country's agricultural workforce. Inevitably, the profits flowing into Portugal from the west coast of Africa caught the attention of Europe's other maritime nations. An edict issued by Pope Nicholas V in 1455 granted the Portuguese exclusive rights to trade with the inhabitants of West Africa (whom they were also supposed to convert to Christianity), but their monopoly was steadily eroded by interlopers. Their mode of operation was to lie in wait for Portuguese ships setting out on their return voyage and then seize both vessel and cargo. In 1562 the English adventurer John Hawkins took things a step further when he acquired 300 slaves from West Africa, "partly by the sword, and partly by other meanes," and sailed them across the Atlantic to the Caribbean islands, where they were set to work in the recently established sugar plantations.

Hawkins's voyage heralded the moment after which Europe's sweet tooth would radically shift the course of history in Africa and the Americas. Sugar was in high demand and Hawkins bears the dubious distinction of starting the triangle trade in the Atlantic. Goods from Europe were exchanged for slaves in Africa that were exchanged for sugar in the Caribbean, which sold in Europe at a profit that returned the initial investment many times over. Hawkins became a very rich man. When he was knighted, he made a point of having African slaves depicted prominently on his coat of arms. Over the next three centuries, more than nine million slaves were shipped across the Atlantic. The largest number, 42 percent, were sold to plantation owners on the sugar islands of the Caribbean; 38 percent were shipped to Brazil (by the Portuguese);

fewer than 5 percent were landed in what is now the United States, while between 10 and 20 percent died en route. Large numbers of slaves from West Africa also were transported across the Sahara for sale in North Africa, and yet more were shipped from East Africa to Arabia.

The Tuareg doubtless participated in the trans–Saharan slave trade. They probably were customers as well, since slavery has always been a feature of Tuareg society. Even today a man will speak unashamedly of his family's slaves, but these days it is slavery at its most benign. Most slaves are destitute farmers and their families who have attached themselves to the Tuareg as a way of staying alive. They do all the hard work but are integrated into Tuareg society at the family level, and their daughters may even marry a Tuareg. It seems that, from the Tuareg point of view, the principal reason for acquiring slaves has been to assimilate them and increase the size of the family unit.

WHILE THE TRANS–SAHARAN trade in gold and slaves brought undeserved misery and death to millions, the Tuareg were also transporting a commodity that helped to sustain life: salt. The Sahara is the greatest repository of salt in Africa. When the lakes and waterways of the wet period began to evaporate, the receding waters leached salts from the soil; the lakes eventually dried out and became vast salt pans. The lake that filled the basin north of Bilma in Niger 10,000 years ago was at least 75 miles long and 12 miles wide. As the water receded, the lake bed became permeated with salt at concentrations of 50 percent to depths of more than 19 feet. The total quantity of salt in the basin is estimated to be several million tons. Similarly, vast Saharan salt deposits are located at Taoudenni and Teghaza in northern Mali and at Tichit in Mauritania. This high-quality salt is located in the heart of

the world's greatest desert, hundreds of miles from the people who need it and have no other source.

The constituents of salt, sodium and chloride, are essential to many functions of the body, but they are excreted after being used and must be replaced. A daily intake of about 0.04 ounce meets the requirements of an average person, even in tropical regions. Most people get enough salt from their everyday diet, especially those who eat milk and meat, which are naturally saltier than vegetable foods. But people everywhere have developed a taste for salt that encourages them to consume more than they need.

Salt is the primordial narcotic, and people have been hooked on it since time immemorial. Throughout the world, salt has been the most widely sought-after food supplement, and wherever salt was not available, the desire for it became a strong incentive for the development of trade. Indeed, the movement of salt from source to consumer in Africa probably marked the world's first long-distance trade routes. They were so clearly defined by the 16th century that Portuguese explorers made a practice of following the salt routes to the interior. And the size of the salt trade by then was impressive.

Given that every person uses a basic 0.4 ounce of salt per day, a rural community of 250 people in Africa needed just a little over one ton each year. Personal taste, medicinal use, and curing of skins and food probably doubled this requirement, and the needs of livestock would have doubled it again. Thus, to cover all its needs, a community of 250 people required at least 4.4 tons of salt per year. One thousand people required 17.6 tons; one million required 17,600 tons. At this time the total number of people using salt in

Between one and six million tons of high-quality salt lie in the Bilma Basin. At the height of the Sahara trade, 70,000 camel loads (about 6,600 tons) were exported from the region each year.

FOLLOWING PAGES: With splayed feet and webbed toes, the single-hump camel can carry heavy loads over soft sands that no other transport could cross.

Africa cannot have been much less than ten million. The total annual requirement was thus 176,320 tons. For the camels that carried the salt from the Sahara deposits to the savanna, it was 800,000 loads.

These rough figures indicate how the demand for salt stimulated trade in Africa. By the 19th century, when European explorers first succeeded in reaching the fringes of the central Sahara, the volume of the trade was vast. One eyewitness account reports that as many as 70,000 camel loads of salt were exported from the Bilma region alone each year. The Bilma salt traveled due south, supplying primarily the salt-deficient Sahelian regions of Niger, Chad, and northern Nigeria, with significant amounts traded onward from there to people in the forest regions of

Cameroon and southeastern Nigeria, where salt was equally scarce. Rock salt from deposits in the western Sahara at Tichit, Teghaza, and Taoudenni also traveled south to join routes supplying the Sahel and forest regions extending from Nigeria to Senegal.

The Niger River was a major artery of the Saharan salt-trading network. Timbuktu, the city of fable poised where the Niger curves eastward in its sweep around the ancient gold-laden rock core of West Africa, was the clearinghouse. Within living memory, tens of thousands of camels congregated at Timbuktu to join the twice-yearly salt caravans. Once on their way, the caravans spanned over 15 miles of the 800-mile desert trail to Teghaza and Taoudenni, and they returned to Timbuktu with between 4,000 and 5,500

The maize is growing well for Suleyman Barka at Timia, Niger. Though the Tuareg are renowned as intrepid desert nomads, economic pressures have persuaded many to adopt a semisedentary life.

tons of salt each year. This was pure rock salt, in the form of slabs weighing about 65 pounds each, white and smooth as marble gravestones.

From Timbuktu the salt was carried by canoe upstream to Jenne-jeno, from there by donkey to the edge of the forest, and then by human porters through the forest to the most distant settlements. At each stage its value was inflated by the costs of transportation and the markups of the middlemen. By the time a slab of Saharan salt had reached Kong in what is now the Ivory Coast, or Gonja in modern Ghana, it had traveled nearly 1,200 miles and was as much an article of prestige as of utility. Arabs visiting Mali in the tenth century reported that to avoid waste, rock salt was always licked, never ground and sprinkled. Even in recent centuries, salt was sold in Gonja for 60 times its price in Bilma.

For every last grain of salt that came into the region, something of equivalent value had to go out. Ivory was one item that found a ready market, providing farmers with an income from the elephants they were constantly chasing from their fields. Another was the kola nut, an addictive stimulant whose bitter taste relieved thirst and became a symbol of hospitality throughout the Sahel and Saharan regions of West Africa. The nut stimulated long-distance trade, and by the 13th century it was regularly carried across the Sahara to markets in North Africa—and thence even farther afield. By the late 20th century the influence of the kola nut had embraced the planet as an ingredient of the world's most popular soft drink: Coca-Cola.

The trade in Saharan salt continues but at a fraction of its previous volume, since cheap manufactured salt is now so widely available. It is uncertain whether it can go on for much longer.

The Tuareg fought the Arabs, they fought the French colonial administrations, and they have constantly rebelled against the governments of inde-

pendent Africa, which have claimed the Saharan regions that they consider their own. But while fighting fiercely to retain their independent rights, they have never at any time formed a single political unit. Instead they have remained seven independent groups, each maintaining political and cultural distance from the others.

Today there are about 1.5 million Tuareg living in the Sahara regions of Algeria, Mali, and Nigeria. The northern Tuareg, custodians of the Tassili-n-Ajjer paintings and the epitome of the blue-veiled warlords of the Sahara, are now comparatively few in number, and their traditional way of life is all but abandoned. During colonial times their seminomadic pastoralism was supplemented by the development of gardens (cultivated by slaves), and the camel caravans that once crossed the desert to the north were replaced by convoys of trucks. For many of the northern Tuareg, satisfying the curiosity of tourists became the only way they could sustain even a semblance of their former proud glory. Hiring themselves and their camels to local tour operators, working as guides and cooks, they earned enough money to carry on a traditional life.

Now even that has gone, along with the tourist industry that the Algerian crisis swept from the region in the 1990s. But although most northern Tuareg now live in villages, perhaps 1,000 still follow a seminomadic existence, largely as a consequence of the government having declared their homelands to be a national park. There was a strong political motive to this move (with so much trouble in the north, the last thing the Algerian government wanted was a Tuareg uprising in the south), but it has brought many benefits to the Tuareg involved. The government provided tents and some cash assistance and employs an estimated 400 Gardiens du Parc who each get about 100 dollars per month. Though not all the eligible Tuareg approve of these arrangements, their traditional way of life probably could not survive without them.

As night falls in the desert between Fachi and Bilma, the temperature drops dramatically. Fires lit to cook the evening meal also provide welcome for the men. The clear skies of the cold desert night enable the leader to check the caravan's position and course.

For the Tuareg in the southern Sahara, the situation is only marginally better. Trucks are beginning to replace camels on the salt routes from Bilma to the markets in northern Nigeria, but most of the trade is still left to the Tuareg and their camels, though even they struggle to cover their costs.

Last year's caravan was a financial disaster for Mahmouda, whose family gave up the seminomadic way of life a generation ago and settled at the Timia Oasis in Niger. They grow maize, vegetables, and fruit, and keep goats and cattle. The family's slaves take care of the farm work, Mahmouda's mother—following the matricentric traditions of Tuareg society—handles the affairs of family and kin, while Mahmouda and his age-mates hanker for the nomadic life they knew as children. They still keep a herd of camels and each year they set out on the 270-mile desert crossing to Bilma, where they buy salt to sell in the markets of northern Nigeria, another 370 miles to the south.

The round-trip takes five months. Ten men and 100 camels must walk up to 30 miles a day, often trudging through the sands for 16 hours at a stretch in temperatures that can rise to 120°F in the shade—and shade is a largely hypothetical concept. Fodder is cut and packed in bales for the camels, water skins and food bags are filled, prayers for success and safe return are offered. The journey is planned with military precision, but things can still go wrong. Last year, on the long trek from Bilma, several of the salt-laden camels died of exhaustion before the caravan reached the markets. Their cargo had to be abandoned with them in the deserts, wiping out all hope of profit as well as everything Mahmouda had invested in the salt. This is the last salt caravan that Mahmouda will lead. He is taking his son, Adam, with him this time, so that he may begin to learn the ways of the Tuareg

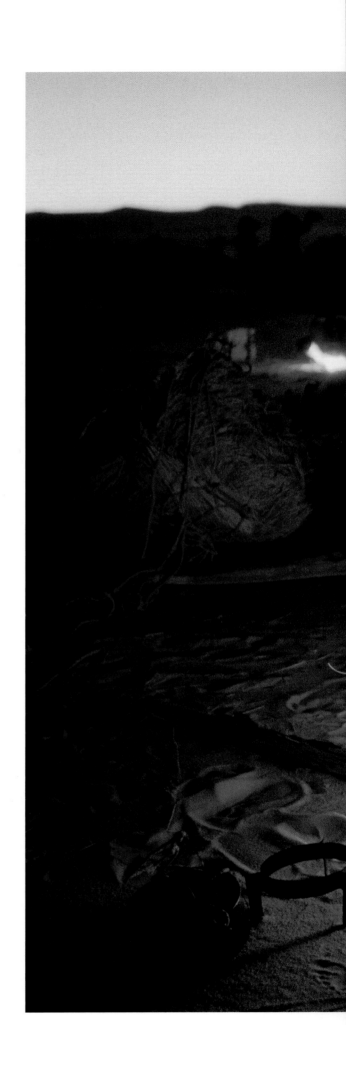

salt trade. Adam is ten years old. No wonder he looks nervous as he leads the head camel away from the mountains and out into the desert.

IN THE FAR-GONE days when Adam's ancestors decorated the cave walls of Tassili-n-Ajjer, the rains that filled the lake basin at Bilma poured even more heavily on the highlands of central Africa, where the Nile begins its long journey to the Mediterranean. Previously, the river had flowed erratically, at low volumes, and parts of the watercourse often dried completely during the hottest months of the year. But the onset of the wet period enlarged the river's catchment area considerably. Rivers from the Ethiopian Highlands joined the flow, eventually contributing more than four times as much water as the central African Highlands. The Nile began to flow freely all year-round, though the volume of the flow still varied with the seasons. The seasonal floods could be huge, sweeping fiercely down the valley and engulfing the plains far beyond its banks. Around 7,200 years ago, for instance, the river rose to heights of 52 feet above the modern floodplain on a number of occasions. This was not an environment that people could inhabit in safety for more than short periods at a time, but as the river scoured a deeper and wider watercourse for itself, the floods became less dramatic, more predictable. The farmers who had retreated into the Nile Valley when the Sahara turned dry settled permanently on a plain enriched with fertile silts washed down from the volcanic highlands of the south.

By 5,000 years ago the river's annual floods had created over 6,900 square miles of cultivable land in Egypt. This narrow strip of fertile land winding through the desert was inhabited by about half a million people, who were concentrated most densely downstream from Aswan, and around the delta where present-day Cairo is situated. In these regions the cultures of the Sahara and the Near East combined to give rise to a unique and stupendous civilization.

The Nile Valley of the ancient Egyptians was essentially a state unified under the control of a single ruler, the pharaoh, and an elite bureaucracy (often members of the ruling family). The pharaoh was regarded as a divine being—the living personification of the sun god Ra and counterpart of Osiris, god of the land of the dead. This link between the living and the dead explains the importance the ancient Egyptians attached to the burial and preparations for the afterlife of pharaohs. The magnificence of the pyramids and the royal tombs of the Nile Valley tells of the human and material resources that the elite had at their disposal. But none of it would have been possible without the Nile flood silt to rejuvenate the fields.

For 3,000 years the Egyptians reaped the benefits of the Nile. They worked the land with the plow, and invented the shadoof (a simple cantilevered water bucket) and the *saqqiyah* (an ox-driven waterwheel) to raise water from the river and irrigate their fields. The empire's surplus production endowed them with time enough to discover the principles of astronomy and mathematics, invent a written language, and create numerous pictures and statues depicting their society, culture, and beliefs. They worked with copper and gold. They hoarded gemstones and made exquisite jewelry. Yet they never advanced beyond the age of bronze. The smelting of iron was delayed in the Nile Valley, despite its proximity to Anatolia, where the technology was first developed. The reason was probably twofold: There was insufficient timber to supply the enormous amount of charcoal required for the smelting process, and they did not really need iron. Bronze farming implements were perfectly adequate for working the soft alluvial soils of the floodplain. The Egyptians were given a lesson in the limitations of bronze when they were overwhelmed between 671 and 664 B.C. by Assyrian forces wielding iron weapons.

History moves on—Assyrians, Greeks, Romans, Turks, French, British, and, finally, Egyptian independence—but none of their heroes would have left a mark on its pages but for the beneficence of the Nile.

Egypt's absolute dependence on the river that gives it life has never been more stark than it is today.

A hundred and fifty years ago, Egypt had five million acres of farmland and five million citizens. Now it has little more than seven million acres of farmland and 69 million citizens. Every nine months there are another million mouths to feed. By 2025 there will be just over 95 million Egyptians—and they will all want food, water, services, a job, and somewhere to live. The trouble is of course that 75 percent of Egypt is barren desert. Few people want to live even on the fringes of the desert, so over 90 percent of the population live where previous generations had grown crops. In the delta and along the banks of the Nile, industrial complexes, houses, and roads are built on the very land that should be feeding the country. In the delta alone, urban areas increased by 58 percent between 1972 and 1990. If this trend continues, Egypt will lose 12 percent of its total agricultural area by 2010. Already Egypt has to import six million tons of grain a year, and the situation is likely to get worse. Egypt is trying to reclaim land from its vast deserts.

Indigo robe, handwoven belt, and distinctive knife are icons of Tuareg resourcefulness in the harsh environment of the Sahara.

At least 9.8 million acres were reclaimed in the 30 years to 1990, for instance, but the total area under cultivation rose by only about 1.2 million acres.

More irrigated farmland, drawing more water from the Nile, seems the obvious answer, but there are problems here too. The Nile's bounty is not unlimited, and other countries upstream also have populations that are growing apace. Sudan, Uganda, Kenya, and Ethiopia all have population-growth and food-supply problems that the waters of the Nile might ease. But any increase in the quantities taken from the river would diminish the amount available to Egypt. The Nile has been at the heart of the regional foreign policy that has been pur-sued by Egypt and its government has never hesitated to use the threat of war. The stakes are high, but the issue is covered by international agreements drawn up when the situation was less critical, and attempts are being made to find a way of satisfying all parties.

When confronted with seemingly insurmountable problems, people have often demonstrated a talent for finding ingenious solutions. The constraints of a desert environment and an unpredictable river inspired the innovations upon which the Nile civilizations were founded. Land and water are still the most pressing issues in Egypt, but while engineers search for new solutions to the old problems and politicians strive to avert conflict, the country abounds with the testimony of past successes. With that ribbon of green, humanity has defied the desert. The monuments of ancient Egypt at Giza, Memphis, and Luxor show what those ancient people were capable of doing, and their legacy persists. In the rural landscape, the essential issues of humanity's relationship with the environment remain unchanged. Every farmer knows that working against the natural order courts disaster. The desert can reclaim all that has been so hard-won.

So there is a measure of hope in the knowledge that many of the plants, animals, fish, and birds that the ancient Egyptians included in their paintings can still be found in the region. Farmers tend their rows of tomatoes and lettuce to the cooing of palm doves, the cries of the crested lark, and the call of the hoopoe—birds that were here 5,000 years ago. Ducks and painted snipe fly into the lagoons at dusk, herons stalk the shallows, and swallows skim the water, taking on fuel for the final stage of their flight from Africa to Europe.

The Tuareg are the undisputed lords of the Sahara. No other people are so at home in the desert's featureless wastes. Swathed in robes of blue and indigo, guided by the stars, they have led camel caravans across the sands for centuries. Fiercely independent, their wanderings knew no boundaries, but only the camel made them possible.

The ships of the desert were introduced to the Sahara about 1,500 years ago. Surefooted, capable of going without water for days on end, camels enabled the Tuareg to become traders who ventured fearlessly into the Sahara's ocean of sand.

Tuareg caravans carried gold, ivory, and slaves across the Sahara from West Africa to the Mediterranean, returning with Arab and European luxury goods, and salt. The salt came from huge deposits left in the Sahara's ancient dried-out lakes and found ready markets in the forests and grasslands of West Africa, where natural supplies of salt are rare.

There was a time when the value of salt increased 60-fold over the 1,240-mile journey from mine to market. Salt from the desert bought gold from the forest. But the value fell as the volume of trade increased. By the 19th century, caravans up to 15 miles long were transporting 5,000 tons of salt a year from the desert. And in its turn, the 20th century brought yet more changes. Nowadays, many Tuareg are settled farmers. Some bring salt from the desert in trucks. But there are still a few who follow the traditional ways.

At Timia, a Tuareg village in the foothills of the Air Mountains in Niger, Salahou is helping to load the camels. Tomorrow the caravan will set off for the Bilma Oasis, a journey of 270 miles across the sands and shifting dunes of the Sahara—some of the cruelest terrain on Earth. At Bilma the men will load the camels with salt, then head south to sell their cargo in the markets of northern Nigeria before returning to Timia. The round trip covers nearly 1,860 miles. It will be months before Salahou sees home again.

Ten-year-old Adam is about to leave his childhood behind (left). This year, instead of merely standing with his father's camels as they wait to be loaded, Adam will go with them into the heart of the Sahara. As the eldest son, it is time for him to join the family business.

Adam has lived on the edge of the Sahara all his life but has never ventured into the brutal emptiness of the desert. He is a tad apprehensive. "I've heard that the devil lives in the desert and that makes me scared," he says.

But it is not the devil that pitches him into a mock battle on the caravan trail (above). The men in masks are his relatives in disguise. "This is Adam's initiation," his uncle Ibouchi explains. "Anyone who does this journey for the first time has this test." Adam has taken a first step toward manhood.

"Every day I pray to God," says Adam's grandmother, Tamakoit.
"I pray that Adam and his father will come back with their
lives. I pray for their deliverance." "We give thanks to God
for our deliverance," says Ibouchi.

Girls from the village (above), looking on as the caravan is prepared for departure, will miss their friends. While the men are away, the women take care of things in the village —praying for the caravan's safe return.

On the night before the caravan leaves, boys from the village join Adam to sing verses from the Koran in his family's nomadic home (left), a little way from Timia. It has been this way for centuries. Every Tuareg journey begins and ends in prayer. The masters of the desert know that they survive in the Sahara only with God's protection.

Rain

forest

The tropical rain forest is a secretive place. Like a protecting veil, a vast green canopy conceals its mysteries from prying eyes, and an awesome tangle of trees, shrubs, vines, and creepers deters those who would trespass in its domain.

But though secretive and forbidding, the tropical rain forest throbs with the primeval essence of life on Earth. Through countless millennia, it has stood wherever warmth and moisture were sufficient, expanding and contracting with the changes of climate, but always preserving a precious store of life's diversity at its core. Unchanging in form while varying in size, the tropical rain forest stands as an icon of the stability and equilibrium of nature—an anchor for the spirit in a rapidly changing world.

Humans evolved from a forest-dwelling ancestor (and our closest cousins— the chimpanzees and gorillas—are there still), but evolutionary adaptations to the savanna environment left humanity poorly equipped for life in the forests. Fewer people live in the Congo Basin forests than in Kentucky, though they are 21 times larger than the state.

A new policy of selective felling may preserve the Cameroon rain forest.

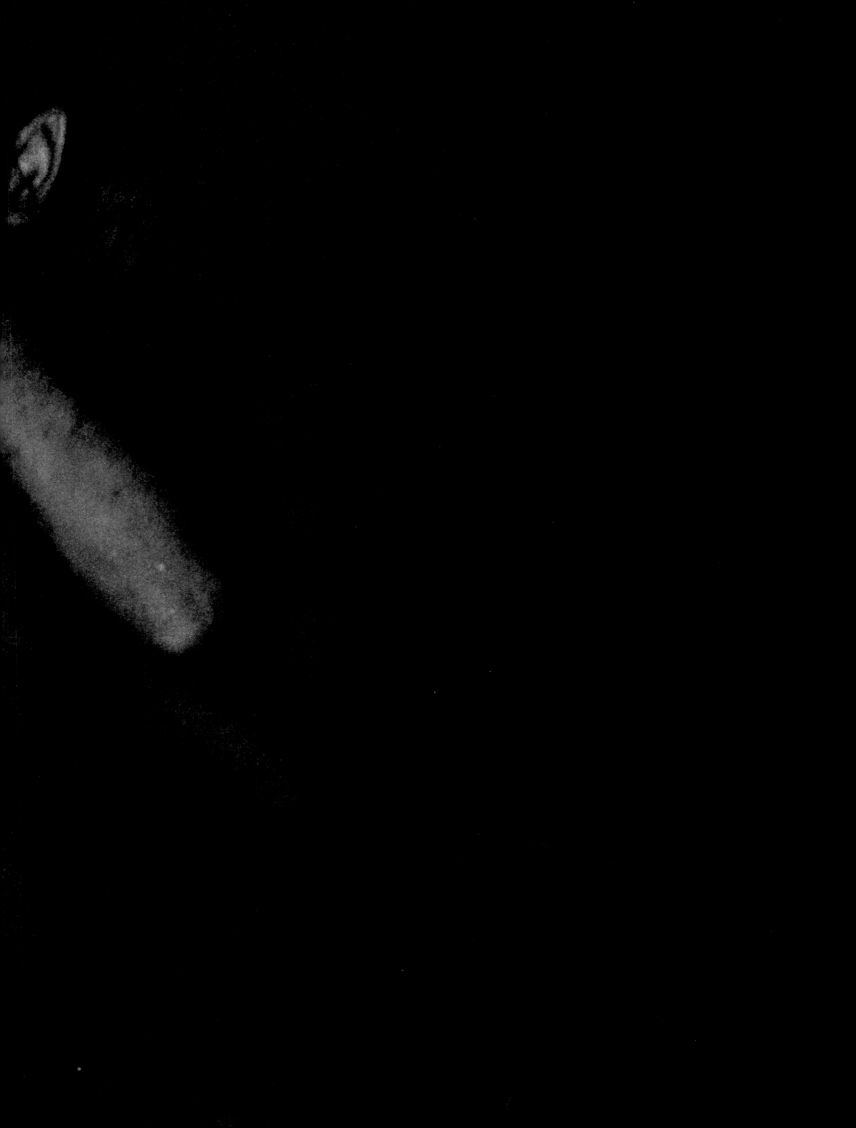

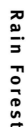
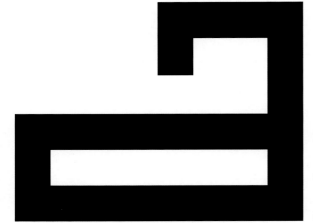

t the height of the last major ice age, about 18,000 years ago, when one-third of the Earth's land surface was covered by glaciers up to three miles thick, much of the remainder was desert. The geometry of our planetary orbit put the Earth at a greater distance from the sun all year-round and kept it there for several thousand years. Global temperatures dropped 14° F to 20° F below today. The volume of water locked up in the ice caused sea levels to fall dramatically.

Along the shores of Africa, the sea level fell up to 425 feet below present-day levels, and the southern tip of the continent was over 60 miles south of its present position. With the Antarctic ice cap covering so much of the Southern Ocean, the temperature of the always chilly Benguela Current, which carries water northward along the Atlantic coast of Africa, plummeted. As a result, ocean surface temperatures all the way to the mouth of the Congo River fell too. Evaporation from the colder water was reduced by up to 70 percent, and the onshore winds were therefore much drier than before. The southwest monsoon, which currently brings almost continuous rain to West Africa,

was suppressed. The Sahara advanced 300 miles along its entire southern front. Lake Chad dried out, rivers ceased to flow, and even the Nile north of Khartoum was dammed by the advancing dunes. The sands of the Kalahari drifted all the way to the Congo River, 1,250 miles north of its present limits.

The equatorial and tropical lowland rain forests occupied barely a tenth of their present range. Not so long before, they had covered most of equatorial Africa. Now they were a string of isolated pockets in West and central Africa.

Africa has never again been as dry as it was during that last ice age. As the global climate improved,

PREVIOUS PAGES: **The designation Pygmy comes from the Greek word** *pygmē,* **meaning "half an arm's length."** ABOVE: **The human line has ancient links with the forest through the gorilla, although our distinctive adaptations evolved on the savanna.**

the forests reclaimed their former range and spread far beyond during the wet period that turned even the Sahara into a landscape of lakes, rivers, and pastures. The forests have shrunk again since then and today cover about 7 percent of the continent's land area. This is a much smaller proportion than the 37 percent of South America that is covered in forest but still equal to almost a quarter of the total land area of the United States.

The fragmentation of the African rain forest considerably narrowed the range of its plant life. Though packed from edge to edge with a challenging tangle of vegetation, there are fewer families, fewer genera, and fewer species of plants in Africa's rain forests than in either South America or Asia. The tiny island of Singapore, for example, has more genera and species of native palms than the whole of mainland Africa. Almost the same number of Africa's fern species flourish on the slopes of a single mountain in northern Borneo (Mount Kinabalu). Even so, Africa's rain forests are bountifully endowed and form a crucial element of global and human affairs.

For anyone accustomed to the managed forests of temperate Europe and America, the tropical rain forest may seem very untidy. There are dead trees lying about, all their fine timber rotting away. Clumps of saplings, thin and whippy as a radio aerial, compete for light and air. Trees of medium height jostle for space, laced together by vines and creepers that weave the undergrowth into thickets only a machete can make a path through. The ground cover is close to absolute. Bare earth shows only on the trails that the forest animals keep open.

My first steps into an African rain forest were taken in the company of Nigerian troops during the Biafran War. Bullets were flying about. Personal safety was my primary concern, and I soon learned that the tactics upon which we depend for safety on the savanna or in a city are less helpful in the forest. You can never see enough to feel safe. The tropical rain forest is a generally dark and gloomy place. Even an occasional burst of sunlight tends to darken the shadows of what lies beyond more than it illuminates the ground it strikes. Trees and leaves are always obstructing the view. A Biafran soldier (or a leopard) could have been waiting behind that thicket, and I wouldn't have known until it was too late. And the vegetation gives no recognizable sense of scale or perspective. Distances are difficult to judge. Move 30 feet in any direction and you could be completely lost. As I huddled with the platoon in a tangle of vines and thick-leaved shrubs, I could imagine that, for forest-dwelling animals, hearing, smell, and touch are probably far more useful than vision.

But although the tropical rain forest is a foreign place to most of us, there are few places on Earth that give such a compelling sense of life's exuberant fecundity. There are good reasons for this. In the equatorial regions the amount of sunshine and the number of daylight hours varies only a little from day to day. Average temperatures are in the region of 77°F throughout the year, hardly ever dropping below 68°F. Some rain falls on most days, adding up to an annual average of between 60 and 100 inches overall and rising to 155 inches (and above) in Liberia and Sierra Leone and on the border between Nigeria and Cameroon. Such constant warmth and moisture has blanketed these regions with the largest volume of vegetation on Earth. The sheer scale of the tropical rain forest, with its massive trees and tangled undergrowth, inspires a sense of the natural world in excess—rampant vegetation, growth without purpose. But like every other living system, the forest is not a haphazard collection of trees and plants. It is arranged with the deliberation and regularity of streets, shop distribution, and energy use in a large city.

Even the so-called impoverished flora of the African rain forest runs into thousands of species. Africa's richest flora is found in the forests that range across southern Cameroon, western Gabon, and parts of Congo. Gabon alone is reputed to have 8,000 plant species, nearly one-quarter of which are found nowhere else in the world. Congo has an estimated 4,000 plant species, and again 22 percent of them are endemic.

The trees are the rain forest's crowning glory. The process of constructing a single tall column of wood requires a great investment of materials and energy—and time. Trees are one of the longest living things on Earth, though it is difficult to know exactly how long rain forest trees live. Most of them do not have annual growth rings that can be counted, and no forester has been around long enough to record the time it takes a rain forest seedling to mature and then die. The best estimates suggest that, as might be expected, the trees that grow fastest are also the ones that die soonest—from 50 to 150 years of age. Many of the slowest growing species could be up to 350 years old, and those that manage to reach the canopy top may live for 450 years.

Soaring high enough to shade the windows of a 21st-floor apartment, wearing a crown of luxuriant green that is home to a host of creatures never seen on the forest floor, each tree in the forest is the winner of endless battles with thousands of other organisms. Every mahogany tree that holds a place in the canopy is the sole survivor from tens of thousands of seeds. The intensity of that struggle is demonstrated by the number of different tree species that are found in the rain forest—though in many cases you would need an experienced botanist to distinguish one from another. The trees are far more varied than their characteristically smooth trunks and almost identical spear-shaped leaves would suggest. In fact, virtually every tree in sight could belong to a different species. More than 200 different species have been counted in a 12-acre block, and the number increases with the size of the area surveyed: 300 in 37 acres, nearly 400 in 60 acres.

Why do so many different species of trees all look so alike? On the face of it, such uniformity defies a fundamental rule of evolution: If two species are doing the same thing in the same place, one of them will evolve a trick that enables it to get more nourishment and reproduce faster—to the exclusion of the other.

The answer lies in the trees' life span. Since they live a very long time, events between them occur slowly. It takes a long time for one tree species even to "notice" the effects of another, and centuries may pass before anything changes. But from the trees' points of view, the forest is no less competitive than any other environment. Their evolutionary experiments are many but result in species that differ by just a little. The massive trees of the rain forest give the impression of stability, but they are actually a potent example of evolution in progress.

Furthermore, although our respect for these awesome trees encourages the belief that the tropical rain forest has much to give the world, it is actually extremely selfish. Self-sustaining and generous to its own, it gives very little away. Indeed, it even makes its own weather, since the massive banks of clouds that form from the water vapor rising from the trees seldom drift beyond the forest boundaries—most of the rain they release falls right back on the forest itself. In addition, the forests capture up to one-third as much rain again from moisture-laden winds blowing in from the ocean. With such abundant water and warmth, the forest has become so efficient at recycling its resources that nothing is wasted. Much of the nutrient content of compost accumulating on the forest floor is rapidly channeled back into the living vegetation by dense networks of shallow feeder roots; the remainder is stored in the ground. The process is so thorough that in one instance the groundwater was found to be purer than commercial distilled water. That's how efficiently rain forest vegetation can remove salts and impurities from water.

By far the greatest proportion of the rain forest biomass consists of standing trees, where nutrients are locked away for hundreds of years in a form that is totally inedible to all but the most specialized insects. Only 2.5 percent of a rain forest's biomass is directly available as food for herbivores, compared with 50 percent in the savanna. This simple fact explains why rain forest mammals, though many in terms of species, are few in individual numbers.

People are the least numerous of all—though the number of Pygmies who thronged to an elephant kill observed by Harvard zoologist Richard Wrangham might have suggested that the forest was bursting with people. Wrangham was studying the food-gathering and social behavior of the Mbuti Pygmies in the Ituri Forest of the Congo Basin when a group of hunters killed the elephant. This was a rare event. Word spread rapidly, and people from camps near and far soon gathered around the carcass. Excitement was intense and appeared dangerously volatile as the animal was skinned and dismembered. The hunters worked feverishly while onlookers surged around them, pushing, shoving, gesticulating, and shouting. Others moved from one hunter to another, grabbing an arm, shaking a shoulder, demanding attention. But amid the din, patterns of negotiation became discernible. The hunters and those with immediate rights to a share were told to honor the obligations of kinship. Old debts and favors were settled in exchange for meat; new pledges were contracted. The talking went on for hours, doubtless reinforcing a web of reciprocal obligation that was fundamental to the social order of the region.

This incident eloquently demonstrates the value of cooperative behavior in human society, especially in the rain forest, where the scarcity of directly edible vegetation and the consequent low density of herbivores have made it difficult for humans to establish a permanent presence. We evolved from a forest-dwelling ancestor, but it was on the savanna that we evolved. While our forest cousins continued to subsist principally on leaves (and retained the large gut needed to process sufficient quantities of these low-energy foods), we had moved on to a diet that consisted predominantly of high-energy foods. The African rain forest is almost totally devoid of the grains and beans, roots and tubers that constitute the greater part of the human diet.

There are more than 30 plants in Africa that people gather and eat often enough to be called a food crop, and none was originally a forest plant. Even the yam, a staple food of people throughout the rain forest regions of West Africa, was originally a savanna plant that evolved large tubers as a means of surviving drought and periodic burning. Only with the introduction of food crops from other parts have people been able to live permanently in the forest. First the savanna crops, then, with the arrival of the Portuguese, maize, cassava, and sweet potato from Central America and bananas and coco yams from Southeast Asia. But even with these introduced crops, human occupation of the forest has always been limited. The rain forests of the Congo Basin, for example, support just over 3.1 million people — which seems alot until one considers that over 700 million live in the same area of land in India.

Elephants are the architects of the rain forest, in their daily rounds of feeding, drinking, and socializing creating trails and clearings, which the rains may turn into streams and water holes.

The people of the arrow were the first to establish a presence in the African rain forest. Their small stature was an advantage for hunters moving stealthily through the tangled undergrowth of shrubs and hanging vines. It also meant they needed relatively less food, which is a help where food is scarce at the best of times; and they could lose heat more quickly by virtue of their high surface-to-volume body ratio, which is particularly useful in an environment where the air temperature often approaches blood heat and humidity is always high. These forest people are known by a number of names, according to the region they occupy, such as the Mbuti in the Ituri Forest of the north Congo Basin and the Baka of the Cameroon forests, but to most of us they are known collectively as Pygmies—a word that comes from an ancient Greek term referring to fabulous dwarfs who were believed to be no taller than the distance between a man's elbow and his knuckles.

The earliest known reference to an actual living Pygmy comes from the records of an expedition sent into the depths of Africa by King Neferkare over 4,000 years ago. In a progress report sent back to Egypt, the Pygmy was described as "a dancing dwarf of the god from the land of the spirits" who had been captured for the curiosity of his stature. On hearing this, the king ordered the expedition:

Come northward to the court immediately; and bring this dwarf with you. When he boards the vessel, appoint reliable people to stay beside him, taking care that he does not fall into the water. When he sleeps at night, have reliable people to sleep beside him in his tent; inspect ten times a night. My majesty desires to see this dwarf more than the gifts of Sinai and of Punt.

The earliest modern reference to the Pygmies is less complimentary. The German botanist Georg

Schweinfurth, who explored the Ituri region in 1869, described the Pygmies as the "remnants of a declining race," the original inhabitants of the forest who once had lived as independent hunters and gatherers but were now so degenerated that they depended upon villagers living nearby for their survival. But years of rigorous research have convinced experts on the subject that no Pygmies have ever lived permanently in the deep forest.

Available evidence suggests that the ancestors of the Pygmies were people of the arrow who lived around the fringes of the forest. They had the best of both worlds: ready access to the staple foods they required from the savanna, and ample opportunity to take advantage of what the forest had to offer. When the people of the stick brought their cattle onto the savanna, and others with the hoe took over the more fertile areas, the Pygmies turned more and more to the forest for their subsistence. They developed links of mutual benefit with the farmers and herders, exchanging honey, meat, and labor for the essential foods the forest could not provide. Of the three items they had to offer, labor was probably the most welcome at first. This became the basis of a bond between the Pygmy foragers and Bantu farmers that enabled both to move deeper into the forest than either could have done alone. They followed the rivers and elephant trails, clearing stands of primary forest to establish villages and gardens where the farmers settled. The Pygmies continued with their more nomadic ways, returning regularly to exchange the produce of the hunt (protein) for the produce of the garden (carbohydrates).

Hunting and farming created a patchwork of secondary habitats that was significantly more

Strips of bark or palm frond are intricately woven into a strong but lightweight basket.

productive—from the human point of view—than the pristine forest they replaced. Some authorities believe that people have been using the African rain forest in this way for so long that the distribution and composition of forest that we see today is often as much the result of human activity as it is of natural processes. This is particularly true of the forest fringes, where islands of forest thought at first to be relics of forest that once covered the entire region are in fact new forest that has grown up around villages—with some trees even deliberately planted by the villagers themselves.

The farming villagers with whom the Pygmies traded were the vanguard of a little-known movement of peoples that is unmatched in human history— the Bantu migration. In the space of a few thousand years the Bantu changed the human landscape of sub-Saharan Africa dramatically, from a region thinly inhabited by scatterings of hunters and gatherers to one that was dominated by farmers living in villages. But it was not a conquest, nor even a migration, properly speaking. It was the dispersal of an expanding population. As one village was established and grew, some of its inhabitants moved on to establish another, farther afield.

The cradle lands of the Bantu people were the grasslands of what is now the border region of Nigeria and Cameroon, where they cultivated the rich soils of the forest margins. Domesticated crops such as yams were an integral part of the diet, supplemented by meat from the hunt. The Bantu began dispersing about 5,000 years ago. As their numbers grew, villagers moved to new sites every five or ten years, selecting promising natural clearings and forest-edge locations. The movement was decidedly slow at first, taking 600 years to advance 600 miles in one instance and advancing at an overall rate of no more than 15 miles each decade. Once beyond the forest, however, the rate of expansion accelerated. Bantu farmers were well established in the Great Lakes region of central Africa by 2,500 years ago and had reached the coast of southern Africa and the limit of their dispersal about 900 years later—in the fourth century A.D.

In little more than 3,000 years the Bantu colonized virtually all of sub-Saharan Africa from the savannas of the Sahel along the southern fringe of the Sahara, where their expansion was restricted by the camel- and cattle-herding people of the stick, to the southwest corner of the continent, which lies about as far south of the Equator as the Mediterranean is north of it and thus has a climate of winter rainfall and dry summers in which the summer-rainfall crops of the Bantu farmers could not thrive. So the Cape region of southern Africa was virtually vacant (except for its indigenous hunters and gatherers) when the first European settlers arrived with their winter-rainfall crops. This was the only part of sub-Saharan Africa well suited to European settlement, and if not for this ecological happenstance, the European presence in South Africa would not have been so firmly established.

IASA VILLAGE LIES on a road through the Ituri Forest that would hardly qualify as a cart track elsewhere. Baruwani was waiting for me, and he was anxious to leave as soon as I clambered down from the truck. Although the Pygmy hunters regularly traded their meat (and labor) for maize, fruit, and cassava, an air of mutual distrust prevailed. The Pygmies never stayed in the farmers' village longer than necessary.

The Pygmy camp was about an hour from Biasa. The women built a hut for me soon after we arrived, lacing large oval leaves onto the dome-shaped framework of fresh saplings so effectively that hardly a drop of rain came through during the storm that afternoon. I soon learned there was a torrential storm every afternoon, during which I would retreat to my hut. Many of the Pygmies, on the other hand, clearly enjoyed sitting out in the rain.

There were seven men and seven women in Baruwani's group, who between them had 11 healthy children—nine less than five years old. In the evening seven fires would burn. While the children continued with their games or made bows to shoot arrows at makeshift targets, the adults were constantly on the move—fetching wood and water, unwrapping their stock of cassava and leaves, preparing forest mushrooms and scraps of meat for the pot. There was little if any discussion, no apparent schedule, but gradually I realized a well-ordered system was in operation. Firewood, water, food—all arrived at each of the fireplaces and was prepared without fuss. When the food was ready, each family group gathered at its fire, eating together from the same pot. Darkness had fallen by the time the meal was finished.

The women piled wood on one of the fires, and all gathered round as Baruwani sang of the elephant to the accompaniment of a rhythm tapped out on a hollow log: "The elephant is a monstrous animal / It moves in herds / It is difficult to kill / Our people are lucky to have brave hunters among them."

Baruwani's group had occupied the camp clearing for nearly two months when I visited, and it was looking distinctly lived-in. The huts were shedding their leaves, the ground was littered with a mess of fireplaces, old leaves, pawpaw skins, and scatterings of palm-nut husks—demonstrating a fundamental principle of the hunter-gatherers' nomadic lifestyle. Staying in one place for too long is unhealthy. Yes, Baruwani confirmed, the group would be moving soon.

FOLLOWING PAGES: **The tangle of vines, saplings, and buttresses of mature trees at ground level in the Bosquet community forest is a hint of the vitality that soars above. Although the rain forest is thick with trees and plants, very little of it is directly available to feed animals and people, thus its thin human population.**

EPIDEMIC DISEASES ARE the scourge of humanity, and they are most prevalent where enough people are constantly in close contact—and thus form a large enough pool of candidates for infectious organisms to move among. Towns and cities are decidedly unhealthy. To give a modern example: Laboratory tests found that a typical Nigerian bank note harbored bacteria responsible for gastroenteritis, boils, sties, and conjunctivitis. If there are not enough people, though, the disease dies out. Measles, for instance, requires a community of roughly half a million people to sustain an endemic infection. The small number and scattered distribution of our earliest ancestors limited the capacity of any infection to become rooted in the population, where it could attack generation after generation.

Agriculture and the establishment of permanent villages swept aside this natural limitation on the spread of disease. Crucially, the Bantu farmers who settled in the forests created the conditions that enabled malaria to get a hold on the human population. Previously the mosquitoes that carry the disease had taken their blood meals from wild animals, but people became a new source as pioneer farmers converted stretches of forest into precisely the kind of open, moist, and well-vegetated environment that the insects preferred. Forest clearings increased the number of breeding places for mosquitoes, and with their generation times measured in days, before long a species evolved that preferred human blood: *Anopheles gambiae.* The newly evolved insects spread like weeds in the gashes that farmers made in the natural environment. Wherever farming became a common

Now the Baka people of the Cameroon rain forest are settled permanently in Bosquet village. Their houses are roofed with corrugated iron, the walls a framework of thin poles plastered with red forest mud.

activity, *Anopheles gambiae* became the most common mosquito. Unhappily for us, *Anopheles gambiae* carries the parasite that causes the most virulent form of malaria: *Plasmodium falciparum.*

The microscopic single-cell organisms of the genus *Plasmodium* are probably among the oldest of human and prehuman parasites. Dating from at least 60 million years ago, they appear to have begun their careers in the guts of reptiles and moved on to birds and mammals when susceptible predators ate an infected reptile. The parasites must have co-opted the mosquito as a means of dispersal not long after blood-feeding insects appeared on the scene 35 million years ago. Once injected into the bloodstream by a feeding mosquito (along with an anticoagulant saliva the insect secretes to keep the blood flowing), the parasites invade the red corpuscles, destroying them by the million. The host suffers bouts of fever and debilitating weakness as successive waves of parasites multiply within the ruptured corpuscles and then set off in search of yet more to invade. Any uninfected mosquito that takes a meal from the host during this time will also ingest parasites, and they in turn will be passed on to the mosquito's next victim. In this way the disease spreads rapidly.

Malaria started in Africa, but today it is a worldwide public health problem. More than 40 percent of the global population lives in areas where they are at risk from the disease. Nor is there any sign that its grip is likely to weaken in the foreseeable future. In endemic regions, nearly all children are infected by the time they are two years old. One child dies of the disease every 30 seconds, and African children under five are chronic victims, suffering an average of six bouts a year. Fatally afflicted children may die less than three days after developing the first symptoms. Those who survive are often drained of vital nutri-

ents, impairing their physical and intellectual development. Malaria is particularly dangerous during pregnancy, causing severe anemia that often leads to the death of the mother and her unborn child. Tragically, many people in affected areas know very little about malaria. A survey in Ghana, for instance, found that half of those questioned did not know that mosquitoes transmitted malaria.

In rural areas the disease hits working families especially hard. Those affected are able to work only 40 percent of the land that healthy families can. Overall, the costs of malaria in Africa south of the Sahara are estimated at more than two billion dollars per year.

In the 1950s the mosquitoes' breeding sites were sprayed with DDT to keep malaria under control. But that was before the environmental cost of using DDT was understood. Since then the mosquito and the malaria parasite have in any case shown a distressing ability to evolve into species that are resistant to insecticides and preventives. The quinine derivatives that kept European travelers alive in malarial regions for much of the 20th century are no longer effective, for instance, and DEET—the repellent developed by the U.S. government 50 years ago and still used by millions of tourists—is typically effective for less than 15 minutes, not the eight hours the packet promises.

The World Health Organization (WHO) has initiated its Roll Back Malaria program, with national plans for reducing or preventing the disease in 80 percent of affected countries. Within ten years every child in Africa should be sleeping under a net impregnated with pyrethrin, a mosquito-killing insecticide. WHO believes the campaign could save half a million lives each year. Skeptics, though, fear the scheme will fail. Doctors warn that by reducing exposure, bed nets could reduce the buildup of natural resistance and end up killing more children than they save. Ecologists believe mosquitoes will begin feeding in the daytime more than at night. Furthermore, past experience suggests that no chemical barrier is likely to keep the mosquito at bay for long.

Meanwhile, the human organism itself has not been entirely passive in the face of malaria. As falciparum malaria attained unparalleled levels of intensity in the rain forests of West Africa, observers noticed that while practically all newcomers to infested regions became seriously ill soon after being bitten, large numbers of people who lived there all the time seemed to escape infection. Further investigation revealed that they possessed a physiological adaptation that gave them a measure of resistance against malaria—the sickle cell. In people with this resistance, genetic inheritance causes their blood cells to contain an abnormal form of hemoglobin that reduces the amount of oxygen in the cells, causing them to become crescent or sickle shaped. These blood-cells rupture when the malaria parasite invades them, thus denying the parasite a place to multiply and reducing the debilitating effects of malaria.

The advent of the sickle cell in populations at risk of malaria infection has been described as an example of human evolution in progress—a genetic response to an environmental threat. It evolved with the advance of farmers into the rain forest and enabled many more of them to survive than would otherwise have been the case. But the advantage did not come without a cost. The distorted sickle cells, which deny parasites a site in which to multiply, also block capillaries and can cause a variety of dangerous conditions, ranging from mild anemia to heart failure. The dangers are particularly high among individuals who inherit the sickle-cell gene from both parents. Most of these victims die in infancy from what is known as sickle-cell anemia. But those who inherit the gene from just one parent are endowed with a degree of resistance to malaria—not immunity, but they are less badly affected. The catch is of course that if all are not to die of sickle-cell anemia, each new generation must contain a high number of individuals who have survived malarial infection but do not have the gene. Indeed, the incidence of the sickle cell in susceptible populations is generally not more than 20 percent.

DESPITE THE PROBLEMS of malaria, Bantu farmers established numerous villages and small towns in the rain forest as they spread from their cradle land. In some instances a combination of history and environmental circumstance fostered the emergence of large states, with an urban center and a single ruler—in a word: kingdoms. The spread of the forest has covered much of the physical evidence, and European influence has colored if not distorted accounts of their history. Yet enough remains to show that these were extensive and sophisticated societies, with a highly productive agricultural base. Archaeological evidence suggests that farmers were settled in the forests of what is now southeast Nigeria nearly 3,000 years ago, and the origins of the city of Benin probably date from that time.

During the centuries preceding the arrival of the Portuguese in the late 1400s, the rulers of Benin were powerful enough to order the construction of a mighty city wall, seven miles in circumference and measuring 57 feet from the bottom of the exterior ditch to the top of the surviving wall. The human effort involved in these earthworks was enormous, equal to that of an army of 1,000 men working ten hours a day for five dry seasons. And the construction did not stop there. In the tangled vegetation surrounding the modern Benin City, archaeologists have uncovered a vast network of enclosures, covering an area of about 2,500 square miles in total and linked one to the other by nearly 10,000 miles of earthworks. All this hints at the process by which a group of villages had developed into a city and constitutes one of the greatest works of urban construction in the non-industrial world. Far more material was moved than was used to build the Giza Pyramids, and on a 40-hour week the work would have kept 1,000 men busy for 150 years.

A Dutch traveler who visited Benin City about 1600 described its main street as "a great broad street, not paved, which seemeth to be seven or eight times broader than the Warmoes street in Amsterdam." Benin by that time was an established city-state, with thousands of residents, and supplied with food by farmers owing obeisance to the *oba*, whose status approached that of a divine king. He was never seen, except as a veiled figure in ceremonies acknowledging his power and authority. His rule was absolute—the life and death of every man, woman, and child was at his whim. Craftsmen were employed to make artifacts reflecting the authority of the state, in stone, wood, ivory, brass, and bronze. Hundreds of bronze plaques— most of them now the prized treasure of museums around the world—adorned the walls of the oba's palace and administrative buildings, depicting scenes of ceremony, ritual, and conquest in a unique stylized manner. Stone figures, abstract representations of the deities, bore an air of divine authority. Ivory tusks, tall as a man, were carved all around from end to end, with images evoking the mannered dignity of the Benin court. The art and the craft employed in the making of these

Benin bronzes 600 years old indicate high levels of cultural sophistication in West Africa well before Europeans arrived.

items clearly drew upon a tradition with ancient roots. The exquisite detail and finish of the bronze plaques in particular denote skills in crafting and casting that may have taken generations to acquire. Such dedication to a specialized craft was possible only in a society that did not expect its craftsmen to be farmers as well—in other words, a stratified society.

For all its glory, Benin's history had a dark side— the slave trade. Slavery was practiced in Africa before the arrival of European traders. Africans were the first enslavers of Africans, and Africans were among the first customers of European slave traders, too. The

10,000 slaves that the Portuguese bought from Benin and other groups on that coast between 1500 and 1530 were sold to dealers on the coast of present-day Ghana, who paid for them in Asante gold.

Asante is the only part of Africa whose inhabitants found both mineral and agricultural resources in abundant quantities. Kumasi, situated near the fringe of the rain forest, had access to both forest and savanna produce. Imported slaves cleared the forest for farming and transported its produce—especially kola nuts—to distant markets. Kumasi became the center of a trading empire that at its maximum extent of more than 96,500 square miles in 1820 was larger than the present-day United Kingdom.

Goods were transported from Kumasi to savanna regions in the north along four main roads (not trails), and another four roads provided for trade southward to the coast. The roads facilitated Asante control of its subjugated territories, but although Asante was always a military society, the kingdom's strength lay in its political institutions. Asante integrated the king and local chiefs in a national council. The Asantehene was king in council, but chosen from among matrilineal candidates by the queen mother and prominent chiefs—a system that averted the dangers of succession disputes that plagued other states in Africa and abroad.

Still, gold was the main reason for the long-term stability of the Asante state. The amount of gold mined is legendary. Even today Asante gold puts Ghana tenth in the league of world producers—

FOLLOWING PAGES: **Celebrating the 25th anniversary of his ascension to the Golden Stool, the Asantehene, Otumfuo Poku Ware II, is carried shoulder high in a pageant of color and gold.**

Dirt roads through the heart of the Cameroon rain forest were made primarily for the logging industry. Regions have been heavily logged, but the forest will regenerate where only mature trees are felled.

only 18 percent of South Africa's production but still enough to be the country's foremost foreign exchange earner. In the early 19th century, various Europeans on the Gold Coast noted that in one group of mines each miner was expected to produce two ounces daily; in another, 10,000 slaves were said to be employed. They dug slanting pits with broad steps to depths approaching 165 feet. The ore dug from the gold seams was collected in calabashes or baskets and passed along a human chain to the surface, where it was crushed, washed, sieved, and packaged as gold dust or smelted and made up into bars or wires.

Quite apart from the gold that went into the state coffers, gold was such a common aspect of commercial life in Asante that the treasury also collected large amounts in the form of taxes, tithes, tributes, and fines. One province was reported to have paid an annual tribute of 18,000 ounces to the state; another poorer province paid a mere 450 ounces. A poll tax of one-tenth of an ounce was collected from every married man in each village. In the courts, gold fines were imposed for petty offenses, and a person found innocent was expected to make a thanks offering to the state. Those found guilty of serious offenses and condemned to death could buy their acquittal for 500 ounces.

Everything, even a few bananas, had its price in gold dust, and merchants carried appropriate quantities about with them, together with scales and ornately crafted cast-brass weights. When converted into slave labor, gold enabled Asante to conquer the encircling forest. When converted into muskets, it defended the kingdom against its enemies. The state was all. The Asantehene assured himself of the allegiance of ambitious followers by binding them to him with loans of gold. Gold accumulated by a chief belonged not to his descendants but to his chiefdom or the state, and heavy death duties prevented rich men from establishing personal dynasties. As an authoritative source has noted, gold gave Asante a means, notably lacking in most African societies, of channeling individual competitiveness into the service of the state.

Eyewitness accounts from the early days of European encounters with the Asante give an impression of so much activity—of a people engaged in farming, mining, manufacture, and trade, with rounds of ritual ceremony filling every spare moment—that readers might be inclined to assume that the region was very densely populated. Asante histories of long-running military campaigns and battles involving armies of 9,000 men and women tend to confirm the assumption. But in fact, Asante and the West African rain forest were always thinly populated. Their way of farming was incapable of supporting large numbers of people.

Biasa village, where the Pygmy hunters traded meat for the villagers' produce, is probably typical of farming communities that have been a feature of the rain forest for hundreds of years. It is home to about 40 families. The recent history of Zaire (now the Democratic Republic of Congo) has left the Biasa villagers pretty much to their own resources, replicating to a greater extent than they would like the conditions of their ancestors. They have no services whatsoever. Their water comes from the river; their fuel from the forest. Paraffin (for lamps) is occasionally available from a passing truck, but few villagers have the money to pay for it.

The houses that line the road are each a rectangular mud-and-wattle structure with two rooms and a palm- or banana-thatched roof. The hard-trodden earth around each house is kept meticulously clear of weeds and rubbish. This is not for any aesthetic reason but to deny hiding places for snakes and scorpions. There is a mission school at Nduye, and 20 children walk the 5.5 miles there and back each day, sheltering under banana fronds during the frequent rainstorms. Like much of the Congo Basin, rainfall in the Nduye region averages 78 inches per year. This,

and temperatures hovering around 86°F, is good for the crops.

But farming is anything but easy in the tropical rain forest. The soils are not rich in nutrients. Farmers must continually clear new land, which they cultivate for 2 or 3 years before leaving it to lie fallow for up to 25 years, while the natural vegetation grows back and rejuvenates the soils. Under the traditional system of shifting agriculture, as it is known, the forest was always a mosaic of cultivated land and clearings in various states of fallow. Because of this, it was thinly populated. Even the 6,500 square miles of the "metropolitan" Asante homeland in the Ghana rain forest—where the population would have been most dense—could have supported only about 425,000 people. The point of this is that farming in the rain forest was extensive, not intensive. A relatively small number of people used a large area of land in one way or another, and in the rain forests of Ghana had been doing so for centuries. This is important because Ghana is frequently cited as the African country that lost the greatest proportion of its forests during the 20th century. Reassessment of the evidence, however, has shown that the original pristine forest was never so large as the baseline for deforestation assumed (much of it was secondary growth and long-fallow cultivated land), and thus the rate of depletion is not as high.

This is not to deny the obvious—over the last 50 years too much of the equatorial rain forest has been cut down—but a less emotional approach to the issue is required. When authoritative journals report that up to 90 percent of the West African rain forest has disappeared in the past century, they not only provoke the despairing conclusion that there is no point trying to save the remaining 10 percent—but they are also plain wrong.

Vast areas of forest in West Africa have been lost to farming, logging, fire, mining, and commercial plantations during the 20th century, but the total may be only about one-third of that widely reported by the popular

media. Moreover, in some places the forest has actually advanced. Ancient termite mounds in the forests of eastern Ghana, for example, point indisputably to the fact that the region had been savanna grassland in the not so distant past, for mound-building termites live exclusively in the savanna. Likewise, archaeological evidence indicates that the city of Kumasi has not always been surrounded by dense rain forest.

Such examples are a demonstration of the rain forest's capacity to regenerate. The rain forest is one of the world's most dynamic ecosystems and is not easily suppressed, as the farmers there have known for generations. Even in modern times, farmers must spend up to half of their time weeding, a greater proportion than weeds demand of farmers in any other part of the world. The problems of rain forest loss are serious, but exaggeration helps no one. Accurate statistics and a fuller understanding of the forest's immense potential to regenerate could engender real-

istic hope and eliminate the prevailing air of despair.

Cameroon is a step in the right direction. Cameroon has had more of its forest logged than any African country. By 1985, loggers had exploited 64 percent of its forest at some time during the previous 60 years. But logging practices in Cameroon generally have been quite selective, taking only mature timber and rarely felling all the standing trees. Some areas have been logged three or four times.

The amount of timber felled increased dramatically during the late 1980s and 1990s as the economy

The Baka say their ancestors were thrown out of heaven for making too much noise, but the soft tunes Felix plays on his homemade harp, called an *ayita*, cannot have been a problem.

FOLLOWING PAGES: **The Baka grow cassava in forest clearings. Introduced to Africa by the Portuguese, the plant's tuberous roots are rich in starch, but contain poisons that must be leached from the flour to make it edible.**

Baka ceremonies follow traditional patterns, especially when someone dies. Western clothes are set aside; body paints are applied; forest plants are brandished; and the *Ebouma* dance urges the spirit of the departed to find peace with the ancestors.

of Cameroon took a downturn. In 1996 alone, 95 million cubic feet of timber were harvested from approximately 670,000 acres of Cameroon's rain forest—about one-seventh of the total. Not all this logging was as careful as it should have been, but not all the forest was completely cleared either. Much of it is capable of regenerating, given the chance. For the most part that means closer control of access to the forests and of methods of cutting. And who better to do it than the people who have lived in the forest longest?

Scientists have concluded that Pygmies derive from three different groups, each of which was isolated from the others for 10 to 20 thousand years—perhaps even going back to the long, dry period when the forest fragmented into three parts. The Baka of Cameroon are arguably the most ancient of these groups. For centuries the Baka have depended for their survival upon sharing everything that the forest had to offer. No one in a group had the right to claim personal ownership of any of its resources. Everyone was aware that survival depended on the judicious husbanding of resources for communal benefit, not private gain.

Their local knowledge of the forest and its resources was encyclopedic. The rain forest was no Eden, but the Baka were supremely well adapted to life in its testing environment. In recent years, however, life for the Baka has been transformed. Government agencies and Christian missionaries have persuaded them to settle in villages permanently. They have adopted the lifestyle of the agriculturalist Bantu, with whom they previously had merely traded. Abruptly, the Baka moved from a way of life based on mutual support and sharing to one based on money and personal profit. At first they were easily exploited and cheated because they did not understand the rules of the game. The forests the

Baka had depended upon for centuries were logged without consultation, and the Baka received none of the vast profits that were made from the timber.

But with the characteristic initiative of the human species, the Baka are adapting to the new circumstances. The villagers of Bosquet have demanded that the government grant the rain forest around their village community forest status, which would mean that they could manage the resources as they wish.

Only they could authorize timber extraction, and already they have thwarted a timber merchant's attempts to enter the forest and fell trees without permission. Formulating plans for sustainable management is going to be a long haul. The timber industry will finance the Baka villagers' adaptation to the new economic order. They—better than anyone else—understand that management is the order of the day, not a blanket ban on logging.

People have been using the African rain forest for centuries. In the past they felled a tree only to make room for crops and houses. Nowadays, the incentive is timber, and demand is high. But the forests can be logged in a sustainable manner to the benefit of everyone—from people who live where the trees are growing to the city dweller whose dining table gleams with the richness of the rain forest.

For the Baka people the mysterious depths of the Congo rain forest are home. The ancient Egyptians knew of these forest dwellers and called them "people of the trees." Early explorers called them "pygmies" on account of their small stature. The Baka say they have lived here longer than anyone knows. They even have a legend that tells how their ancestors were thrown out of heaven for being too noisy and sent to liven up the forest. Ever since, their voices, laughter, and music have brought the warmth of humanity to the forbidding forest.

The rain forests of the Congo Basin are built on a scale that humbles the human spirit. So big, yet offering so little opportunity for people. Warmth and ample rainfall keep this equatorial heart of Africa thumping with deep, enduring power, but nearly all the forest's bounty is locked up in huge trees that only insects can eat. And the trees use available resources so efficiently that the ground on which they stand is virtually devoid of nutrients. Little is left to sustain other living things. Only ingenuity and a long history of custom and tradition have enabled the Baka to thrive in the forest, generation after generation.

But now the Baka's traditional way of life is threatened. The huge forest trees that stood for centuries as the unchanging reality of their very existence are being felled for the global market in exotic hardwoods. The demand is high, but the Baka have turned it to their advantage. Having successfullly petitioned the government for community control of their forest, they now plan to manage it for sustainability as well as profit.

Humanity has been its most resourceful in the rain forest. Fired from his crossbow, the slim dart Richard Kadjama holds in his mouth will slip swiftly and silently through the undergrowth to spear the unsuspecting target —a bird or small mammal.

Food has never been easy to obtain in the rain forest, so when the Cameroon government encouraged the Baka to move out of the forest in the 1960s it seemed like a good idea. Most Baka now live in villages on the red-dirt highways that have been cut through the rain forest, where they have the benefits of permanent housing, access to medical care and schooling, and the chance to trade.

The boys above and Pascal Kokpa (right) were born in Bosquet, a roadside village in the heart of Cameroon. They have never known another way of life but like all Baka firmly believe the encircling rain forest is their true home, where the Baka alone have the right to hunt and gather forest produce.

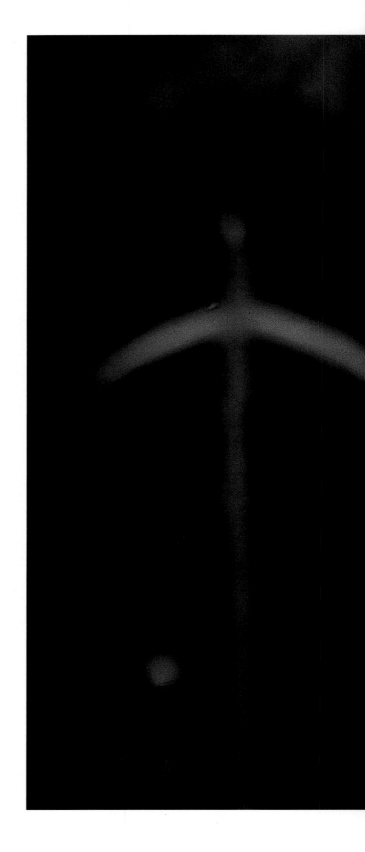

"It is known throughout the land that the Baka live in the forest,"

they say. "We were the first to live here—it is ours by right."

"The state moved us to the edge of the forest near the road," they point out, so "the state should now give our village the forest in return."

Without the Baka's consent or knowledge, a massive tree has been felled in their tract of forest. The road that brought so much good into their lives has brought trouble—loggers, who will take the most valuable trees regardless of whose forest they are in. The Baka petitioned the local government, pleading that the state should attribute the forest to the villagers so they can protect it.

With their request granted, the villagers mark out the boundaries of their forest (left). An inventory of the trees will be made, and a program of controlled felling will ensure the long-term survival of the forest, bringing employment and revenue to the Baka.

The timber above was salvaged from trees felled and abandoned by loggers in the forest.

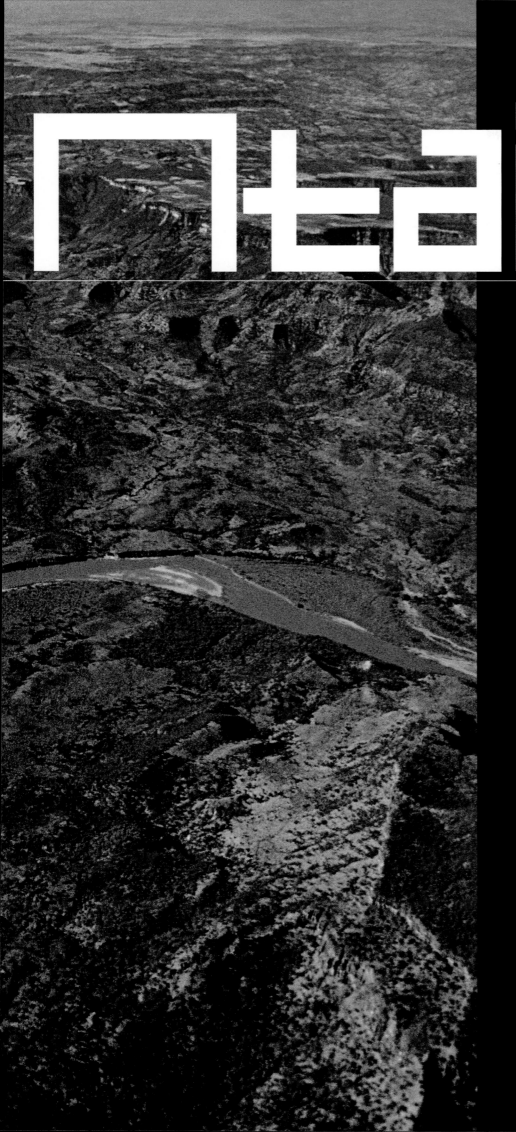

ntains

Africa's high mountains stand li[ke] far-flung islands in a sea of sava[nna] and lowland forest—grand relic[s of] the Earth's ancient turmoil, whe[re] altitude and isolation conspire t[o make] taxing environments for all form[s of] life. Equatorial sun and thin air [bring] scorching summer every day an[d freez-] ing winter every night to the hei[ghts] of Africa's highest mountains. O[n] Kilimanjaro, a climb from the sa[vanna] foothills to the summit glaciers [is akin] to traveling from the Equator to [the] Pole in the space of a few miles.

Forests of heather and alpine m[eadow-] lands studded with giant groun[dsels] and lobelias are some of the pla[nt] kingdom's wondrous adaptatio[ns] to these extreme environments[.] the bleeding heart baboon and [the] Ethiopian wolf are two animals [that are] uniquely adapted to life on the [windswept] heights. Among people, social [and] cultural adaptations are often a[n] response to environmental cons[traints,] and a remarkable history of hu[man] fortitude and resilience has spr[ung] from the isolated mountain fortresses of Ethiopia.

The Blue Nile carves a winding canyon through the high mounta[in] landscape of Ethiopia.

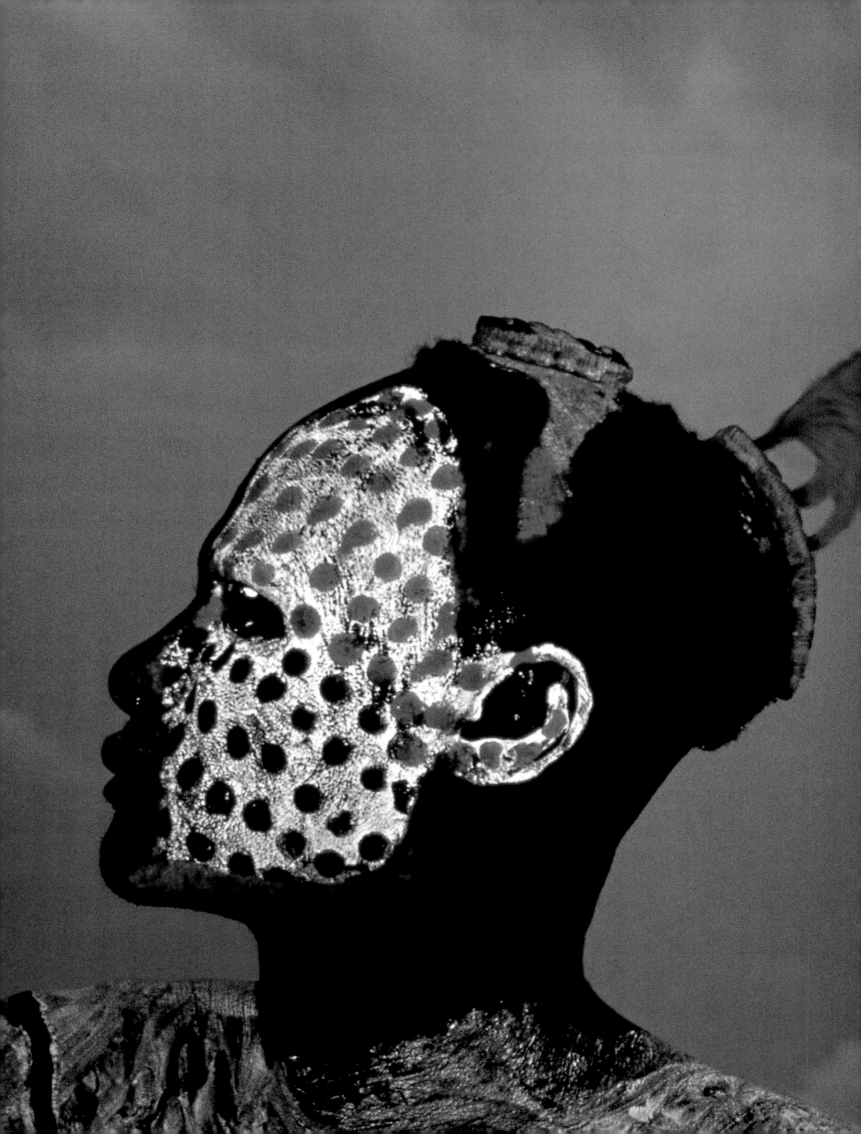

awn, and as the sun breaks through the piercing chill of night on the plain outside Korem, Ethiopia, it lights up a biblical famine, now, in the 20th century. This place, say workers here, is the closest thing to hell on Earth. Thousands of wasted people are coming here for help. Many find only death. They flood in every day from villages hundreds of miles away, felled by hunger, driven to the point of desperation. Death is all around.

The BBC television news report of October 23, 1984, was broadcast around the world.

Famine had struck in Ethiopia—again. Memories of the Ethiopian famine just ten years before were evoked by pictures of cruelly emaciated children, of mothers brushing the flies from the eyes of dying babies, of fathers digging graves. Once again makeshift refugee camps sprang up around aid distribution centers. Thousands of people—most of them farmers and families with a proud history of growing enough food for themselves and the nation—were reduced to the indignity of holding out begging bowls. The world responded generously, contributing millions of dollars to famine relief. But what was going on? Was the famine simply a consequence of drought, or were farmers abusing the land in their attempts to feed an expanding population? Was the drought a consequence of climate change, and perhaps a first sign of the global warming that scientists were warning of? Or was something more sinister afoot?

In recent times, drought and famine, political upheaval and civil war have made Ethiopia an icon of human distress, but in the distant past, its location and unique ecological circumstance fostered the evolution of an especially resilient set of living and cultural characteristics. These include plants and animals that, in their adaptations to the high, isolated environments of Ethiopia, are unlike anything else

PREVIOUS PAGES: A clay hair bun crowned with an ostrich feather denotes a man's high reputation and courage for the Karo farmers of southwest Ethiopia. ABOVE: Ethiopia's present population of nearly 66 million is expected to double in the next 25 years.

in the world. Among people, the trials of life on the high plateaus created traditions of robust faith that—among other things—became the rallying points for opposition against despotic rulers.

In 1973, the Welo Province of Ethiopia suffered a famine in which an estimated 100,000 to 200,000 people died. The government of Emperor Haile Selassie refused to acknowledge the problem, as indeed it had ignored famines in 1958 and 1966. But this time the famine was more serious. Though the imperial government tried to conceal the scale of the emergency until the media reported it and the emperor's official itineraries were rerouted to avoid the disaster zones, civil administrators could not hide from the Ethiopian tradition of mass supplication.

Thousands of famine-stricken peasants marched to the towns in protest. There were no food riots and no violence to start with—but things turned ugly when city dwellers, students, and junior army officers seized upon the famine as a symbol of the need for political change. The government was

overthrown. Emperor Haile Selassie was assassinated. Government ministers and administrators were imprisoned. Col. Mengistu Haile Mariam became the head of government. Soon thereafter, new legislation stripped wealthy landowners of their traditional rights. Their lands were distributed among the peasants who until then had farmed for their masters in conditions of feudal penury, never far from starvation.

Mengistu, whose hatred for the old regime was the very embodiment of the revolution, was said to have "emerged out of the belly of the Ethiopian masses." His reputation as a man of the people was further embellished with rumors that he was descended from slaves. But Col. Mengistu Haile Mariam was not the man he had been made out to be. He rapidly fell from favor as he murdered rivals and assumed political powers in excess even of those whom the revolution had displaced. Before long, rumors were spread saying that Mengistu came from aristocratic stock. He even began comparing himself with the 19th-century emperor Tewodros II. But his time would come.

In the afterglow of the revolution, the Marxist ideology, which brought the benefits of land reform to feudal Ethiopia, also caused changes in all corners of the administration. Political ideology reached even the National Museum. The directors were persuaded that museum displays should stress themes of national identity and unity. In the time-honored fashion of using visual images to illustrate political themes, it was decided that a painting of some symbolic moment from the nation's history should be commissioned. An artist was officially approved, and in due course the museum was adorned with a painting that showed the felling of a massive ancient tree. The painting was said to symbolize "the people's triumph over feudalism and backwardness."

ASSIVE TREES ARE rare in Ethiopia. The forests of stately cedar and juniper that once adorned the valleys and high plateaus have disappeared. Their straight-grained and termite-proof timber went into the buildings and the fireplaces of an expanding population. At one time forest and woodland covered an estimated 87 percent of the Ethiopian Highlands, but latest surveys give a figure of just 2.4 percent. The destruction is said to have begun before the 16th century, but it proceeded at a relatively low rate until 1900, when forests still covered an estimated 40 percent of the highlands. The massive destruction that occurred during the 20th century has been due to an explosion in the number of Ethiopians and their intensified exploitation of the highland environment. The highlands constitute less than half of Ethiopia's land area, but they are home to nearly 90 percent of the country's population. Furthermore, almost all of Ethiopia's cropland is situated in the highlands, along with two-thirds of its livestock.

The destruction of the forest was causing concern by 1900. A major program of planting new trees was started, but the aim was not so much to replace the natural forest as to ensure that Ethiopia would have a continuing supply of timber. The emperor, Menelik II, sought foreign advice and was persuaded that eucalyptus was the answer to Ethiopia's looming timber shortage. Throughout the country, government forestry departments established plantations of eucalyptus and encouraged private landowners and villagers to do the same.

Eucalyptus grows fast, and a plantation—with its rows of trees neatly spaced—takes up less room than a natural forest. But eucalyptus is a selfish tree that drains the soil of available water and nutrients and gives very little back.

Specialized invertebrates and microorganisms had evolved with the eucalypts in their native Australia, where they help to compost its fallen leaves and thus

Muhajure Taju is warden of the government eucalyptus forest—planted over a century ago as a source of wood for fuel and construction—on the hills above the Ethiopian capital, Addis Ababa.

hasten the return of nutrients to the soil. In their absence even the eucalypts' leaf litter lies for years in Africa—untouched by the continent's decomposers, which cannot deal with the tree's pungent resins. Not much else grows where eucalyptus has been planted, so that while a natural forest will hold water like a sponge, most of the rain falling on a eucalypt plantation will run straight off, creating erosion problems and delivering hardly any moisture to the water table that keeps springs flowing through the dry season.

One of Menelik's predecessors, Zera Yakob, who reigned from 1434 to 1468, appears to have recognized the beneficial influences that forests have. Or at least he was aware that the uncontrolled felling of forests could be detrimental. To protect important watersheds, Zera Yakob declared the Wof-Washa and Jibat Forests, 90 miles north and west of Addis Ababa, respectively, to be forest reserves. Closer to the capital, he ordered that the forests that had once clothed the Yerer and Wechecha Mountains, 15 miles east and 12 west of Addis Ababa, respectively, should be reestablished. Seeds from junipers were collected in the Wof-Washa Forests and planted on the mountains. All the reserves were designated as crown lands in which the random felling of trees was banned. The forests are there still. Massive junipers up to 400 years old stand tall among the naturally regenerating younger trees—eloquent testimony to Zara Yakob's success.

Elsewhere in Ethiopia, where an ancient juniper survives it is nearly always behind the protective walls of a church compound. Religious authority is no less strict than royal edict, and cutting a tree standing on holy ground is akin to desecration. Still, these trees are a sorry sight. Standing alone, with their spindly branches reaching out like wasted limbs, they look like elderly citizens silently lamenting their fate.

ETHIOPIA IS THE most mountainous corner of Africa, a continent that is not well endowed with mountains, even though it stands relatively higher than the other continents. The greater part of Africa's land surface is between 1,600 and 3,200 feet above sea level, but less than 1.35 percent of it rises to 6,500 feet or more, and only 0.10 percent is higher than 9,800 feet. Many of Africa's mountains are the product of volcanic activity and correspondingly young in geological terms. Kilimanjaro, for example, one of the world's best known mountains—and Africa's highest (19,341 feet)—is little more than a million years old. Kibo, its central cone, did not exist when our ancestors ranged across the plains at its feet.

High tropical mountains do not make life easy. Summer every day and winter every night is not an

scoured the heights. Where distant peaks host identical plants that occur nowhere else, there can be little doubt that a climatically induced corridor of such vegetation must once have linked the two. Thus the vegetation of Mount Kenya is affiliated with that of the Congo Basin, while the younger Mount Kilimanjaro has more in common with the Usambara range standing nearby.

But the high mountain landscapes are few and far between—they stand like a widely spaced archipelago of islands in a sea of savanna and lowland forest. Although Ethiopia represents barely 4 percent of the continent's land surface, it has 50 percent of the land above 6,500 feet and just under 80 percent of the land above 9,800 feet. It all began with a mushroom-head plume of abnormally hot material from the Earth's mantle that began rising under that corner of northeast Africa between 20 and 30 million years ago. The plume was about 1,200 miles across, centered on what is now the Afar region of Ethiopia, and it forced the landscape upward into the form of a huge dome. Surface tension kept the skin of the dome intact for millions of years, but eventually it split under the strain, creating three rays. One is now the Red Sea, a second became the Gulf of Aden, and the third was the Great Rift Valley, which from that moment began unzipping the continent of Africa southward.

For millions of years, volcanoes spewed sheet upon sheet of lava from the edges of the fracture, eventually piling enough volcanic rock to cover the entire United States to a depth of about 60 feet. The volcanoes began to quiet down five million years ago, leaving a high, mountainous landscape that was virtually devoid of life but now subject to the depredations of climate. Glaciers scoured the heights

exaggeration of conditions challenging life in the afroalpine zone of Kilimanjaro, for instance. One form of senecio (a family to which groundsel belongs) has evolved into a giant form with thickly insulated stems, leaves that close in around the growing bud at night, and the capacity to exude a thick slime that offers protection as an antifreeze.

All of Africa's high mountains pose similar challenges, and so they share many features. Each is ringed with ascending belts of similar vegetation that rise from lowland forest, through moist montane forest, to bamboo, heath, and finally the afroalpine flora of the highest zone. The differences among their populations of plants and animals reveal just how much the continent has been affected by the Earth's wide swings of climate. Where the number of different plant species found on a mountain is low, it is certain they became established there only since glaciers last

FOLLOWING PAGES: A necklace of cowrie shells gives a poignant note to the confident gaze of a farmer's wife in the Ethiopian Highlands. Cowrie shells, dredged from the lagoons of the Maldive Islands, were once the currency of the slave trade.

during the ice ages. The sun baked the lava fields of the plateau. Wind and rain eroded the steep cliffs of the escarpment, sculpting a mesmeric landscape of peaks and canyons, precipices, and jagged fans of ridges and gullies. As with the Grand Canyon, a first sight of the Ethiopian mountain landscape evokes a humbling sense of awe. The Earth's internal forces piled up huge mountains over millions of years, and equally irresistible forces have been whittling them down ever since.

Rugged escarpments on the north, east, and west sides of the massif and deserts to the south have compounded the isolation of the Ethiopian Highlands. By virtue of its young age, geologically speaking, the Ethiopian massif is considered to be impoverished in terms of its plant and animal life, but isolation and a unique environment have made an ecological vacuum of the region, into which colonists were drawn from other parts and rapidly evolved into species that are found nowhere else. Ethiopia is home to a number of endemic animals and plants. Of the 219 mammalian species identified in the region, 28 are found only in Ethiopia. Similarly, 23 of Ethiopia's 665 breeding bird species occur nowhere else on the continent, along with significant numbers of insect, amphibian, reptile, and plant species.

The highland rose (*Rosa abyssinica*), which has sweet-smelling leaves as well as flowers, is found only in Ethiopia. Likewise, the African primrose (*Primula verticillata*) adorns only the shaded mossy seepages of Ethiopia's highland valleys. The blue-winged sheldgoose (*Cyanochen cyanoptera*) also is endemic to Ethiopia, its ancestors having flown in long ago from the cradleland of the sheldgeese on the alpine grasslands of South America. And then there is the Malcolm's earless toad (*Nectophryonoides malcolmi*), an endearing little creature found only at altitudes of between 10,500 feet and 13,000 feet, where it is often very cold and mostly dry. Survival under these conditions called for some adaptations to the amphibians' customary reproductive procedures. Instead of laying

spawn in pools to be fertilized by the male, the toad's eggs are fertilized in the female's body (which negates the risk of their being frozen to death) and laid in soil where the tadpoles feed only from the yolk sac until emerging as miniature adults (which deals with the problem of drought). Related species of earless toad are known from the mountain forests of Tanzania and Liberia, leading naturalists to suggest that they were widespread throughout Africa when the cold and dry conditions of the ice ages prevailed. Now eliminated from moist lowland Africa, they may be a depository species, locked into a small area from which they may be released one day. When cold and drought return, the unique adaptations of the tiny toads should permit them to regain their former territory—the rare and local could become common and widespread.

On a considerably larger scale than the earless toad, the mountain nyala also thrives in the Ethiopian Highlands, where it feeds on herbs whose pungent aromas other herbivores find distasteful. Another endemic species, the Walia ibex, likewise split off from its ancestral stock (the Nubian ibex) in the relatively recent past but found a niche for itself on the precipitous cliffs, where it clambers about with astonishing agility in search of the grazing that only it can reach. And the cliffs of the northern massif are where Ethiopia's most colorful animals are found on wet, chilly evenings, safe from predators, huddled together for warmth in their thick waterproof coats as they prepare for the night—gelada baboons.

Also known as "bleeding heart" monkeys for the distinctive patch of bare pink skin on their breast, the gelada is a grass-eating monkey that has to devote most of its waking hours to the business of eating —preferably undisturbed—if it is to get all the sustenance it needs from a very low-quality diet in a very cold environment. Fossils from other parts of Africa indicate that five or six gelada species were common about two million years ago, but now only the species found in the Ethiopian Highlands survives. The other ancestral lineages probably became extinct as they were evicted from the savannas by larger and more adept grazing species (our ancestors also may have been a factor in the eviction). The Ethiopian Highlands have proved to be an ideal refuge for the gelada. There is plenty of grass, and few other animals competing for it.

Because they must spend so much time eating, gelada troops are remarkably peaceful and orderly. There is little of the squabbling seen among other monkeys, and no quarrels over food or space. There is enough for all; only the time in which to eat is limited. Gelada often gather in the hundreds and purposefully strip a patch of grassland so bare of its leaves, stems, and roots that they are known by local people as gelada fields. But the devastation is not an altogether bad thing, for the fields are soon invaded by a host of opportunistic and fast-growing plants.

Geladas eat sitting down, which saves energy and conserves warmth. As naturalist Jonathan Kingdon points out, the practice has had extraordinary evolutionary consequences. All primates show great interest in the genitals, but not all are interested primarily in sex. In monkeys and apes especially, genital gestures replicating sexual submission (presenting, as ethologists put it) are part of the everyday social order, used to appease aggression and as friendly greetings. Of course, it also enables males to keep an eye out for the reddened and swollen vulva that indicates a female coming into estrus.

By sitting down to save energy, the geladas have lost an important means of keeping the peace and monitoring the sexual readiness of females. But in a remarkable instance of evolutionary ingenuity, the gelada females have made up for the loss by developing an area of bare skin around the breasts and up to the neck that reddens and swells at the same time as the vulva swells and reddens with the onset of estrus. The breast ornamentation mimics the swollen vulva. It is triggered by the same hormones, and there can be no mistaking the message: This female is primed to reproduce. Hence the name—"bleeding heart" monkey. Males also develop the bare pink breast, but in them it serves only as a means of attracting or repelling individuals of both sexes.

The bare pink breast of the gelada baboon, an adaptation to their environment, gives them their popular name: bleeding heart monkeys.

Gelada baboons are primates, like us, and fossils discovered in the Afar depression reveal that our ancestors also lived in the Ethiopian region four million years ago. At that time the highlands were bleak, raw mountains, and the lowland savannas were well enough endowed to satisfy needs. Hunters doubtless worked their way up and into the mountains as the forests took root. Around 7,000 years ago, when changes in climate brought prolonged drought to the plains, farmers and herders took to the heights. Here they found an environment that was highly conducive to human settlement. The temperature range is congenial in tropical regions at altitudes of over 6,500 feet and the diseases common in the lowlands, such as malaria, trypanosomiasis, and bilharzia, are absent. The tsetse fly, which makes cattle raising impossible in much of Africa, is not found in the cool highlands. Furthermore, the elevated landmasses also force moisture-laden winds up to the heights at which clouds form and rain falls. The hot and damp winds that the coastal deserts draw from the Red Sea rise as they strike the Rift Valley escarpment, just 37 miles inland, and ample rain falls on the plateau beyond.

Teff is a tiny grain full of goodness—one daily portion is enough to sustain life; two will ensure good health. Equally important, teff will produce a harvest when other crops fail. Because teff evolved in the Ethiopian Highlands, it is perfectly adapted to the region's testing conditions and was domesticated by local farmers long ago.

By the time people arrived, the vegetation included a number of endemic plants that might have been expressly intended for human exploitation. The Ethiopian Highlands contain more indigenous plants used for food by people than in any other part of Africa. In fact, the region is described as "one of the world's greatest and oldest centers of domestic seed plants." Ethiopia also has the endemic false banana, ensete (*Musa ventricosa*), whose starch-rich rootstock has for centuries been the staple diet of people on the southern portion of the highlands. The oil-producing nug (*Guizotia abyssinica*) is another that was brought into human use in Ethiopia. So too is the Oromo potato (*Plectranthrus edulis*), which grows wild but is also cultivated as a crop. The seeds of the safflower (*Carthamus tinctorius*) are roasted and ground to produce a thickening for soups and drinks. The pungent-smelling leaves of sensel (*Adhatoda schimperiana*) are used to treat malaria and as a pot scourer. It also makes a good hedge. Then of course there is coffee (*Coffea arabica*), an indigenous, straggly bush, hidden away in the lower reaches of the forest, whose berries the Ethiopians have been using as the ingredient of a refreshing beverage for 2,000 years. Coffee was virtually unknown in Europe until the early 1600s, but it soon caught on. By 1675 there were 3,000 coffeehouses in London alone, and today coffee is the United States' single largest agricultural import.

But while coffee stimulated the mind, it was the cereals that did most to feed the body. Finger millet (*Eleusine coracana*) probably originated in Ethiopia (although the earliest evidence of its cultivation comes from India), and distinct types of wheat, barley, and sorghum were developed locally from stock introduced from elsewhere (probably from the Nile

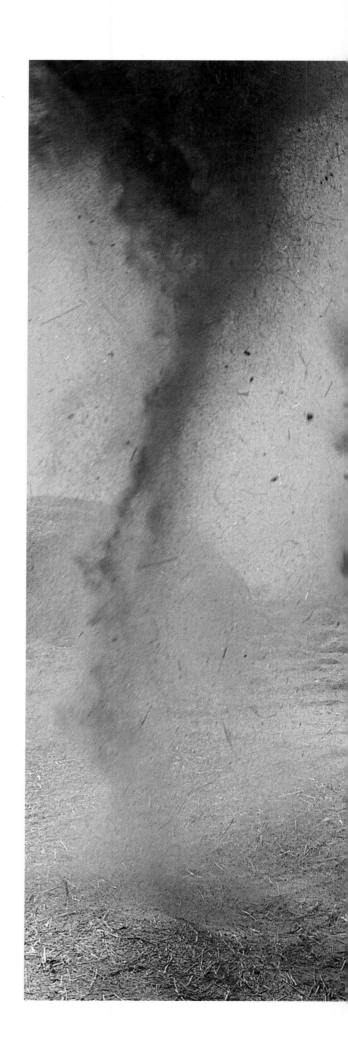

or across the Red Sea). The cereal that contributed most to the historical development of the region, though, was of purely Ethiopian origin. First cultivated on the plateau, 2,500 years ago, it fueled the growth of a civilization whose size and sophistication was unmatched in sub-Saharan Africa. That cereal was teff (*Eragrostis tef*)—with a seed smaller than a pinhead.

Even today, teff is sown on more land than any other crop in Ethiopia, and for centuries it has been grown there exclusively. There is no evidence that teff was ever grown in southern Arabia, for example, which invites the conclusion that teff was being cultivated before the eighth century B.C., when southern Arabian influence first reached the Ethiopian plateau. It is more likely that wheat and barley were introduced to Ethiopia from southern Arabia around that time, along with the plow, perhaps, and the techniques of terracing and irrigation. But wheat and barley could never supplant teff as the preferred crop,

simply because teff had evolved in the region and was best adapted to the climate of the highlands.

The fields of teff dominating the landscape of northern Ethiopia in the aftermath of the rainy season look more like hay meadows, rippling in the wind, than a cereal crop just a few weeks from harvest. The plant is light and delicate, and the grain it produces is tiny. But size is no measure of quality. In its value as a human food, teff is superior to any other cereal grown in Ethiopia. Carbohydrate and protein content matches and in some instances surpasses that of maize, sorghum, wheat, and barley, and even more important, its amino acid composition is closer to human dietary requirements. It is particularly rich in the amino acids that cannot be made inside the body and must therefore be ingested. A single daily portion of teff supplies enough of these essential amino acids to sustain life without any other source of protein, while two daily portions are enough to ensure good health.

Injera is prepared for a wedding feast. Teff contains more essential minerals than are found in other grains; its nutritional value is enhanced by preparation, which generates additional vitamins.

FOLLOWING PAGES: At a wedding in Addis Ababa, young congregation members wear homespun cotton shifts and crowns of satin.

During the 19th and 20th centuries, when drought and famine have periodically brought devastating calamity to Ethiopia, the particular value of teff has been not so much its nutritional value as its capacity to produce a harvest when other cereals fail. Because teff is uniquely adapted to the region's climatic conditions, it will develop and ripen grain from every pollinated flower even when no further rain falls while the plant is maturing. Other cereals commonly grown in Ethiopia will either ripen none (maize) or only some of the grain (barley and sorghum).

The most dependable portion of the region's rainfall blows in from the Red Sea during August and September, so farmers planting teff that flowers on the strength of those rains can be sure of a harvest, even if the rest of the year is dry. High-yielding cereals perform well only in years when conditions are good. For the subsistence farmer, an adequate yield even in a bad year is far more important.

With farms extended by terracing of the hillsides and the advent of the plow (pulled by oxen bred from cattle brought by pastoralists from the west), a sound agricultural base was established on the northern plateau by 500 B.C. Monumental temples were built at Yeha, Haoulti, and Mantara, with altars dedicated to a pantheon of deities almost identical to those known from the southern Arabian kingdom of the period. At Haoulti, an elaborately decorated throne carved from a single block of fine-grained local limestone has been recovered. Among the remarkable quantity of metal objects found at the sites generally, there are axes, adzes, sickles, and daggers of bronze, and scissors, rings, daggers, and swords of iron.

The large buildings, the tombs, sculptures, and altars, the elaborate stone carving, the metalwork, and the use of writing at these sites all indicate that a complex society, most likely a state, was firmly established on the northern Ethiopian plateau by the third century B.C. at the latest. Social stratification is implied, and since some inscriptions tell of kings ruling over groups of people distinctly identified as "red" and "black," it may be concluded that the population was also divided on racial grounds.

A town called Aksum was the center of these developments. Nestling beneath a semicircle of low wooded hills, Aksum was beautifully sited—both in strategic and natural terms. A river flowed in from the north through a narrow cleft that was dammed to store water for the dry season, when the river often ceased to flow. There was open ground for crops and grazing in the immediate vicinity of the town, while the woods on the hills above provided timber for building and fuel. The layout of the town was as stratified as its society. The dwellings of the wealthy occupied the higher elevations, which caught the cooling breezes, and the artisans and lower classes lived down below. Stone, quarried from the nearby hillside, was the material of choice for wealthy residents. Everyone else used mud-and-wattle construction, with roofs thatched with straw.

What we know of Aksum is derived from archaeological digs, the detailed examination of ancient land surfaces, and careful estimations of the prevailing climate. No eyewitness reports of everyday life in the town exist, but its modern counterpart, Axum (this alternative spelling is often used when referring to the modern town), is far enough away from the developed world to give an impression of what Aksum was like.

"Biblical" was the word that immediately sprang to mind when I visited Aksum. The roads are unmade, there are more carts and donkeys than motor traffic, and the people wear rough homespun cloaks, with sandals on their feet and a staff in the hand as they trudge through the loose sand. Voices and the sounds of human activity predominate—a striking contrast with the cacophony of mechanical noise that most

St. George's Church is one of 11 hewn from the living rock—a relatively soft volcanic tuff—at Lalibela in the Ethiopian Highlands. Lalibela was chosen by a 12th-century ruler to be laid out as a new City of Zion.

urban dwellers must tolerate. Away from the main thoroughfare, narrow paths wind between the houses, giving glimpses of courtyards in which women are grinding teff and preparing *injera* over charcoal stoves. Their husbands work the fields, and their children tend the goats.

By the first century A.D. Aksum was the commercial and administrative center of an empire whose influence extended across the Red Sea to southern Arabia. Its rulers maintained close ties with the eastern Roman Empire, and in the third century achieved international prominence by issuing their own coinage, in gold, silver, and bronze. Persian leaders of the day described Aksum as one of the world's four most important kingdoms (the other three were Persia, Rome, and Sileos—possibly meaning China).

Though situated high up on the plateau, about a hundred miles from the nearest eastern access to the Red Sea, and then still some 20 miles from Adulis (a difficult eight-day journey down the escarpment), Aksum exported goods from the plateau and the Sudan as far as India, China, the Black Sea, and Spain. Pliny the Elder, writing in the first century A.D., specifies ivory, rhinoceros horn, hippopotamus hides, and slaves as goods from Aksum. Other sources refer to gold dust, frankincense, civet cat musk—and even live elephants. One classical author describes a herd of about 5,000 elephants "pastured on a broad field" in the vicinity of Yeha.

The goods Aksum exported were acquired locally or from the hinterland in exchange for cattle, iron, and salt. Iron probably was smelted on the plateau, but salt had to be collected from evaporation pans at the coast or dug from deposits in the Danakil Desert and carried up the escarpment. Hence salt was an especially valued commodity on the plateau and beyond, and it remained an important medium of exchange well into the modern era.

But while Aksum's commercial and territorial influence expanded, the capacity to grow food and its population remained finite. By A.D. 500 the city of Aksum covered an area of 185 acres and housed about 20,000 inhabitants. The city was more extensive and more densely populated than its modern counterpart—and has never been larger. Meanwhile, its rulers had developed what has been aptly described as a "mania for the gigantic."

Conspicuous consumption is commonplace behavior of wealthy people, and it was evident at Aksum in the size and grandeur of their residences and in the variety and quantity of imported luxury goods that have been recovered from among the ruins of the buildings. These included glassware and ceramics, articles made of precious metals, fabrics and clothing, wine, sugarcane, vegetable oils, and aromatics and spices. Most of the luxury goods were imported from the eastern Mediterranean. The ruling elite lived well, and even more conspicuous consumption was dedicated to them after death.

At an early stage in its development, Aksum adopted the practice of burying its rulers in stone-walled tombs and marking their graves with monumental stelae (or obelisks). Over 120 stelae have been located in the city. All but a few have fallen. Some lie like stranded whales beside dry, dusty streets. Others clog narrow ravines. Fragments of some that broke have been incorporated in church walls.

Most of the stelae are irregular in shape but perfectly smooth, with rounded edges and curved sides and shallow undulations along their length. Like works of sculpture, these stelae might have been carved to enhance the form of the natural stone. The six largest are very different, more indicative of an intention to revise rather than respect the natural form. Each is precisely hewn, rectangular in section, and the surfaces are elaborately decorated with bas-relief representations of multistoried buildings.

One of the larger examples still stands among a number of smaller, undecorated stones in a neatly

tended park in present-day Axum. It is a single block of granite 68 feet high, carved with geometric precision to represent a ten-story building, with a false door at the base. The fallen pieces of an even larger stela (78 feet overall), similarly decorated, were taken to Rome in 1937 during the Italian occupation of Ethiopia and reerected near the site of the Circus Maximus. (There is talk of this stela being returned to Axum.) The largest of all—108 feet long,

9 feet by 6.5 feet in section at the base, and carved on all four sides to represent a 13-story building, lies broken in five huge pieces, with smaller fragments scattered about the point of impact. Whether this massive decorated piece of stone ever stood upright is uncertain.

Whatever the case, the massive Aksum stela weighed over 700 tons and was probably the largest single block of stone ever quarried, carved, and set up

Priests carry the Tabot in procession through the streets of Lalibela. The Tabot is a replica of the Ark of the Covenant, the chest that contained the original Ten Commandments. Each of Ethiopia's 20,000 churches has a Tabot. Guarded by priests, these icons of faith are seen only on ceremonial occasions. This occasion is Timkat, which celebrates the baptism of Christ.

FOLLOWING PAGES: Lalibela landscape, site of the rock-hewn churches, lies over 6,500 feet above sea level. Rugged and afflicted by drought, the region is noted for the deep religious conviction of its people.

The church displays its finery during the Timkat procession in Lalibela. Many young men aspire to join the priesthood for a life of prayer and poverty. They pledge themselves to serve the community through the church.

in the ancient world. Its production called for technological expertise and labor resources comparable with those that built Egypt's Great Pyramids. The granite block was cut from a hillside about four miles west of Aksum, where the marks of quarrying are still evident. Dressing the stone with the unsophisticated metal or stone tools of the time and cutting bas-relief designs between four and eight inches deep into its entire surface area (roughly 3,550 square feet) would have kept a sizable corps of masons busy for years.

Exactly how the stone was moved from the quarry to Aksum and erected is a matter of conjecture. Rollers would have been employed, and elephants may have been used. Still, transporting such a massive stone over a distance of four miles and then raising it to a vertical position was an undertaking that would strain the ingenuity and technical resources of modern engineers.

No two of Aksum's six great stelae are identical, but when arranged in order of increasing size, each one is more elaborately decorated than the one before. This "mania for the gigantic" appears to have ended with the greatest of the six stelae; possibly because its fall was interpreted as a bad omen, possibly because its manufacture demonstrated the sheer impossibility of hewing, transporting, and raising anything larger. In any event, by the fourth century A.D. developments at Aksum were moving in a direction that made further pursuit of the gigantic impossible. The city-state was destined to become a victim of its own success.

During the period of conspicuous consumption, the region's woodland and forest had been stripped to fuel the charcoal-burning furnaces of iron smelters and local glass, brick, and pottery manufacturers; people needed wood and charcoal for cooking and heating, and timber was also used in house building and for furniture. The landscape was denuded, and

Behind the door at Narga Selassie Church, Lake Tana, decorated with guardian angels, lies the Tabot, the replica Ark of the Covenant. The original ark was the chest containing the tablets on which God had written the Ten Commandments. Legend says that it was brought to Ethiopia by an early ruler and is kept in the Church of St. Mary, Axum.

while clearing the forest initially made additional land available for crops to feed a growing population, it also exposed the soils to over-cropping and erosion. Ironically, the good rains that had nourished the growth of Aksum now hastened its decay. Nutrients were leached from the land as soil was washed from the hillsides. Rain that had been a blessing was now a curse.

"The breakdown of Axumite civilization was the result of a chance concatenation of mutually reinforcing processes that led to environmental degradation and precipitous demographic decline," wrote Karl W. Butzer. Aksum's problems of food production at home were compounded by the commercial and political difficulties abroad. During the late sixth and early seventh centuries, war in the eastern Mediterranean reduced the market for luxury goods in the increasingly impoverished Roman Empire. Then Persia gained control of southern Arabia (threatening trade routes to India), and by the early eighth century Arab forces had destroyed Adulis.

Aksum was cut off from the Red Sea trade. Gold coinage ceased to be issued. Centralized power collapsed. Within a few generations Aksum and its satellite communities were reduced to loose clusters of villages. By A.D. 800 Aksum had almost ceased to exist. People abandoned the impoverished landscape in favor of settlement on the virgin soils to the south, where they spurned the luxury grains—wheat and barley—brought in from southern Arabia and relied again on the food crop that had evolved in the region: teff. This move laid the foundations for the emergence of the modern Ethiopian state. In it Aksum would become a symbol of ancient royal and religious authority—which it remains to this day.

Aksum converted to Christianity only in the fourth century A.D., but Ethiopian tradition claims that its connection with biblical events dates back to the ninth century B.C., when the Queen of Sheba is said to have traveled from her Ethiopian palace to meet King Solomon in Jerusalem. Their meeting is described in the tenth chapter of the Book of I Kings:

And she came to Jerusalem with a very great train, with camels that bare spices, and very much gold, and precious stones: and when she was come to Solomon, she communed with him of all that was in her heart. . . .

And she gave the king an hundred and twenty talents of gold, and of spices very great store, and precious stones: there came no more such abundance of spices as these which the queen of Sheba gave to king Solomon. . . .

And king Solomon gave unto the queen of Sheba all her desire, whatsoever she asked, beside that which Solomon gave her of his royal bounty. So she turned and went to her own country, she and her servants.

Ethiopian tradition interprets the last verse as meaning that Solomon had spent the night with Sheba, so that his gifts to her included the son to whom she gave birth on her return to Ethiopia. The child was named David, and in due course he ascended to the throne as Menelik I, founder of the Solomonic dynasty of which Haile Selassie was the last incumbent. In later times, the link between Ethiopia and Christian religion was strengthened by a legend telling that while still a young man, Menelik had brought the fabled Ark of the Covenant to Aksum.

The Ark of the Covenant was the most sacred object of Old Testament times—and the most precious. A strongbox covered and lined with gold, it was made for the tablets of stone on which the Ten Commandments had been written by the finger of God. After its construction at the foot of Mount Sinai around 1250 B.C., the ark accompanied the Israelites through the wilderness, helping them to victory in every encounter, including the conquest of Palestine.

King David took the ark to Jerusalem, and his son Solomon installed it in the temple he was building when the Queen of Sheba made her visit. Legend tells that David, son of Solomon and the Queen of Sheba, spent a year at the court of his father as a young adult. On his departure he stole the Ark of the Covenant from the temple and carried it back to Aksum, where it has remained ever since.

So the story goes. It is a good story, but only because there is no other explanation for the ark's disappearance. Even the Bible is silent on the subject. However, claims of its presence in Aksum are contradicted by historical fact. The legend of Solomon, Sheba, and Menelik has no historical basis. The Queen of Sheba is a mythical figure. Aksum did not exist as a political entity while Solomon was alive, and the city of Aksum itself was founded several centuries after Menelik was supposed to have brought the ark from Jerusalem.

But belief is a powerful force. With the collapse of the Aksumite state, the church became the font of influence and authority in Ethiopia. Kings acquired divine status—the priest-king—and before long fabulous tales of Ethiopia and its monarchs reached Europe. The earliest known European reference to a king of Ethiopia appears in a manuscript from 1145, which refers to Prester John as a powerful Christian priest-king ruling a vast empire that was then presumed to be somewhere in middle Asia. A letter said to have been addressed to the Greek emperor Manuel by Prester John himself in 1165 claimed, among other things, that the wonders of his empire included the fountain of youth, a river whose bed consisted entirely of gemstones, ants that dug gold, pebbles that gave light or could make a man invisible, and a mirror that enabled Prester John to see anywhere in any one of his many kingdoms.

However much credence was given to the more fantastic elements of these stories, the rulers of medieval Europe decided that Prester John might be willing to help them repel the Arab forces that seemed determined to conquer all Europe. The prospect of being able to attack Islam from the rear was appealing. The Portuguese fleet that sailed from Lisbon under Vasco da Gama in 1497 carried letters from King Manuel I addressed to Prester John that were surely written in hopes of forming a military alliance with the Ethiopian monarch. Vasco da Gama rounded the Cape of Good Hope and sailed up the East African coast to Malindi before tacking east across the ocean to India. At ports along the African coast he picked up reports that confirmed the existence of Prester John, but he did not manage to deliver the letters. In any case, the Europeans could not have known that the Prester John of the day maintained friendly relations with the Arabs. His predecessor had given shelter to followers and family of Muhammad when they fled Arabia in A.D. 616. Islam and Christianity have coexisted peacefully in Ethiopia ever since.

The European interest in Africa was reciprocated. Africans regularly ventured out from the East African coast via trading routes to the Red Sea and India. Indeed, Ethiopians were exploring the city streets of Europe long before Europeans visited Ethiopia or any other part of sub-Saharan Africa. The first European to visit Ethiopia was an Italian, Pietro Rombulo, who made the long and arduous journey in 1407. Remarkable, one might conclude, but in fact Ethiopians had visited Italy in 1306—100 years earlier. The evidence is scarce and always brief, but a document chanced upon by historians delving through medieval archives describes how a priest in Genoa had interviewed a group of 30 Ethiopians who were returning home from visits to Avignon and Rome, but had been forced to wait at Genoa for a favorable wind. The account suggests that the Ethiopian travelers were fairly commonplace.

If the Ethiopians were on a mission to the Pope at the command of Prester John, presumably with interpreters or able to converse in a common language (probably Latin), this suggests that their journey had been preceded by other fact-finding missions.

It is known that Ethiopians regularly visited Egypt and Cyprus, and made pilgrimages to the holy sites of Palestine, where they established links with the rest of the Christian world. These contacts gave Europeans exaggerated notions of the role the Ethiopians could play in an alliance against Islam. It was commonly believed, for instance, that the Ethiopians controlled the flow of the Nile. A typical report stated that "if it pleases the Prester John, he could very well make the river flow in another direction."

In the year 1400 King Henry IV of England sent a letter to the "king of Abyssinia, Prester John," evidently seeking King David's (the then Prester John) participation in a crusade against Islam. It is not known if Henry's letter reached Ethiopia, but in 1402 King David himself sent envoys to Italy asking for technical aid (apart from any political purpose) and duly received a number of Florentine craftsmen at his court. Vatican records show that letters of safe conduct were given to at least three parties of Italians who traveled to Ethiopia between 1451 and 1453 alone, and a traveler who visited Ethiopia in 1482 reported on his return that he had met ten Italians there who had been in the country for 25 years. The French sent missions to Ethiopia too. During the 1420s the Duke of Berry dispatched a Neapolitan by the name of Pietro who not only reached Ethiopia successfully but also married an Ethiopian and remained there for some years.

These fragments of evidence add up to a clear indication that continuous relations were established between Ethiopia and Europe during the first half of the 15th century. There was extensive interchange, much of it initiated by the Ethiopians. Furthermore, the extent of Europe's knowledge of the land of Prester John is shown on two contemporary maps: the Egyptus Novelo, probably drawn in Florence circa 1454, and the Mappa Mundi, drawn in Venice in 1460. Though the Egyptus Novelo shows only northeast Africa while the Mappa Mundi gives a representation of the entire world, both contain details of Ethiopian geography and the location of towns that must have come from firsthand sources. Even more significantly, the Mappa Mundi shows Africa surrounded by ocean, ostensibly confirming the assumption that sailing around the continent was a practical idea.

MANY OF THE stories about Prester John were myth, but the kings of Ethiopia were real enough. Their brand of religious nationalism united the people of the Ethiopian Highlands in the Christian faith, setting down roots from which a nation of remarkable durability has grown. They were cruel despots, some of them. Warlords ruthlessly exploited feudal peasants. Civil wars ravaged the country—but none of this could destroy the state. Rulers and ruled alike believed in the ultimate sanction of the divine, transcendental authority that was vested in the church. The words of God, written in stone and preserved in the Ark of the Covenant, lay in the dark recesses of the sanctuary at Aksum. No human eye has ever seen them, but no Ethiopian is beyond their authority.

A replica of the ark is enshrined in each of Ethiopia's more than 20,000 Christian churches. Known as Tabots, these replicas play a central role in major religious events—particularly at the feast of Timkat, when the Tabot is carried in procession from every church and the faithful bow and pray as it passes. A replica of the ark is used in the Timkat procession even at Axum—where sceptics might expect to see the real thing on display. People flock to Axum in the thousands for the Timkat festival. Crowds surge past the stelae, those huge hewn stones offering tangible evidence of the region's ancient history, but there are no gestures of respect—much less reverence—for the relics of an ancestral civilization. Ancient Aksum is forgotten. The relics of the past are highly visible, but the crowd today strives for just a glimpse of the Tabot—a replica relic—and is more concerned with the promises that faith and belief offer for the future than with the evidence of the past.

The power of faith was something the new regime attempted to ignore when it took control from Haile Selassie in 1974. The ambitions of the new Communist-inspired rulers soon proved to be no less oppressive than those of their predecessors. They introduced reforms that were designed to sweep away many aspects of the old order—including religion. Some aspects of reform were welcomed, especially land reform, but attempting to reduce the influence of the church was a step too far. As the dictatorial nature of the new regime began to show, religion would provide a network of shared belief through which dissent and opposition could spread and consolidate.

Like history repeating itself, it was once again a famine that set the grounds for the regime's collapse. The BBC television news report of October 23, 1984, focused world attention on the Ethiopian crisis, but unlike Haile Selassie's government in 1975, the Mengistu regime welcomed the international attention that the famine of 1984 attracted. It suited them. The foreign media were only too ready to attribute the famine to drought (and even global warming), and so the Ethiopian leaders were able to direct attention away from the wholesale, government-directed population resettlement, economic upheaval, and civil war that had done more to precipitate the disaster than the drought. Moreover, the large amounts of food aid flooding into the country provided a ready source of supplies for the Ethiopian army, which was fighting the secessionist Eritrean and Tigrean forces. The army provided transport for the relief agencies, but only a fraction of the food they carried

His grip on life as slender as his wasted limbs, a young victim of famine in Ethiopia is examined at an intensive-feeding facility.

reached the famine victims. In December 1984, acting Foreign Minister Tibebu Bekele told the U.S. chargé d'affaires, probably with more candor than he intended, that "food is a major element in our strategy against the secessionists." In 1985, Ethiopia received about 1.37 million tons of food relief, of which a mere 99,000 tons were distributed in non-government-held areas of Eritrea and Tigray, where between one-third and one-half of the famine-stricken population lived.

In the aftermath of the 1975 famine, land reform and restructuring of the agricultural industry had led to unprecedented well-being for millions of rural Ethiopians. The revolutionary government showed a serious commitment to tackling the causes of famine—rather than relying on relief—that was widely welcomed. But disillusion set in as the government became steadily more concerned with defeating the secessionists in Eritrea and Tigray than with the welfare of the rural population. The ever expanding army had to be fed. So did government supporters in the cities. Before long the peasants were being forced to supply strict quotas of grain to agents of the central government in much the same way as they had before the revolution. Some were even obliged to pay a famine relief tax. Farmers were made to move away from their land to live in communal villages; large numbers were resettled from the north to the south of the country. Selling grain other than through government agencies was restricted, and the number of grain dealers fell from 20,000 to 30,000 to less than 5,000 in ten years. These measures caused massive impoverishment; even more significantly, they were a powerful disincentive to production. Why bother to produce what the government would take away?

Still, prospects seemed good in the early 1980s. The northern region had suffered two sharp droughts in the late 1970s, but 1980 and 1981 were described as normal, while 1982 was a bumper year. Some regions suffered drought in 1983, but others enjoyed above-average rainfall. The UN satellite images of the vegetation showed that conditions on the ground were improving throughout 1983 and early 1984. Even so, in early 1983 a trickle of destitute migrants began arriving at relief feeding centers, pleading for help. The trickle grew into a steady stream during the course of the year and became a flood in late 1984. There had been a widespread drought early in the year, but this was not the direct cause of the famine. It merely turned a serious problem into a disaster. The rural population had been bled dry by the government. The peasants had nothing left, and it is no coincidence that the most severe famine was in the war zone and that the phases of the developing famine corresponded with the major military campaigns.

Hundreds of thousands died in the Ethiopian famine of 1984–85, and millions more were left destitute, homes gone, families decimated, and the lives of children irreversibly blighted. The world responded to the catastrophe with unprecedented generosity, stirred by Band Aid and countless other fund-raising campaigns. The scale of the response seemed to herald a new era of global concern for those who have been afflicted by calamities that were no fault of their own. That makes all the more tragic the heartless chicanery of the Mengistu government, which worked to ensure the world's humanitarian effort actually prolonged the suffering more than alleviated it. In Tigray in particular, aid supplies fed soldiers and not rural people.

Overall, the relief program helped to keep Mengistu in power longer, but other factors he could not resist. The crumbling of Communist power in the Soviet Union in the late 1980s reduced the military assistance Ethiopia had been receiving from that quarter. In cities and towns across the country, opposition to his rule was mounting, with the church as the rallying point of protest. Church attendance soared, and religious authority strengthened as priests—almost without exception—led their congregations in demonstrations of what appeared to be religious fervor but were also coded messages of political opposition. The government could do nothing about them. A priest who connived with the authorities in an attempt to remove the Tabot from his church in Addis Ababa in the dead of night was set upon by his outraged congregation and killed. At Timkat each year during the final years of Mengistu's rule, the crowds straining for a glimpse of the Tabot were huge and determined—their devotion an expression of religious nationalism that could not be suppressed.

Mengistu slipped away from Ethiopia one day in May 1991 to Zimbabwe, where he is officially regarded as a refugee. Like weary travelers relieved of their heavy burdens, Ethiopians paused briefly after the fall of the Mengistu regime, then began tackling the country's problems with characteristic vigor. Korem, known around the world as a symbol of disaster, soon became its former self—a small, peaceful trading village that served a far-flung community of farmers. Returning home was not easy for the many thousands who had crowded the refugee camps. They trudged back to their farms, weakened in body and spirit, with painful memories of the children and relatives they had left behind in graveyards. But even the climate was generous in the aftermath of the famine. A sequence of exceptionally good rains helped the long-suffering farmers to regain their former proud and honorable status. They turned the soil, sowed the seed, and reaped the harvest. Before long they were on the road to Korem again—but this time not as refugees. Now they were successful farmers, with bags of grain for sale.

The high, craggy mountains of Ethiopia are the last refuge of the rare Walia ibex, gelada baboon, and endangered Ethiopian wolf. They also have been a haven for the world's major religions. Judaism, Islam, and Christianity have all found a home here. Their legacy has left a land replete with holy places.

Ethiopia embraced Christianity less than 400 years after the birth of Christ—while Europe was still in the Dark Ages. The church became the font of influence and authority throughout the country. Kings were accorded divine status—and became so famous that tales of the priest-king Prester John reached distant Europe. The Ark of the Covenant, the chest containing the tablets on which God wrote the Ten Commandments and therefore Christianity's holy of holies, is said to be in Ethiopia, taken from Solomon's Temple by a legendary Ethiopian king. A replica of the ark, called the Tabot, is kept in each of the country's 20,000-plus churches.

In the 12th century, a replica City of Zion was built at Lalibela. A hill in the city was named Calvary, and a stream flowing through it was called the Yordanos. Over the centuries, the devout have carved 11 churches from the solid rock at Lalibela. Each year, thousands flock to the town for the celebration of Timkat, the feast of Epiphany, when the Tabot is ceremoniously paraded from the churches to the baptism pool. For most who take part, a spray of holy water is the joyous culmination of Timkat. But for some young men, a place in the formal procession is a first step on the road to becoming a priest.

Ethiopia is a deeply spiritual country, where the authority of the church is widely respected by the country's 24 million Orthodox Christians.

Sixteen-year-old Kebkab Wube Wodemariam (on the left) is training to become a priest, like his late father and his brother, Liku. The scriptures he must learn by heart are written in Ge'ez, Africa's oldest written language. Here Kebkab copies out a page under the watchful eye of his elder brother.

"My goal is to complement my church education with modern education,"
he says. "I would like to graduate from theology college, then I want
to come back home to serve the church here."

After Sunday morning service Kebkab is in a thoughtful mood (left). While following ancient tradition, he has new ideas. He wants to study abroad.

Meanwhile, Kebkab takes an important step on his spiritual journey when he is chosen to participate in the annual Timkat ceremonies. Here, robed in white (above, right), he joins priests preparing for the procession.

As a trainee priest, Kebkab depends for food upon the local village communities, which sometimes have little to give (above). "The training and way of life is difficult," he says, "but it is the only way to qualify as a priest."

Timkat celebrates the Feast of Epiphany—the baptism of Christ— which culminates with the spraying of holy water over the crowd (right).

"Many people come here to be baptized and are cured by the holy water," says Kebkab. "This is a great inspiration to me."

SaheL

Sweeping imperiously across the continent from the Atlantic to the mountain fortresses of Ethiopia and the Indian Ocean coast of Somalia, the Sahel's unbroken ribbon of arid savanna grassland—4,300 miles long and 185 to 700 miles wide—is a corridor along which people, animals, and plants have mingled and migrated for millennia.

Sahel is the Arabic word for "shore," and this is the shore of the Sahara Desert. Like a high-water mark that advances and recedes with the tide, the Sahel has moved south as climate change caused the desert to expand, and north again as the desert contracted. But throughout, the Sahel has endowed Africa with a ribbon of life-giving opportunity.

Cattle herders are the masters of the Sahel—the Fulani of Senegal and Mali, the Peuhl of Niger, the Dinka of Sudan, and the Samburu of Kenya. These are the nomadic pastoralists whose cattle graze on distant Sahelian ranges, converting a scanty crop of grass to a harvest of meat, milk, and calves that will enrich their home villages.

Harmattan winds fill the Dogon region of Mali with the promise of rain.

The cluster of huts was situated on the southern edge of the El Barta Plain, 6,500 feet above sea level. The low, windowless huts maintained a comfortable temperature day and night, and there was a body of warmth among the cows crowded into the thorn enclosure, but the air was cold in the early morning. In preparation for milking, Nankarusi first warmed her hands in a stream of urine flowing conveniently from one of the cows, then laid the crudely stuffed skin of a calf killed by cheetahs the previous day before its mother, which nuzzled the surrogate form and obligingly let

down her milk. Nankarusi massaged the teats, then directed the milk into the long polished gourd. She collected just a few cupfuls, for the small Samburu cattle seldom give large quantities of milk. When the milking was finished and the herd had left the enclosure, the women took handfuls of the fresh, wet dung left behind and plastered it over the walls of the huts, filling cracks, patching holes.

At the brink of a gully the leading animals of the herd suddenly shied back, all together—like leaves caught in a gust of wind—and soon afterward their alarm was explained by the appearance of two *moran* (warriors) bearing a fresh lion skin wrapped around

the pole they carried between them. The previous day three lions, two females and one male, had killed and eaten a cow while the young herd boy had looked on helplessly. When the moran had tracked down and confronted the culprits late in the evening the females had run, but the male had stopped to fight and died with seven spears in him.

Across the plain some groups of zebra were grazing. They lifted their heads from the scant grasses as the herd approached, then strolled peaceably out of its way, not greatly disturbed. As the day advanced, a band of quivering white heat rose from the ground, slicing the distant Ndoto hills from the landscape.

PREVIOUS PAGES: **Three young women head for the Daral festival in Diafarabé, Mali.** ABOVE: **The Niger River—artery of the western Sahel—has been traveled for centuries by traders between the cities and villages.**

There was no sign of rain. Red sand, humps of gray scrub bush, acacia trees with thorns standing out from the bare branches like bleached fish bones— amid all the dryness the cattle somehow found something to eat. But they had to drink too.

Lesipin, a man whose ability to interpret the juxtaposition of the stars was widely respected, had said that if rain did not fall before the horn of the Pleiades dropped below the horizon, there would be no rain at all that season. For the past week the clouds had been gathering and growing thicker over the Ndoto Mountains and the summit ridges of Mount Nyiru, but they had thinned out again, and the horn of the Pleiades had disappeared below the horizon the night before. There were still some heavy clouds piled up over the highlands to the south and tumbling back from the western escarpment of the Rift Valley, but the prospect of rain on the El Barta Plain was slim now, and the next chance of rain was four or five months hence.

Several herds were already drinking at the much depleted dam pond below Koitokol when Linolosi arrived there with his cattle, and not all of them were Samburu. Koitokol marks the point at which the Samburu territory merges with that of their neighbors, the Rendille and the Turkana in northern Kenya. From the retaining wall of the dam, other herds could be seen approaching across the plains, raising clouds of swirling dust, Turkana from the west, Rendille from the north and east, Samburu from the south and east.

When the rainfall is adequate, these three groups are kept apart by the different rangelands used by the different livestock they keep. The Samburu are able to keep cattle as well as sheep and goats in the highlands they occupy, due to the relatively high rainfall. In the drier lowlands of the Koroli and Kaisut deserts to the north of the Samburu territory, the Rendille can maintain only camels. The Turkana, who range around the southern end of Lake Turkana and into the furnace of the Suguta Valley, lead a much more opportunistic life, subsisting largely on sheep and goats but keeping cattle when they can—stock that is often stolen from neighboring communities.

Basically, it is ecology that keeps the three groups apart. Each subsists on the most productive stock that its territory can support. Yet for the people themselves the distinctions are first and foremost cultural.

The Rendille, or "people of the camel," share many affinities with the Samburu, "people of the cattle." The two groups are traditional allies against the Turkana, who are noted primarily for their lack of social cohesion. They do not circumcise, and they have few food taboos. They will even eat fish, Samburu elders point out.

Now, at the height of a drought, both the Turkana and the Rendille were invading Samburu territory. The pastures they had vacated were virtually devoid of nourishment for their stock. Grazing in the highlands was running short for the Samburu cattle, but there was still enough for camels and goats, which browse on bushes more than they graze. From the Rendille and Turkana point of view there was no choice. They had to move onto Samburu territory or watch their stock die. Their intrusion was not welcomed, though.

At the dam stories were told of similar instances in the past when bloody skirmishes broke out between Turkana and Samburu warriors. Already in this drought several Turkana encampments had been established in Samburu territory; spears had been thrown and men wounded near the town of Isiolo. Feelings ran particularly high at the few remaining sources of water, where the herds and herdsmen had to mingle. The diplomatic skills of the elders were exercised time and again as Samburu moran became increasingly agitated, calling for the order to take up their spears and repel the invaders.

In scattered outbreaks of fighting, some warriors were killed, but the elders managed to keep the peace. At the critical moment, pressure in the lowlands was relieved as the Samburu moved large herds of cattle up the tortuous tracks to the summit plateaus of Mount Nyiru, 9,000 feet above the plains. Here in the grassy forest glades of their sacred mountain, the cattle flourished. Meanwhile Rendille camels quickly moved in to browse on the scrubby vegetation the Samburu had left behind, and the Turkana herded their livestock onto the territory vacated by the Rendille. But if the pasture on Nyiru is so lush—even in the dry season—why did the Samburu not keep cattle there all year-round? Because they get diarrhea if kept too long on a rich diet, Linolosi explained, because ticks and disease build up rapidly in the damp pasture, and because a dry-season reserve that is used throughout the year would be less useful in a really severe drought. And so, with Nyiru as a reserve and each group moving a step up the ecological gradient, the Samburu, Rendille, and Turkana were able to keep more of their animals alive during the drought.

**EEPING A BIG** enough herd of domestic animals watered and well fed enough to sustain the people looking after them is a challenge at the best of times. On the plains of the African Sahel, rainfall is

erratic and the distances between grazing and water critical. That challenge makes for a way of life in which the connection between people and the environment is very direct. Until relatively recent times only a very narrow margin separated success from failure. Nowadays the margin has been broadened by the availability of supplementary foods and the cash economy. The pastoralists are no longer so absolutely dependent upon their livestock. Health care—from childbirth to old age, from the treatment of illnesses and snakebites to the removal of arrows from cattle raids—keeps more people alive. But pastoralists are still a very small fraction of the national populations, though they occupy a huge fraction of the land area.

Among a total of 200 ethnic groups in East Africa, for instance, only 15 are pastoralists, of which 12 range across the semidesert Sahel of northern Kenya. These 12 groups constitute just 6 percent of Kenya's population, but they occupy a full 85 percent of the country's land area.

The different population densities of the two regions are of course directly related to rainfall and agricultural potential. Kenyan farmers have always been inclined to look upon herders as little more than dangerous and wasteful vagrants. This point of view derived initially from their conflicting land-use strategies, and it has compounded in the years following independence by the views of Western experts trying to introduce development aid projects. The question of what to do with the herders seemed very straightforward to African politicians of an agricultural background and Western experts with limited experience of Africa. As they saw it, the herds were too large and the cattle consequently of inferior quality. Smaller herds of better fed animals was the answer. Selling those animals would provide a cash income to

The fine work of Mali's expert goldsmiths is beautifully displayed at the Daral festival in Diafarabé.

replace the traditional dependence on milk. For the pastoralists, development meant settling down on land that they would own and concentrating on the raising of high-quality beef cattle. They would send their children to school, grow a few crops, and service the tourist industry. They could even consider hunting the game animals with whom they shared the plains and which consumed so much grass.

In a word, maximization was the strategy of the development planners. But on the Sahel rangelands survival is the strategy that the pastoralists must respect. Their way of life is regulated by the natural ebb and flow of climate and environment. These can be evaluated only by considering the evidence of the past, particularly in terms of the worst that might happen in the future. Every aspect of the pastoralist lifestyle is a measure of human ingenuity trying to assess their ever changing environment.

In regions where the rainfall ranges widely in the course of a few years, with no reliable forecasts available, the size of a herd is in effect a measure of the rainfall of previous seasons. The pastoralists' aim must always be to raise as many animals as possible, for next year it might not rain at all, or the year after that. Their determination to maintain large herds is often criticized on the assumption that they regard livestock as a form of wealth and that large herds are therefore a sign of avarice. This is wrong. A large number of livestock represents insurance in case of disaster. Lepusiki had 200 cattle when the 1984-85 drought set in, for example. He lost 80 percent of them, and so still had 40 animals—the best of his stock—to

FOLLOWING PAGES: **Cattle are the wealth of the village, sent away to graze the Sahel's wet season flush of grass while crops are raised on the village lands.**

Farmers on the inland delta of the Niger River plant a succession of crops as the flood rises and falls over their fields—rice on the rising waters, sorghum and millet when the receding flood leaves saturated soils.

keep his family alive when the drought broke. Had he started out with 40 (a number the agroeconomists might recommend to maximize cash returns from the land) and lost only 50 percent, Lepusiki and his family would have found it hard to survive and rebuild the herd from the remaining 20 animals.

Small stock—goats and sheep—are another important aspect of the pastoralists' survival strategy that is often criticized. Goats are especially denigrated because they are said to breed too fast and degrade the environment. But goats are a vital safety net. They are extremely hardy and able to survive where other animals die off. Most important of all, they continue breeding when larger stock have turned barren. Goats are the last to stop giving milk as a drought intensifies and the first to begin again when rain does at last fall. Their gestation period is short, and pregnant goats start producing milk within days of the first good rains. The Samburu built up large flocks of sheep and goats during the dry years of the 1970s. Many of these animals survived the 1984-85 drought that killed their cattle, and large numbers were subsequently traded for the Ethiopian and Somali cattle with which the Samburu replenished their herds.

Over the centuries, pastoralists have developed feasible strategies to sustain themselves in the Sahel. Their population density is low, but that is due to the land, not their strategy. But what of the future? It is unlikely that any other means of exploiting the food potential of these regions would support more people. Enterprises such as large-scale ranching or irrigated farming might produce more cash for a few individuals, but neither activity would employ as many people per square mile as pastoralism supports. Meanwhile, the population is growing and resources remain finite. There are more people and more livestock than ever before in the Sahel, despite

recurrent drought, famine, and civil strife. Clearly, these expanding populations cannot all be accommodated within the narrow margins of survival that traditional pastoralism has developed. That system has expanded and intensified to its limits. Selling livestock has already begun to take a regular percentage from the system. More schools and more economic growth in the Sahel might foster alternative skills and create jobs that take a regular percentage of people from the system too. As ever in African affairs, the story of the Sahel is one of adaptation to circumstance.

THE **SAHEL SWEEPS** imperiously across Africa south of the Sahara, from the westernmost cape of Senegal on the Atlantic coast to the ramparts of the Ethiopian massif, then south and east across southern Ethiopia, northern Kenya, and Somalia to the Horn of Africa—the continent's easternmost point. It is a 4,300-mile ribbon of unbroken savanna grassland, never less than 185 miles wide and extending up to 700 miles wide in some places. Sahel is an Arabic word meaning "shore"—the shore of the Sahara Desert. Like a high-water mark that advances and retreats with the tides, the Sahel has moved north and south with the climatic changes that have changed the Sahara from bone-dry desert to savanna and back again over the millennia. In similar fashion, the vegetation of the Sahel becomes richer from north to south with the increased rainfall that the Equator brings. It ranges from sparse scrub on the desert fringes to wooded grasslands in the south. But regardless of its variations north to south, the Sahel has

The West African rice *Oryza glaberrima*, here being hulled, is the staple of the Sahel. Domesticated by Sahelian farmers thousands of years ago, it is distinct from the Asian rice *O. sativa* and exists in numerous varieties, each suited to a particular range of soils and water depths.

always been an unbroken east-west corridor across Africa through which countless generations of plants, animals, and people have migrated. No other part of Africa demonstrates such uniformity of environments and inhabitants across such a wide expanse of territory. The cheetahs of northern Kenya could be the progeny of populations now so rare in Senegal. The elephants of Mali are probably related to those living in the southern Sudan. The antelope species found across the Sahel share a common ancestor from the recent past. Their predators—the lions, hyenas, wild dogs, and jackals—are identical throughout.

Indeed, of all the creatures that inhabit the Sahel the people who live there appear to differ the most. The region hosts an impressive variety of cultures and languages—the Fulani of Senegal and Mali, the Peul of Niger, the Dinka of Sudan, and the Samburu of Kenya, to name but a few. But although the differences among these groups may seem significant, they reinforce more than they disguise the overriding importance of the one thing they all have in common. All are herders—people of the stick—and most are cattle herders. The ability of the cow, in particular, to convert grass into a renewable source of food has inspired people to exploit resources that otherwise would have been unusable. It is not too much of an exaggeration to say that the cow has underwritten the history of the Sahel.

The total number of people living in the ten countries that are either wholly or partly within the Sahel (from west to east they are Senegal, Mauritania, Mali, Burkina Faso, Niger, Chad, Sudan, Ethiopia, Kenya, and Somalia) amounts to about 195 million, which is roughly 29 percent of the entire population of sub-Saharan Africa. Of that 195 million, some 51 million live in cities. This means that at least 144 million people raise families and live out their lives (for generation after generation) in a region the textbooks describe as semiarid. Their ability to survive ought to inspire widespread admiration for the strength and ingenuity of the people living there, but the Sahel is most widely remembered as the scene of human disaster. In 1984, after several years of poor rains, a severe drought brought the Sahel to world attention. Dubbed the Stricken Land, the Sahel has since become synonymous with drought and desertification and the plight that threatens the world if global warming becomes a reality. Some of the concern is justified, but not enough of it is tempered by a proper understanding of the Sahel environment, its vegetation, animals, and people. And especially the importance of cattle.

LL DOMESTIC CATTLE are descended from the extinct wild aurochs *Bos primigenius*. The earliest evidence of their being domesticated comes from southwest Asia and southeast Europe, where cattle bones have been found at sites dating back to 8,000 years ago. The identification is made primarily on the basis of size, since domesticated animals generally are smaller than their wild progenitors, probably as a result of inadequate feeding and because people have tended to select and breed small animals that are easy to handle and house. Though the aurochs originated in Eurasia, they migrated into North Africa a million years ago and may have survived there until Roman times.

The remains of six very large wild aurochs found at a site in the Nile Valley dating from 19,000 years ago show that people were hunting them at that time. The discovery of 10,000-year-old human burials in the Sudan with cattle skulls as headstones shows that people had developed a close attachment to the animals by then. This suggests that cattle may have been domesticated independently in Africa, and the complete skeleton of a domestic cow found in a central Saharan site dating from 6,000 years ago seems to confirm the theory. Or domesticated cattle may have been brought into Africa from the Near East. There is no doubt that domestic goats and sheep came into Africa via that route, since their progenitors were never present in Africa.

Whatever the case, cattle thrive in temperate regions. Cold suits them better than heat, wetness better than aridity. In the Sahel cattle confront conditions that are frequently both very hot and very dry. They survive, but only within the limits of an animal that evolved in temperate regions. Cattle generally must drink every day to remain healthy, and at least every few days simply to stay alive. And in the tropics they use the water they drink much less efficiently than do the animals that evolved there. A wildebeest or a kongoni, for instance, needs far less water than a cow. When cattle are hot, they drink not only to avoid dehydration but also to cool themselves by passing huge volumes of water through their systems. One study recorded an instance in which urine output increased fivefold, rising from 26 to 132 quarts per day as the temperature rose. Selective breeding has produced cattle that can go without water for two days or more, but water deprivation puts a significant strain on the animals. They eat less and lose condition rapidly. And for pastoralists on the Sahel, keeping their herds in good condition is crucial—their lives depend upon it.

Like most Sahelian pastoralists, Lepusiki will occasionally provide meat for his wife, Nankarusi, and their family (especially at feasts and as a protein tonic after childbirth or illness), and in times of hardship they will drink blood taken from living animals. In modern times, their diet has been significantly supplemented by cereals of various kinds, but milk remains their staple food. To maintain a constant supply of milk, Lepusiki's herd must always contain a critical number of cows that have recently calved, along with some that are pregnant and will thus begin to supply milk when the others have ceased. But cows will conceive and raise calves successfully only while

they are sufficiently well nourished—no mean feat on Lepusiki's home range, where grazing is sparse at the best of times. Western agriculture reserves its lushest pastures for milk production and grazes only beef cattle on its rangelands, but Lepusiki produces enough milk from what is little better than semidesert.

The advantages of basing their survival on milk rather than on meat are considerable. Milk protein is produced five times more efficiently than meat

protein. Milk can be obtained daily, whereas a cow supplies meat only once in its lifetime. Also, milk production resumes within days of a drought breaking, while muscle tissue takes months to regenerate. But the difficulties of keeping cows well nourished demands a good deal of effort and expertise from the herders, and imposes heavy burdens of responsibility on the men who lead them. The leaders of every group must have profound knowledge of the land-

For the people of Diafarabé, the Niger River crossing that ends their cattle's eight-month trek through the Sahel is a moment of concern as well as excitement. Calves born on the trek, too young to brave the waters, are carried across the river by canoe.

FOLLOWING PAGES: The mosque at Diafarabé is built in traditional fashion from mud-brick. When the rains have been heavy any eroded walls must be replastered—hence the protruding poles, which serve as scaffolding supports.

scape and its climatic cycles, of their herds, and of the people who tend them. It is not enough to know where there is grass today. They must know where it can be found in the days, weeks, and months ahead; how long it will sustain how many cows; where there will be sufficient water; and when the herds must be taken to the sparsely distributed salt pans. The leader must calculate when the herd should leave for fresh pasture, always bearing in mind the quality of grazing en route and the dangers of hurrying the herd. They must know when calves are due and which cows will come into estrus next.

Samburu society has been described as a gerontocracy—one that reveres its elders. And no wonder. They are an indispensable source of knowledge based on the experiences of a lifetime. They know their environment, their people, and their animals intimately. They note the phases of the moon and watch the movements of the stars and planets. They use these celestial markers as a calendar of the seven seasons during the year when rain might fall, and of the periods in between, which are known as the long and the short hungers.

There is nearly always a period of drought and hunger between one rainy season and the next, but when the rains fail to rejuvenate pastureland for more than nine months (the gestation period of people and cows), then the elders begin to speak of the killing cycles. First is the calf killing, which can come twice in every seven years, when fetuses are aborted, udders dry, and calves die. Then there is the cattle killing, which a man can expect to suffer three times in a lifetime of 74 years. In this period, rains are poor or absent for seven successive years, cattle die, and the Samburu increasingly depend on their sheep and goats. Finally, there is the bull killing. When the drought is so severe and prolonged that bulls die, it is certain that people will die too. Even to speak of the bull killing is considered a bad omen. This tragedy can be expected to recur every 100 years. Drought and epidemics of smallpox and rinderpest all but eliminated the Samburu toward the end of the 19th century. During the mid-

1980s the Sahel experienced 24 months of continuous severe drought. Along with over 80 percent of their cattle, the Samburu were among the pastoralists of northern Kenya who lost 40 percent of their sheep and goats and 5 percent of their camels. Many people died too, and deaths would have been much more numerous without the famine relief that humanitarian agencies made available.

Beyond what they know of the land and what they can see in the stars, the Samburu believe their fate lies in the hands of their deity, Nkai, whose name also happens to be the Samburu word for "rain." This belief conditions everything they do. The Samburu live in a marginal environment, often at the edge of starvation, and yet where one might expect to find a hard, intolerant manner, an air of grace prevails. When elders meet, their greetings take the form of responses—asking after the family, the settlement, the livestock, the land. The replies are always positive, accompanied by a slight bow of the head and the words "*Nkai, Nkai*" repeated in supplicatory tones (any matters to the contrary that need to be discussed will be broached later). On parting, elders will offer blessings to their juniors, and again the response is "Nkai, Nkai." A young man will ask for a blessing when he feels the need. Children walk up to newly arrived elders and stand silently awaiting the blessing of some quietly spoken words and the right hand placed lightly on the head, to which, once again, the response is "Nkai, Nkai." The name of God and the word for rain are constantly repeated in the Samburu community; they always speak of rain with reverence.

Nkai is said to reside in a cave on Mount Nyiru, high above the arid Sahelian plains at the southern end of Lake Turkana. Indeed, as a haven from the trials of a scorching drought, Nyiru is close to paradise. The slopes are cloaked with forests of cedar and yellowwood. Burbling brooks lace the glades and meadows of the summit plateau. There is honey and wild fruit, and the cattle give rich milk when drought drives them up from the plains. The Samburu have ritualized the significance of Mount Nyiru in their lives. A man returning from the mountain will wear a sprig of cedar in his hair, and in distant parts a sprig of any cedar is worn as a sign of reverence for the mountain. The direction in which Nyiru lies is always known. God and rain have blessed Mount Nyiru, the Samburu believe, however devastated the land around may be.

THE SAMBURU ARE a small group in northern Kenya. Farther west, the Fulani constitute one of the largest cattle-raising peoples in the world. Nearly 16 million strong, the Fulani are one of West Africa's largest groups and unique among all people of Africa in how far they are scattered. In every country from Senegal to Sudan, there are people speaking Fula languages. They have different names—the Peul in Mauritania, for instance, or the Wodaabe in Niger—but they share a common heritage and are known collectively as the Fulani. They originated along the banks of the Senegal River less than 2,000 years ago; their expansion has therefore been fairly recent, leaving little time for their languages to diverge one from the other.

Just as the rainfall increases southward across the width of the Sahel, so too the human population thickens. The Sahelian fringes of the Sahara are very lightly populated, and most people live where the rainfall is sufficient to support agriculture. Here, farmers produce the cereals the pastoralists trade in exchange for dairy and other animal products. More than half the Fulani do not raise cattle, and of those who do, only a small fraction are true nomads—people with no fixed home base whatsoever who move constantly from place to place and live entirely off the produce of their herds. The remainder are what has been termed "semisedentary," following a way of life that combines both herding and agriculture.

The semisedentary Fulani have settled villages, often along rivers or around a well or other perma-nent source of water. They farm, with millet as the staple crop, and keep large herds of cattle. Unlike pastoralists whose cattle are herded far and wide in search of grazing during the dry season, the herds of the semisedentary Fulani are kept at home during the driest part of the year, and range widely during the wet season. The system is not as perverse as it sounds. Sending the cattle away from the village during the wet season leaves the land free for the farmers to cultivate. The crops are harvested by the time the cattle return, and the stubble provides fodder while the cattle manure the land.

Meanwhile, by leaving the village during the wet season the cattle are able to make use of pastures where no water is available at any other time of year. Again, it seems perverse that most of the people are cut off from their cattle at the very time when their animals are most productive (though they do keep a few milk cows at home). But the milk from the roaming herds is not going to waste, for it feeds the herdsmen and—most crucially of all—feeds and fattens calves that would get much less sustenance if their mothers were being milked in the village. Indeed, the herds are expected to grow in number and the animals to improve in condition while they are away. Thus the semisedentary Fulani get the best of both worlds during the rainy season. While their farmland is producing its bounty of grain, their herds are gathering the fat of the land from far afield.

Grain and calves are the reproductive output of field and fold and are crucial to the continued existence of the community, nurturing the children and nourishing the young adults who will in their turn produce the next generation. The future of every community depends entirely upon its reproductive success, though few people see this as an overriding purpose in life. Couples fall in love, marry, and have children with hardly a nod to the greater order of things. Love and marriage are solely the concern of individuals and their families, it seems, initiated by personal attraction or parental arrangement, con-

Rice and cattle are two mainstays of life along the Niger River. Fish is the third. From canoes and across the floodplain, prodigious quantities of fish are taken from the river. Most are species that produce huge numbers of young each year.

firmed by social practice, and consummated by mutual commitment to the not inconsiderable responsibility of raising children. But among the herders of the Sahel, the biological imperatives of reproduction are close to the surface. A fickle environment leaves smaller margins for error. How young people perform in their allotted roles can be a measure of their suitability for marriage.

When Errou and his companions set off with the cattle from Diafarabé on the northern edge of the Niger River's inland delta, they take with them the hopes as well as the accumulated wealth of the village. They will be gone for eight months on a search for pasture that covers hundreds of miles but should fatten and increase the herd. The villagers expect that their wealth will grow while Errou is away. For his part, Errou looks forward to marrying the love he left behind. He aims to do so with his reputation as a herdsman enhanced, thus fulfilling his role in his community.

MILK IS A vital source of calcium for people whose diet does not include enough vegetables. But many Africans are denied the calcium-rich benefits of milk by virtue of their genetic predisposition. All people can digest lactose—milk sugars—as infants and children, but only some retain that ability as they became adults. As might be expected, the pastoralist people are universally lactose tolerant while the non-pastoralist farmers are lactose intolerant.

The lactose molecule is too large and complex to pass through the walls of the small intestine in one piece. It first must be broken down by an enzyme, lactase. But lactase serves no function other than to break

Sunset, and the dancing of the Daral festival at Diafarabé is under way. Beautiful women, rich swirling silks of exotic color, gold, and mesmeric music do more than simply celebrate the return of the cattle and the herdsmen. This reunion reaffirms the stability of the community and the depth of shared belief in its enduring values.

down milk sugars. From a physiological point of view, lactase production becomes superfluous once infants have passed the age at which they are weaned from their mother's milk. Accordingly, as this stage is reached, the gene activating lactase production is switched off in all mammalian species except one. The exception, of course, is humans. Large numbers of people continue to produce lactase beyond infancy and remain able to digest lactose throughout their life—but not all. A significant number experience extreme discomfort if they drink so much as a single glass of milk.

A strong hint that milk might not be universally "good for you" was noted by Western nutritionists during the 1960s, after international aid programs had shipped millions of tons of dried milk around the world and found their generosity greeted with less than total enthusiasm. While Americans and Europeans were drinking milk by the gallon in the firm belief that it maintained good health, the inhabitants of impoverished countries were complaining that it made them ill. In West Africa, villagers told a Peace Corps volunteer that the powdered milk supplied by the United States contained evil spirits and was therefore avoided. Elsewhere, large shipments were used to whitewash houses after first adding some clay to give the wash a more desirable off-white shade.

At first the donors attributed the problem to poor hygiene, dirty water, and lack of experience with a new type of food. But while shipping mountains of powdered milk abroad, the United States government was also distributing surplus whole milk to needy Americans. By the mid-1960s blacks in the ghettos were also complaining of discomfort and diarrhea after drinking milk. After the issue was researched, the lactase-deficiency problem was identified. Sub-

sequent tests found that 70 percent of American blacks could not digest lactose, while 85 percent of American whites could. These findings imply that lactose tolerance differs among ethnic groups. This was subsequently confirmed by studies in Africa that found the difference between the cattle herders and the farmers. Indeed, it has been concluded that the vast majority of humankind is lactose intolerant. Far from being the norm, the ability to digest milk as adults is a distinctly abnormal and a recently evolved characteristic of some groups.

This tolerance can only have begun with the domestication of cattle around 10,000 years ago. Clearly, the rise of lactose tolerance and the spread of pastoralism went hand in hand. No herding community could have existed without it, while no agricultural community would have had much need of it. By genetic selection, if one parent is tolerant and the other nontolerant, only

the gene for tolerance is copied when they have children. Thus the use of milk as an adult food has spread beyond pastoralist communities.

As generous as the cow has been to Africa, though, its temperate origin makes it susceptible to a terrible disease residing harmlessly in the continent's indigenous wildlife. This is trypanosomiasis—sleeping sickness in humans, nagana in cattle. It is caused by single-cell parasites (trypanosomes) that invade the bloodstream, disarm the immune system, and remorselessly build up to numbers that the body cannot sustain. If left untreated, the most virulent forms of the disease can kill in weeks. Although less virulent forms may linger on for years, all attack the central nervous system in their final stages, invading the brain and inducing seizures, delirium, sleepiness, and coma—hence the name, sleeping sickness.

Thousands succumb each year. The disease of Justin,

one of its sufferers, began with a headache and a slight fever, aching joints, and a persistent weariness. A few weeks later, Justin simply did not want to wake up. He was one of a hundred patients being treated for advanced sleeping sickness in Tambura Hospital in southern Sudan. He lay listlessly on a bed, painfully thin, wearing just a tattered pair of blue shorts and a thin necklace of blue beads. His sandals had been placed on the windowsill above his bed. Justin was 12 years old, and the doctor could not say that he would live another 24 hours. She asked him his name and if he knew where he was. Justin nodded and mumbled a reply as she tried to lift his head—but it was too stiff, and his entire back was rigid as well.

Justin had been brought to the hospital five days before. For three days, nurses gave him a drug that had reduced the number of parasites in his body, but Justin had suffered a reaction. Now his brain and spine were awash with dead parasites, and his immune system was frantically attacking the debris and inflaming the surrounding tissue. Justin whimpered, as though in a bad dream, as the nurse gave him an injection of steroids. The hope was that by reducing the inflammation, the steroids would ease the pressure on Justin's swollen brain.

The hope was fulfilled. Justin was still alive when the doctor made her rounds the next day. In fact, the swelling of his head and neck had gone down, and he was propped up on his elbows, sipping broth from a bowl. Though he didn't smile or talk to her, the doctor was relieved to find him so much better. It meant that he probably would survive.

The microscopic parasites that had taken Justin to death's door were injected into his bloodstream by a fly—the tsetse fly, a member of the genus *Glossina*—which in turn had ingested them with the blood it had taken from a wild animal. The tsetse's only source of nourishment is blood. They feed every day, locating their host by sight and smell, and with a rapierlike proboscis capable of piercing even the hide of a rhinoceros, there are few animals they do not dine

upon. Antelope, buffalo, warthog, and bushpig are popular choices; people and cattle are inevitably bitten because the preferred habitat of the tsetse is the same as for humans and domestic animals—a warm and well-watered mosaic of trees, bush, and open grassland. The regions in which these conditions prevail amount to nearly half of all the land in sub-

Saharan Africa, distributed through 36 countries. At least 50 million people live in these regions, with a similar number of cattle.

About 300,000 people are infected with sleeping sickness each year in Africa. About 20,000 succumb to the disease, which means trypanosomiasis has a devastating effect on the well-being of the continent

The bridge over the Bani River to Djénné carries women to market and children to school and provides a shaded mooring spot for fishermen. Founded by eighth-century merchants, the town was a center of Islamic learning and pilgrimage.

the tsetse fly or the disease it carries.

A five-million-dollar project spearheaded by the International Atomic Energy Agency succeeded in eradicating the fly from the island of Zanzibar, off Tanzania on the East African coast, by rearing millions of males made sterile by irradiation and then releasing them to mate with females. No offspring were born, and eventually the population died out. But this success on an isolated island would be difficult to repeat in mainland Africa. Not least because the tsetse is so widespread and its reproductive strategy so ingenious. The female literally keeps all her eggs in one basket and hatches every one successfully.

Unlike most insects—houseflies, for instance—which lay hundreds of eggs over a span of weeks and leave their survival almost entirely to chance, the female tsetse produces just ten eggs in a life span of about 100 days and does everything she can to ensure that they all mature into adults. She mates only once, a few days after her emergence as an adult fly, and stores the sperm to fertilize one egg at a time within her body, where the newly hatched larva feeds from the fly's internal milk glands. After a few days the mother's abdomen is almost completely filled by the larva and she locates a shaded patch of damp soil in which to relieve herself of the burden. As soon as it is born, the larva burrows into the soil and pupates. An adult emerges about a month later and repeats the cycle all over again.

Once inside the human body, the trypanosomes breach the immune defenses, which normally fight intruders, by constantly changing their coats. Trypanosomes are enveloped in a protective layer whose antigenic character can be changed to frustrate the antibody response of their host. The host's immune system may destroy one wave of the parasites,

as a whole. Experts have estimated that without the tsetse fly Africa would be between two and five billion dollars per year better off. Calculations like this have encouraged the World Health Organization, the United Nations Food and Agricultural Organization, the European Union, and others to devote millions of dollars to the search for a means of eradicating either

but the population quickly recovers as survivors with different antigenic characteristics reproduce. Trypanosomes are capable of producing at least a hundred antigenic variations, and this quick-change artistry thwarts efforts to produce vaccines against sleeping sickness and nagana. For the time being, treatment of infected individuals and control of the tsetse population offer the best hope of relief from trypanosomiasis—the "scourge of Africa."

Treatment is most successful when the disease is identified in its early stages. For this reason the World Health Organization coordinates a screening and treatment program in ten African countries. The disease can usually be cured if it is detected before entering the central nervous system, but after that the treatment of choice is almost 20 percent arsenic, and it can be as toxic to the patient as it is to the parasite. Treating infected cattle is not feasible, and they simply die. Protecting them from the tsetse costs between $34 and $77 for each animal, every year. Such an annual expenditure would soon mount up to more than the value of the animal.

Fula women are renowned not only for their beauty and elaborate hairstyles but also for their embroidery skills.

Paradoxically, the most effective way to control the tsetse fly seems to be by bringing in even more people and their cattle. Wherever enough people have moved into tsetse-infested regions, they have largely reduced the fly's presence. One reason is that people scare away or kill the fly's wild animal hosts. Another is that their farms destroy the fly's natural habitat. The expansion of Nigeria's road network, for instance, encouraged people to establish villages along the new roads. Their buildings and farms made the environment drier and less shady, and generally unsuitable for the tsetse fly. When there are more than 100 persons per square mile, tsetse infes-

tation falls below threatening levels. Furthermore, historically the herders and their cattle created environments that repelled the tsetse.

No animals clip the grass as thoroughly as a herd of cattle under human control. From the first flush of green until the dry season, cattle keep the pastures very short. Heavy grazing ensures that no tree or shrub seedling can grow to more than a few inches high. With tree cover restricted, the tsetse were kept at bay. This natural check was destroyed during the rinderpest epidemics that wiped out between 90 and 95 percent of all cattle in Africa between 1887 and the early 1900s. Once rinderpest had removed the cattle and their herders from the landscape, the woody vegetation quickly regenerated. Within a season or two, open pasture was transformed into woody grassland and shady thickets, creating ideal conditions for the spread of the tsetse fly. As Europeans poured into Africa a century ago, this tangled, tsetse-infested landscape, now teeming with wildlife, became the archetype of "unspoiled" Africa. The idea of turning over large areas of empty African savanna for game reserves, first for hunting and later for conservation, took hold around this time. The conventional wisdom of the day was that all ecosystems marched toward a climax form that remained the same forever after. The settlers and colonial administrators therefore assumed that the country they found packed with animals and empty of people was the pristine climax environment of the savannas and set about trying to preserve it.

They created Africa's game reserves and national parks: the Serengeti and the Maasai Mara, Tsavo and Selous, Kafue, Okavango, Kruger, and the rest. They decreed that humans and their cattle had to be excluded from these parks permanently, not realizing that a few decades earlier these regions had been open grassland with grazing herds of cattle, not antelope. "A National Park must remain a piece of primordial wilderness to be effective.... No men, not even native ones should live inside its borders. The Serengeti cannot support wild animals and domestic cattle at the same time," wrote the German biologist Bernard Grzimek, author of the influential *Serengeti Shall Not Die*. But pastoralists had been herding their cattle in harmony with wildlife for thousands of years. Rinderpest gave the system a severe kick toward bush at the expense of open grassland, and in its aftermath the misconceived edicts of conservationists have created two distinct ecosystems: one in which people reign and the bush and tsetse are tamed, and another where the West's vision of "wild" Africa holds sway and the bush runs wild and tsetse flourish. The truth is that the precolonial population of Africa had learned how to work with the environment—usually to the mutual benefit of all parties concerned.

 S THE NILE lays a green ribbon of prosperity through the eastern Sahara, so the Niger River pours the life-giving opportunities of abundant water across a vast swath of the southern Sahara—the Sahel region of Mali. Farmers, fishermen, herders, and hunters have been exploiting the rich environment for thousands of years, their activities tuned to the seasonal rise and fall of the flood, their lives drawn together by bonds of mutual need and respect. At Jenne-jeno, archaeologists are unraveling the evidence of a unique history. A wall of the excavation trench reveals 1,600 years of continuous occupation. The evidence consists of broken pottery, clay net weights, spinning whorls, grindstones, fireplaces—the remnants of everyday life that can speak so eloquently of people making a way for themselves, living and dying, generation after generation.

Their descendants are there still. From the trench I could see the skyline of modern Djénné, a half or one mile to the north. Dust raised by the strengthening wind had softened the landscape to a series of gray planes. In the near distance, beside the causeway that raises the main road to Djénné above the flood, three women were firing new pots. The kiln was a huge heap of rice straw burning at a slow smolder, its internal heat apparent only when the wind brought a sudden flush of orange flame to the surface.

The Niger River, which has sustained this long, unbroken history of human endeavor in the wetlands of the Sahel, rises from a highland massif in Guinea, near the border of Sierra Leone. Although this is little more than 150 miles from the Atlantic Ocean, the river flows inland and, supplemented by its tributaries, takes a grand circuitous route to the ocean: northeast through the Sahel to Timbuktu, then curving east and southeast across Niger and through Nigeria to its estuary on the Gulf of Guinea. In its journey from the Guinea Highlands to the Atlantic, the Niger covers a distance of 2,600 miles.

The highlands and the adjacent Tingi Mountains in Sierra Leone are among the world's most ancient, and when they were heaved from the Earth's primeval mass, about 3.6 billion years ago, their rocks were laced with veins of mineral ores. Over millions of years, erosion stripped huge quantities of rock from the ancient formations, washing away the mineral residues. As a result, iron and aluminum ores are commonplace throughout the region, along with rich deposits of gold and diamonds. Sedimentary sands and clays have accumulated to the north of the mountains in such quantities that their weight has caused the underlying basin floor to subside. This feature, known to geologists as the Taoudenni Syncline, is one of the largest of its kind in the world.

The landscape through which the Niger River flows across the Taoudenni Syncline is notable for its sandstone outcrops and escarpments, elevated riverbanks, and expanses of gentle undulation. The diversity of

A corner of a Diafarabé home is where a Fula woman keeps the items she will take to marriage. Mats woven of reeds and palm fronds, embroidered blankets, baskets, dishes, and decorated calabashes—all await the day when she and her husband will establish their own family home.

these landforms belies an underlying uniformity. In effect, the sediments filling the basin have settled like sugar in a bowl. Over its total expanse the surface is remarkably level. Where the Niger veers northeast around the Bandiagara Plateau, the river drops just 32 feet over a distance of more than 125 miles. Over this broad and gently sloping section, the Niger assumes the character of a delta. It spreads in a tangle of meandering streams that shift their course from time to time but are always reunited near Timbuktu, where the Niger joins in a single course once again.

Like the Nile, the Niger is powered by high seasonal rainfall in the mountains where the main stream and its tributaries originate. With the onset of the rains, the river swells substantially, rushing toward the level expanse of the basin. Here the meandering streams soon fill to overflowing and the rising waters steadily inundate the adjacent flat, dry land. In a year of average rainfall, the Niger flood transforms nearly 12,000 square miles of parched Sahel into an intricate lattice of channels, flats, ponds, marshes, and lakes. Interspersed are tracts of dry land and islands on which groups of houses are packed tightly together. This is the inland Niger Delta—as big as the country of Belgium.

Because it starts in a region of ancient rock, the Niger brings very little silt to the inland delta. The Nile carries about 20 ounces of sediment per cubic yard from its catchment basin. By contrast, the Niger carries only about two ounces. Annual sedimentation in the Egyptian Nile Valley can be measured in inches. In the inland Niger Delta it amounts to less than .0039 of an inch. The Nile is a turbid river; the Niger and its major upstream tributary, the Bani, run clear.

The volume of water, however, is tremendous. Ninety-one billion cubic yards of water pour into the inland Niger Delta each year. Only about half of that flows out the other end near Timbuktu. The other half is lost to evaporation, absorption by the soil, and percolation to the groundwater reservoir. That means the annual flood creates a vast, diverse, and immensely productive ecosystem.

The flood begins to rise in September, but because the area it covers is so vast and the slope away from the main channels so slight, the waters take time to reach the most distant and elevated parts of the delta. These parts are flooded for only a month or two. The lowest ground, on the other hand, may be submerged for more than six months under ten feet of water. The height of the flooding is reached in early November, and levels everywhere then begin to fall. By May the delta is so dry again that even the main channels are less than ten yards across and barely knee-deep in water.

As the flood spreads over the parched delta floodplain, the water is enriched with nutrients released from the breakdown of decaying vegetation and the droppings of grazing animals. The nutrients fuel an explosive growth of bacteria, algae, zooplankton, and vegetation. In areas flooded for six months or more, the growth of highly productive grasses known collectively as *bourgou* keeps pace with the rising waters. Their photosynthesizing surfaces and seed heads always stay at the surface of the water. Bourgou produces up to seven tons of forage per acre in one season. In areas flooded less deeply for three to six months, the indigenous African wild rice (*Oryza barthii* and *O. breviligulata*) produce about 4.4 tons of forage and grain per acre. By contrast, most of the Sahel, watered only by rain, rarely produces more than 2.2 tons per acre.

The prodigious richness of the inland Niger Delta offers people several ways of making a living. Farmers sow the domesticated West African rice *Oryza glaberrima* on soils moistened by the summer rains as the flood approaches. During the flood they harvest wild rice and the bourgou cereal species *Echinochloa* from canoes. As the flood recedes, millet and sorghum are grown as *décrue* crops on the newly saturated soils.

(*Crue* is French for "flood;" *décrue* refers to the recession of the waters after the flood.) For pastoralists the retreat of the flood coincides with the advance of the dry season in the Sahel regions they had been exploiting to the north. Their herds graze upon exposed bourgou pasture and crop stubble as they draw close to their home villages after the long wet season trek.

A third major way of life, surprising on the verge of the Sahara Desert, is fishing. In the dry season, the delta's fish are confined either to the bed of the river, where the flow may be broken into pools, or they are trapped in small, isolated lakes, ponds, and swamps on the floodplain. Either way, their numbers are very low. But this changes dramatically when the arrival of the flood releases them from their dry season retreats.

The flood stimulates the production of enormous quantities of their food: algae, plankton, aquatic plants and insects, even other fish. As the fish disperse through the delta, they grow very rapidly. They spawn, and the eggs of most species hatch within two days, thus ensuring that the juvenile fish are born when food is plentiful and plant cover offers maximum protection from predators. High water is the main season of feeding for nearly all the delta fish species. Their growth is very rapid and they build up fat reserves to see them through the dry season ahead, though most will not live that long. As the flood subsides, the aquatic habitat shrinks. Fish gather in channels that run back to the rivers. Food supplies dwindle and a mass exodus begins.

The large carnivorous fish are the first to move downstream. They lurk at the exits of channels through which the abundant young-of-the-year must pass. This is also the main fishing season for other hunters, such as birds (which have young to feed) and people.

According to an FAO report, over 50,000 professional fishermen each landed an average of 1.8 tons in a typical year—a total catch of 99,000 tons. The report was compiled from catches recorded in sales only. Probably half as much again was caught and eaten by people fishing for their families.

Yet more fish are stranded in the rapidly shrink-

Okra, picked here in a Diafarabé garden, is a native African plant. Also known as lady's fingers, or gumbo, it features in tropical dishes. It can be boiled, fried, dried, or pickled, or used to thicken stews.

ing pools on the floodplain. Mortality is also very high in the dry season refuges, where food and cover are limited. The inland Niger Delta fishery survives this massive loss year after year because only 10 percent of the juvenile young-of-the-year are needed to sustain the breeding population.

Archaeological evidence indicates that herders, farmers, and fishermen began making concerted use of the inland Niger Delta about 4,000 years ago, probably as part of the southward movement of people that began with the drying out of the Sahara. They made iron tools and began cultivating the wild West African rice, which became a crucial element of the remarkably stable lifestyle that remains dominant to this day.

Wild West African rice was almost certainly domesticated in the delta. It has successfully held off the diffusion of the higher-yielding Asian varieties, largely because of its capacity to produce a crop under a wide range of conditions. More than 41 distinct varieties of *O. glaberrima* are known, some of which will grow in as much as nine feet of water, compared with a maximum of three feet for the Asian rice *Oryza sativa*. The delta's rice farmers sow a mixture of varieties in the same field, each with different growing periods (from 90 to 210 days). Multiple sowings are made at intervals of days or weeks in long and narrow fields that cut across several soil types along a progression of potential flood levels. The procedures and timing of this rice cultivation are determined by a variety of factors—including intricate cosmological observations—and this specialized knowledge is not readily shared.

Specialized knowledge is also employed by the herders and fishermen, and the integration of their skills enables each group to sustain a larger population than either one could on its own. The integration has always been complex. Once population densities had reached a critical point, the different groups were living cheek

by jowl, often using the same piece of land at the same time. The potential for interethnic strife was considerable. The inland Niger Delta might have been a morass of interethnic hostility, like Israel today. But what distinguishes the early history of people in the delta is not frequent conflict, but a total lack of it.

The absence of conflict is reflected in the villages and towns. The people who first settled in the inland Niger Delta left no monumental public architecture, extravagant burials, or incised tablets praising kings and recording feats of conquest. The history of Jenne-jeno appears to have been extraordinarily peaceful. While evidence of dwellings destroyed by fire is commonplace at urban archaeological sites

elsewhere, with level after level of burning, not a whiff of such occurrences is evident at Jenne-jeno.

The reason for this is principally environmental. Although the inland Niger Delta is a well-watered paradise for a few months of the year, it is still part of the Sahel. When the water that poured in from the Guinea Highlands has evaporated, soaked into the ground, or flowed on downriver, the people of the delta are dependent upon whatever the Sahel has to offer. Like Lepusiki in Kenya and people throughout the Sahel, surviving the bad times is what matters. The true history of the Sahel is an account of battles against the environment, not people. It is a harsh and unforgiving environment. One that rewards cooperation, not conflict.

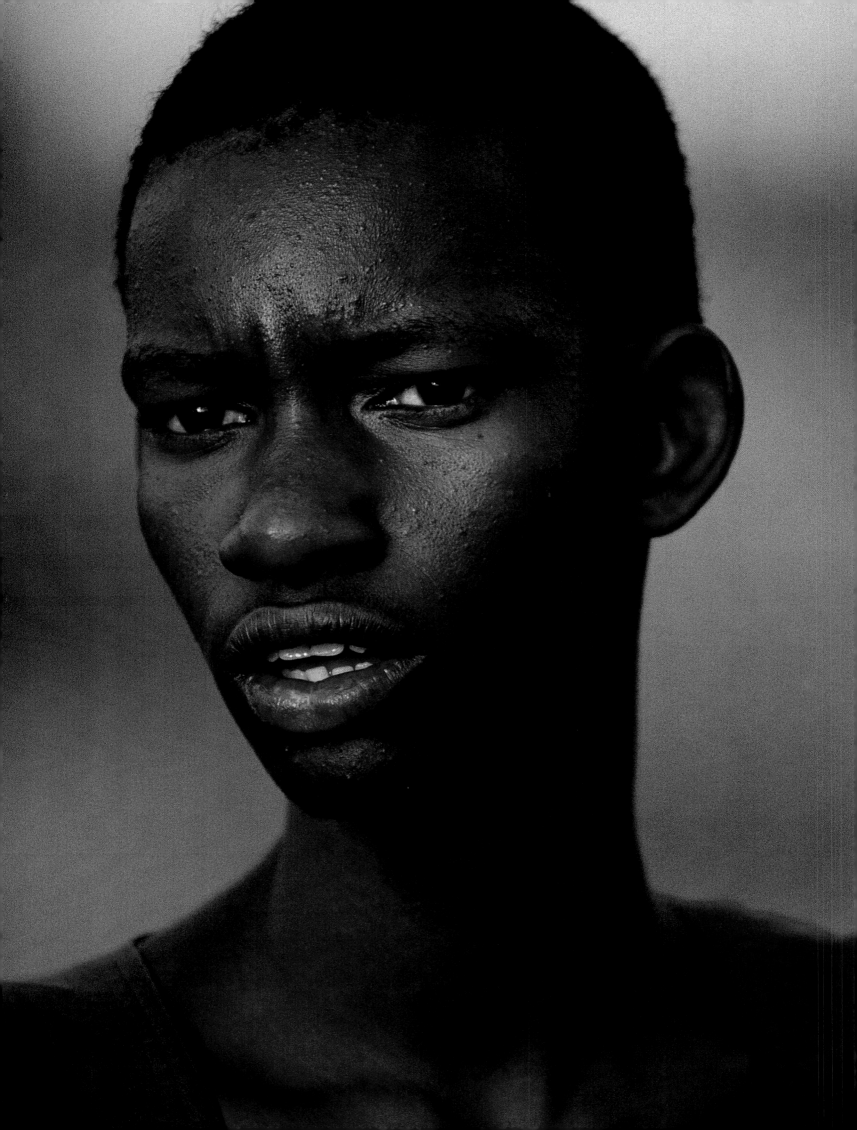

iafarabé, on the banks of the Niger River in Mali, is abuzz with excitement. The cattle and the young Fulani herdsmen are returning at last—after eight long months. Across the river the cattle are plunging into the water. The herdsmen swim alongside, urging the snorting, floundering beasts forward. All emerge joyfully on the Diafarabé shore—the men laughing, the cattle fat and sleek. This moment is the climax of the year. The future of the community is secure.

Numbering nearly 16 million, the Fulani are probably the largest group of pastoralists in the world today. With their traditional way of life dominating the Sahel region, they are found in every country from the Atlantic to the Nile, united in their descent from people who began herding cattle on the grasslands of the Sahel less than 2,000 years ago. The rigors of herding created the enduring nature of Fulani society and culture, while the Sahel enabled the Fulani and their cattle to spread far and wide.

Sahel is the Arabic word for "shore," but this is the shore of a desert—the Sahel marks the southern edge of the Sahara—where there is just enough rain to produce a broad ribbon of sparse bush and grassland. Waterholes are few, and although the Sahel range is huge, the grazing is spread thin. But each generation of Fulani herdsmen learns how to reap the distant harvest.

Errou is nearly home. He and his companions have brought the cattle safely to the banks of the Niger River after a long and arduous trek through the Sahelian grasslands. "It's a tough job," he says. "We walk from sunrise to sunset. We get very thirsty, and the cows get tired. You constantly have to find new grazing. That's what's always in your head. In the bush you have to be completely focused...your mission is to bring back fat cattle."

The wealth and identity of the village are invested in its cattle. Errou hopes to be praised for bringing them home fat and healthy. But first they have to cross the river.

Thousands of animals take the plunge. The crossing is a day for rejoicing and celebration. Ready for the festivities, Errou (second from left above) and his friends pose in their best gear.

"It can be really dangerous in the water. I swim with my cattle across the river," Errou says, "and I try to keep them apart so they don't get injured."

Ica Bar (above) is Errou's girlfriend. He will be back today. "I can't wait to see him again," she says. "We'll celebrate with the festival and singing and dancing." There may even be talk of marriage.

Men from the village gather on the riverbank (left), astutely assessing the condition of the cattle as they come ashore. Errou's chances of marrying depend very much upon how well he has looked after the herd. "I'll be pleased if my cows are the fattest and most beautiful," he says.

Great

Lakes

Born of the upheavals that created the Rift Valley, the Great Lakes stand high in world rankings of significance and spectacle. Lake Victoria is the world's second largest freshwater lake. Lake Tanganyika is so deep that it holds one-hundredth of all the world's freshwater—enough to inundate all of North America.

The region's rainfall is abundant, its soils are fertile, and the climate is warm. Of all Africa, the environs of the Great Lakes are the most richly endowed with the combination of land and climate that fosters the growth of human populations. Bantu farmers first settled here 3,000 years ago. Their numbers grew steadily, multiplying with the introduction of the banana, maize, and cassava.

Rwanda, Burundi, and western Uganda constitute the most densely populated region on the continent—Africa's Garden of Eden. But as the tragic history of the region has revealed, there are serpents in the garden.

Lake Kivu lies on the border of Congo and Rwanda in Africa's Garden of Eden.

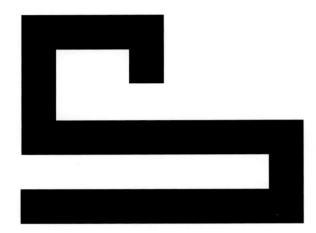eated comfortably in the shade of orange trees, with the child on his knee eating a banana freshly plucked from the grove behind the house, Constantine Maneke announced that yes, he would be very happy to spend a few days explaining the ins and outs of agriculture on Ukara, an island lying off the south-eastern shore of Lake Victoria. Though only 30 square miles in area, Ukara has supported a population of no less than 16,000 people ever since they were first counted, more than a century ago. That gives the island an average population density of 530 per square mile, nearly

six times that of Tanzania as a whole. Clearly, the farmers of Ukara must be doing something right.

With so little room for expansion, intensified production was the secret, Maneke explained. As we toured the island, he pointed out that every available scrap of cultivable land was used to maximum advantage. Irrigation and terracing kept land lying close to the island's streams in continuous production. The lakeshores, where the danger of flooding was a threat to food crops, had been dug out and converted to water meadows, providing a steady harvest of grass for the island's livestock. Maneke himself had five cattle, and was keen that I should

see them. I expected to be taken to some common grazing land but instead found that each family kept their cattle in the household compound. The animals spend their lives in shallow circular pits, with a low surrounding fence and a thatched roof, and they seemed perfectly healthy and content. They were watered and fed regularly, and the manure accumulating in the pit was cleared out every six months or so and spread on the millet, maize, and cassava fields.

Irrigation, terracing, water meadows, manuring; People had worked out how to sustain high population densities on Ukara's limited land area long before any

PRECEDING PAGES: **The Equator crosses Lake Victoria at Entebbe, Uganda, the site of this weekly market. Farmers here can produce all year round.**
ABOVE: **A little egret fishes on Lake Victoria. Though a relatively young lake, more than 400 species of fish evolved here.**

agricultural advisor arrived on the scene, showing that—in Africa as everywhere—people always thrive where conditions are amenable.

Abundant water and fertile soils rarely occur together in Africa. Most regions have unreliable rains or poor soils—or both. The heart of Africa is different. Here the shudders of earthquakes and volcanoes that rippled down the Great Rift Valley 20 to 30 million years ago left a string of lakes and piled up the makings of fertile volcanic soils. If the Garden of Eden ever existed on Earth, it should have been in the Great Lakes region of central Africa. Measuring about 1,200 miles from north to south and about 340 miles wide, the region includes the highland countries of Burundi and Rwanda and the grasslands of western Tanzania and Uganda that reach to the shores of Lake Victoria. The Equator crosses Africa at this point, but since no part of the region is less than 3,200 feet above sea level and much of it stands above 6,500 feet, conditions here are never as hot and humid as in the equatorial lowlands. Furthermore, the elevated landmass draws in moisture-laden winds and so

receives more dependable rainfall. According to locality, the rainfall is relatively high and equably distributed throughout the year. Even the two short dry seasons rarely are without rain.

Verdant hills soak up the rain, and streams and rivers carry the off-flow down into some of the world's most exceptional freshwater lakes. Only Lake Baikal is deeper than Lake Tanganyika, and only Lake Superior is larger than Lake Victoria. Lake Kivu fills the spectacular green encircling crater basin of a long-dead volcano in the Virunga Mountains; Lake Edward lies in the shadow of the legendary Mountains of the Moon; Lake Albert channels the waters draining from the highlands of the eastern Congo into the Nile. From its source in the Luvironza River in Burundi, the twists and turns of the Nile on its journey to the Mediterranean make it longer than any other river in the world—at 4,160 miles longer even than the Amazon or the combined Mississippi-Missouri Rivers.

The landscape is picturesque, and within living memory it was still the home of the wild animals that for millennia had teemed in the region of the Great Lakes. Gorilla and chimpanzee flourished in the forests. Hippopotamus and crocodile were common in the lakes and rivers. Elephant, buffalo, rhinoceros, giraffe, zebra, eland, wildebeest, and a host of smaller herbivores inhabited the wooded grassland and savanna. Lion, leopard, cheetah, hyena, and wild dog preyed on the herbivores large and small. Serval cat, caracal, jackal, genet, and mongoose fed on spring hare, ground squirrel, and mice. Aardvark and pangolin mopped up the ants and the termites. The past tense is significant here, because the wildlife of the Great Lakes no longer roam so widely or so plentifully as in the recent past. Today wild animals are found mainly in the national parks and reserves, displaced from their former ranges by the unrelenting invasions of the region's most recent immigrants: people.

The experiences of the colonial period left the countries of the Great Lakes ill prepared for independence. The dream of democracy soon became a nightmare of corruption, bad government, collapsing economies, hatred, civil war, and even genocide.

Of all Africa, the Great Lakes region is most richly endowed with the resources that encourage people to settle. It was a point of consolidation in the Bantu migration—that little-known population movement, remarkable in human history. In the space of a few thousand years, it changed the human landscape of sub-Saharan Africa from one that was inhabited by scattered groups of nomadic hunter-gatherers to one dominated by farmers living in villages.

Bantu settlers began arriving in the Great Lakes region 3,000 years ago, bringing with them the iron-smelting expertise that contributed to both the clearance of the forests (with the demand for charcoal) and the development of agriculture (with the production of hoes). The soils were fertile, the climate was congenial, and the people were industrious. It is no accident that Rwanda, Burundi, and western Uganda are the most intensively farmed and densely populated regions in Africa.

The hills are meticulously cultivated. Banana groves stand tightly packed, dark and somber green. The simultaneous presence of flowers and fruit betokens a crop that produces a harvest all year-round. The maize does well; the cattle supply milk, manure, and meat as well as bullocks to pull the plow; and a small plantation of coffee trees brings in the cash that is needed for the purchase of household essentials. Though this is an idealized picture, nonetheless the village land-use system in the Great Lakes region is capable of supporting ten times more people per square mile than Mozambique or Sweden. Burundi has a greater proportion of its land area under permanent cultivation and pasture than any other country in the world: 87 percent. Rwanda has less, 75 percent, but even that is more than in all but two African countries (Lesotho and Nigeria).

But as the world knows, the 1990s laid a pall of unspeakable cruelty and slaughter over Africa's most bountiful landscape. Genocide. Like most people, my experience of the terrible events in Rwanda and Burundi was limited to the horrors of television and press reports, but the days I had spent on Ukara lent a chilling touch. The island was as densely populated as the Rwandan villages. Maneke and his neighbors had lived cheek by jowl for their entire lives—as had generations before them. It was simply beyond belief that they could have slaughtered one another. And yet it had happened in Rwanda. Why?

Between 800,000 and 850,000 Tutsi plus between 10,000 and 30,000 Hutu were killed in the Rwanda genocide. In the space of just 100 days the Tutsi population was reduced from 930,000 to no more than 130,000. For every Tutsi that remained alive, six had died. The reverberations of fear spread abroad, inciting spasms of killing in neighboring Burundi and the Congo (then Zaire). A massive exodus eventually led to nearly two million people living in refugee camps sponsored by the United Nations in Tanzania. Most have gone home, but the region is still traumatized.

This most horrifying episode in a history of ethnic antagonism has its roots in Europe's ideas of racial superiority, which administrators brought to Africa during the colonial period. The Berlin Conference of 1884-85, at which the European powers had carved up Africa among themselves (the notorious Scramble for Africa), made Ruanda-Urundi (as the region was then known) part of German East Africa. Ethnographers were among the first visitors to the new colony, and subsequently they reported that Ruanda-Urundi was inhabited by three distinct ethnic groups: the Twa, the Hutu, and the Tutsi. The Twa were described as Pygmy hunters and gatherers who had lived in the region since time immemorial. The Hutu were Bantu-speaking farmers who came later, they said, while the Tutsi were pastoralists who were believed to have migrated to Ruanda-Urundi from a homeland somewhere in northeastern Africa, where they had been the beneficiaries of Egyptian, Arabian, or even European civilizing influences.

The ethnographers concluded that the Tutsi had become established in the region gradually and peacefully, over a long period of time, during which they had accommodatingly abandoned their own language and taken to speaking the Bantu language of the Hutu (as had the Twa), so that all three groups spoke the same language. In appearance, however, the three groups were said to be strikingly different. The Tutsi were described as tall, handsome, slender, and well proportioned, while the Twa were looked upon as grotesque little creatures and often referred to as dwarfs. Between the Twa and the Tutsi stood the stocky aboriginal Bantu.

The Hutu and the Tutsi share a common origin and language, but were already distinguished by lifestyle and numbers when Europeans first encountered them. The Tutsi were predominantly (but not only) herders, while most of the Hutu (but not all) were farmers. The Hutu farmers outnumbered the Tutsi herders by about eight to one. As with the Kikuyu and Masai, the Fulani and the Hausa, the relationship between herder and farmer was largely symbiotic—doubtless antagonistic at times, but also mutually supportive. In the fashion of late 19th-century social science, however, German ethnographers were more inclined to stress the factors that kept people apart than to recognize the practices that bound them together.

The cattle culture of the Tutsi, with its haughty conceits and apparent dedication to the accumulation of wealth, gave the pastoralists an aristocratic demeanor with which the German colonial administrators readily identified and upon which the Tutsi were only too keen to capitalize. They told the colonizers that they wielded almost total political and economic power over the Hutu (and of course the Twa), owning all the cattle in the region and, theoretically at least, all the land as well. The country was ruled by Tutsi princes, who in turn answered to an absolute and semidivine sovereign whose symbol of

authority was a drum hung with the genitals of slaughtered enemies, the Germans were told. Predictably, the colonizers saw the regal status claimed by the Tutsi as a means of facilitating German control of the region. They introduced a system of indirect rule, governing the territory according to the Tutsi claims of authority. Though the Tutsi made up a mere 12 to 15 percent of the Ruanda-Urundi population, they effectively ruled the country—

primarily for their own benefit. This did not augur well for the future.

During World War I, Belgian troops took Ruanda-Urundi, and the territories were ceded to Belgium after the war. A League of Nations mandate required the new colonial power to govern the countries as a "sacred trust of civilization" until they could "stand on their own feet in the arduous conditions of the modern world." The Belgian response was to increase

The future of a country rests with its children. A generation lost the chance of education during the decades of horror (many lost their lives too). But in Uganda at least, the government has made education a priority.

FOLLOWING PAGES: In the Ruwenzori—fabled Mountains of the Moon—the equatorial sun brings summer every day, and the thin air brings winter every night. Under these conditions a species of ground-sel, a common garden weed, grows to the size of trees.

the authority of the Tutsi by giving more of them government jobs and allowing only Tutsi children to attend school. Since the Tutsi were racially superior, they argued, educating the Hutu would be a waste.

But sometimes it was difficult to tell who was Hutu and who Tutsi. The stereotypically tall, slender Tutsi and the short, stocky Hutu were easily identified, but between these extremes were thousands, if not the majority of the population, whose appearance was no clue at all. Generations of intermarriage, migration, and changes in occupation and economic standing had blurred the distinction. But no matter. In 1926 the Belgian authorities introduced an identity card to clarify the issue. By law, the card had to specify which tribe the holder belonged to. Where appearance was indecisive and proof of ancestry lacking, a simple formula was applied. Those with ten cows or more were classified as Tutsi, those with fewer were Hutu.

Throughout the period of Belgian colonial rule, the Tutsi tightened their grip on every aspect of social, economic, and political control. While pursuing colonial government instructions to extract more taxes and labor from small farmers, mostly Hutu, local Tutsi chiefs also used their increased authority to seize cattle and land from rivals and vulnerable farmers. But opposition was growing, especially as the independence movement gained impetus throughout Africa. Independence implied democracy, and with the Tutsi composing only a small minority of the population, a Hutu victory was guaranteed. Confronted with this stark reality, the Belgians abruptly changed sides. After years of conniving with the Tutsi's subjugation of the Hutu, they began dismissing Tutsi chiefs and appointing Hutu to the newly vacated posts. Wherever they could, the new chiefs promptly organized the deliberate persecution of their former masters, precipitating a mass exodus of Tutsi.

Rwanda and Burundi became independent in 1962. In the interests of peace and harmony, the new government, though Hutu, might have been expected to advocate reconciliation, to do away with identity cards and proclaim that the people were no longer Tutsi or Hutu but Rwandan. But in this case, nationalism had not been aroused by aims to drive out a colonial regime; it had been inspired by ambitions to take over an oppressive indigenous hegemony that the colonial government had installed and supported. Once in power, the Hutu elite sought not national unity but absolute supremacy.

Soon after independence, an official policy of ethnic quotas was introduced. Since the Tutsi made up only 9 percent of the population, they were allocated only 9 percent of the school places and no more than 9 percent of posts in the civil service or any other area of employment. This oppression was reinforced with officially sanctioned physical persecution. There were killings and mass exoduses. Furthermore, with events repeated in both Rwanda and Burundi, the two countries became partners in a terrible dance. When Tutsi were killed in Rwanda, the Tutsi in Burundi feared for their lives. When Hutu were killed in Burundi, the Hutu in Rwanda became more afraid.

Fear fed hatred and reprisal into a cycle of violence. The genocide that erupted after the presidents of both Rwanda and Burundi were killed in a plane crash in April 1994 was deliberately planned. The organizers of Rwanda's final solution are known and have been named. Local mayors ordered the rural population to "clean the fields." A radio station urged them on: "The graves are not yet full." The Hutu gangs slaughtered businessmen, journalists, priests, students, children, and whole families by the thousand before exhaustion finally brought the violence grinding to a halt.

Now Rwanda has 90,000 suspected killers awaiting trial. Justice alone cannot solve the problems of political instability, poverty, and displaced masses, but it is a start. Meanwhile, the history of the Tutsi and the Hutu stands as a terrible indictment of the concept of tribalism that the colonial era brought to Africa.

N ZAMBIA, THE chief of a little-known group once remarked: "My people were not the Soli until 1937 when the Bwana D.C. [Mr. District Commissioner] told us we were." Indeed, ethnic thinking was rare in Africa before it was applied by the colonial authorities. Contrary to popular assumption, tribalism was not a cultural characteristic deeply rooted in the African past. It was a consciously crafted ideological tradition that was created during the colonial period. Colonial administrators believed that every African belonged to a tribe, just as every European belonged to a nation. Tribes were defined as cultural units, with a common language, a single social system, and customary laws. In Tanganyika, which became a British mandate after World War I, the incoming British administrators, convinced that the Germans had destroyed every vestige of any pre-colonial African social systems, devoted considerable effort to identifying tribes and finding their chief. "Each tribe must be considered as a distinct unit . . . . Each tribe must be under a chief," a provincial commissioner told his staff in 1926.

These concepts bore little relation to Africa's kaleidoscopic history, but they were the shifting sands upon which colonial administrators imposed a new political geography. Once the process was set in motion, it was enthusiastically reinforced by the Africans themselves. These invented histories seemed to offer a hope of more order and certainty in their lives. "Europeans believed Africans belonged to tribes; Africans built tribes to belong to." And with the tribes came the chiefs. There were always individuals with personal motives for collaborating with the colonial administrators. Throughout Africa, tribal identity became the catalyst that enabled ambitious individuals and groups to achieve positions of status, dominance, and wealth. Tribes became the bases from

which politicians launched the drive for national independence. Tribes were also an ideological refuge in times of stress—during famine, elections, or even in the matter of getting a job—when tribal sentiment polarized into a sense of "them and us" that too often erupted in bloodshed.

A second introduced factor—namely the staple foods that would sustain such large populations—came much earlier. The indigenous African crops, such as sorghum, millet, and yam, offered limited opportunity for exploiting the well-watered, fertile soils of the Great Lakes region. The absence of a dry season impeded their growth, their cultivation was very demanding, and they rarely produced more food than could feed the people required to grow them. But the banana and its cousin, the plantain, introduced an entirely new dynamic, boosting both the population growth and economic development of the region.

Though the banana that Maneke had given his son when I called at the homestead was primarily intended to keep the child occupied while we talked, it was also a clue to how readily available the fruit is in the Great Lakes region and its importance as a staple food. Africa produces 35 percent of the world crop, and where bananas and plantains are the staple diet, Africans each eat about 550 pounds (in the United States average consumption is about one banana per week—roughly 24 pounds per year). Bananas and plantains are an excellent energy food, well ahead of most root crops, and between two and three times more productive than cereals. They are also a good source of potassium and vitamin C, though very low in iron and calcium and practically devoid of protein and fat; a good supply of supplements is essential. The value of the banana as a staple crop is not limited to nutrition. The small amount of labor it demands is equally important. Subsistence farmers can produce a regular and dependable supply of bananas in large quantities. Bananas are a perennial crop. A well-maintained banana grove will produce good crops for 30 years or more.

Such ease of cultivation has enabled generations

Bananas were first domesticated in Southeast Asia and introduced to Africa about 2,000 years ago. Nowadays Africa produces over one-third of the world crop. Bananas (with their cousin, the plantain) are a staple food of people throughout equatorial Africa.

of African farmers to subsist upon the banana. A young man wishing to establish a household for himself and a wife clears two or three acres of vacant land and plants it with banana rootstocks, from which several stems will soon sprout. In 10 to 18 months, each stem bears fruit, and he is set up for life. Maintenance of the grove primarily involves composting dead vegetation. Stems that have fruited are cut down and split lengthways to make a continuous floor, a straightforward operation that smothers weeds, prevents erosion runoff, and also preserves fertility. The growth of the suckers in a mature grove can be manipulated so that there are stems at every stage of development all year-round. Feeding the family then consists of cutting a bunch that is ready for cooking. Unlike grains and tubers, bananas do not need to be pounded before they are cooked, and the energy thus saved can be used for preparing leaf vegetables, cowpeas, meat, or dried fish, which compensate for protein and fat deficiencies.

The banana can survive a moderate drought but does not fruit if the soil remains dry for more than a short while. So although it is grown throughout much of Africa, it can be relied upon as a year-round staple food crop only where rainfall is more or less continuous and temperatures are always relatively high—equatorial conditions, in other words, and especially those prevailing in the Great Lakes region.

Precisely how and when the edible banana and plantain were brought to Africa from their point of origin in Southeast Asia is still a mystery, but they are known to have been grown in the region for about 2,000 years. Furthermore, people have been growing bananas and plantains here for so long, and so intensively, that the African varieties constitute a larger pool of diversity than anywhere else in the world. Of the banana cultivars grown in the Great Lakes region, for example, 60 are exclusively African.

West of the Great Lakes region, where the banana is predominant, the diversity of the plantain is even more impressive. From the lakes to the Atlantic coast, through the entire breadth of the equatorial rain forest, the plantain grows profusely in every village. About 120 cultivars have been developed, most of which are not found anywhere else. Plantains, even more than bananas, are perfectly adapted to equatorial rain forests. Unlike the indigenous yam (initially a savanna plant), the plantain is not affected by the absence of a dry season. Indeed, it flourishes in drenching, year-round rainfall. Forest need be only partially cleared, as compared with total clearance for yams, and the plantain requires far less attention after planting. In all, the plantain produces ten times more food than yams from the same area of land with only a fraction of the labor input.

Overall, bananas and plantains had a tremendous impact on the human demography of equatorial Africa. The boost to agricultural productivity lifted population growth rates and increased the size of settlements. Increased productivity raised the birth rates and attracted hungry immigrants from less successful communities. The banana gardens were islands of fertility and wealth that their owners used to attract and support large followings. But banana production was not the only activity that rose to distinctive heights of achievement in the Great Lakes region. While some farmers established their firmly rooted islands of wealth, others began using the intervening seas of grass as a means of accumulating a more mobile form of wealth: cattle.

Pastoralists such as the Fulani and the Samburu developed the skills necessary to keep their stock alive on minimal resources. This is a survival strategy, though, designed to supply basic needs under even the worst conditions. Pastoralists herding cattle on the Great Lakes grasslands, however, were not totally dependent upon their stock for survival and could therefore afford to rear cattle as a form of wealth. The cattle raised on the grasslands were a surplus resource, a luxury, in fact, and destined to become symbols of wealth and power among the people owning them.

These grasslands are among the lushest in Africa. They are better watered than the Sahelian savanna yet fortuitously avoid the scourge of the tsetse fly. The high productivity of the Great Lakes grasslands enabled people to maximize the breeding potential of cattle with little concern for their ability to withstand drought.

The cattle of the Great Lakes region are not the utilitarian creatures familiar to Western eyes. There are few hornless Friesians producing milk by the churnful, nor are there many Herefords being fattened up for slaughter. The most treasured herds on these rich grasslands are bred to be admired more than to be used. They are magnificent beasts. As the herd approached in the evening light, their sleek coats rippling over well-fleshed bulk, the herdsman walking alongside—so self-assured in his poise—veritably glowed with the pride of possession. He knew his worth and flaunted it, unashamedly, arrogantly. I could only smile and offer the obligatory admiration, while thinking that his herd and his manner helped to explain why the early colonial administrators had so readily granted the herders superior status over their farming neighbors. They reared such magnificent animals; they stood so straight and tall, while the farmers were bent toiling in the fields.

Cattle were already established as a major presence in the Great Lakes region by A.D. 1000, and throughout historical times they have been accorded a degree of prestige seemingly out of all proportion to their relevance as a source of food. Indeed, herding came to be regarded as a noble pursuit, and cattle were objects of adoration—bred more for their aesthetic qualities than for utilitarian purposes. From the basic long-horned and humped zebra stock (*Bos indicus*), the herders bred for size—not only body size, but also the size of the horns. In modern times, horn spreads of over six feet have been noted, and the shape as well as the size is

important—lyre shaped, bow shaped, curving upward, curving downward, pointing forward or backward. The varieties of horn shape and configuration are many, and each has a name, a history, and its passionate admirers. In folk history and legend, cattle were elevated to almost reverential status, becoming the wonderful companions of royal heroes, and attendants to the godlike beings of antiquity from whom the herders believed they were themselves descended. And of course the herders ultimately became rulers whose powers were measured in the size and quality of their herds. Several such herders found themselves elevated to the status of kings in the system of indirect rule that the British brought to their colony in the Great Lakes region—Uganda.

Bunyoro, Toro, Ankole, Acholi, and of course Buganda, from which came the name of the territory itself. All were designated as native kingdoms, each with a royal lineage (and a multitude of princes and princesses). Primogeniture, as is found in European monarchies, with the eldest son inheriting all the incumbent ruler's wealth and status, was not widely known in Africa until the colonial administrations introduced the concept. In most cases, several members of the ruling line were considered eligible to take over. Sometimes the choice was peacefully arranged by an inner circle of councillors, but sometimes it was decided by warlike means. Indeed, in the BaGanda language the only word that approximates the word reign is *mirembe*, which actually means "a period of peace between succession struggles." All of which suggests that any semblance of a European-style monarchy that existed in Africa before colonial times was likely to have been a short-lived deviation from the standard pattern. But when Europeans encountered particularly powerful and cooperative leaders, they frequently regarded them as kings in the European fashion. They gave their lineage power and a right to rule that broke with the standard pattern and all too often led to disaster. Uganda is a case in point.

Buganda, with a common language, customs, clearly defined territory, clan structure, and—above all—a titular head, the Kabaka, was bigger and more unified than any other group in the Great Lakes region under British control. Furthermore, although Buganda was but one of four kingdoms and 15 provinces, the British colonial administration considered the BaGanda people to be superior to other groups. They consolidated control of the territory by extending the Buganda model and naming the entire country Uganda. The political institutions of the BaGanda were imposed upon the rest of the population. The BaGanda were employed as agents of the administration, and the colonial headquarters were established in the Buganda heartland.

The BaGanda were the first beneficiaries of European influence, thereby gaining a head start in the race for development. They were the first to be educated and the first to hold senior positions in the civil service. The BaGanda soon became the richest group in the country, and they liked to flaunt their wealth. While the rest of the country saved for months to buy a bicycle, they developed a taste for motor cars and dinner jackets. The BaGanda regarded themselves as an upper ruling class, an observer remarked, and the rest of the population as their servants—the hewers of wood and drawers of water. Inevitably, all this upset other groups in the territory, encouraging the formation of an anti-BaGanda movement.

The united opposition was easily large enough to defeat the BaGanda in the elections that followed independence in 1962, but instead of tackling the problems of inequality by building up the economies of the other provinces, the government under Milton Obote chose to break down the monopolies of the BaGanda. Where opposition was most concerted, Obote sent in the army, undisciplined and led by a brutal general, Idi Amin, thereby sowing the seeds of his own eventual downfall. The political system of the BaGanda was attacked and destroyed, their Kabaka, fondly known as King Freddie, was exiled to London, where he died an alcoholic. Obote brought the regions under his own centralized control. In 1967 he enacted a constitution giving himself dictatorial powers. In 1969 he nationalized major private enterprises and effectively made himself the sole judge of who should be wealthy and who should not. Predictably, none of these politically motivated tactics helped the economic development of the country in any way or eased social tensions. Indeed, they made matters worse. As the economy faltered, competition increased for access to whatever was available, leading to social conflict and violence.

A military coup brought Idi Amin to power in January 1971. After a few months of rosy hope, Uganda lost its way completely. Violence, and the fear of violence, became endemic. The country endured eight years of despotic rule under one of the most repressive and destructive military regimes that Africa has known. The horror ended with nearly three years of full-scale war, which finally deposed Idi Amin and reinstalled Milton Obote. That step backward in turn sparked a guerrilla war from which the government of Yoweri Museveni emerged to take control of the country in 1986. By then the "Pearl of Africa," as Churchill had once described Uganda, was a shattered and fiscally bankrupt country.

A symbol of colonial conceit, Queen Victoria presents a Bible to an African chief kneeling at her feet.

How does any government rebuild a nation after more than 25 years of such turmoil? A realistic assessment of the scale of the problem and massive injections of international aid are very important, but education is fundamental to the process by which wounds will heal. A generation lost its chance, but in 1997 over five million children were enrolled at primary school (compared with fewer than three-quarters of a million in 1970). More than 33,000 students attended high school (compared with just over 4,000 in 1970). The hope must be that these children will learn, above all else, that a government that ignores regional inequalities is courting disaster. Meanwhile, another Herculean task confronts the country as Uganda stands at the forefront of Africa's battle against AIDS.

THE SCALE OF the AIDS problem confronting sub-Saharan Africa is so great that it renders superlatives meaningless. Sub-Saharan Africa has only about 10 percent of the world's population but has 70 percent of the people infected with HIV. In the year 2000, of all the people in the world who have died of AIDS, 80 percent were Africans. A total of 17 million Africans died by the year 2000, and another 10 million are expected to die within five years. In Kenya 500 people die each day. In Zimbabwe one cemetery alone conducts 70 burials a day. AIDS is now the leading cause of death in Africa. Furthermore, it is estimated that 90 percent of the illness and death that AIDS will bring to Africa are still to come.

As the new millennium dawned, it offered little new hope to the 25.3 million African adults and chil-

Nile perch were introduced to Lake Victoria in the 1950s, transforming both the lake and the lives of people around it. Forty-four thousand tons of perch fillets were being exported annually by the mid-1990s. Thirty million people around the lake were employed in some aspect of the industry. But the perch, being carnivorous, has eaten some of the lake's indigenous stock.

dren who were already living with HIV and AIDS. Overall, 8.8 percent of the region's entire adult population is infected. More than half of them are women whose babies will inevitably acquire the virus in the womb or at the breast. In seven sub-Saharan countries, at least 20 percent of adults are infected. Botswana has the world's highest adult rate, with 36 percent infected. South Africa has the highest number of people infected—4.2 million—with an adult rate of 20 percent, up from 13 percent just two years before.

AIDS in Africa is heterosexually transmitted in over 90 percent of the cases, and hits young and sexually active people very hard. In some areas nearly half of all young adults are infected. Twelve million African children under the age of 15 have already been orphaned by the loss of their mother or both parents to AIDS—92 percent of all the world's AIDS orphans. In Zimbabwe, where one in four adults is infected, a 15-year-old boy has only a 25 percent of living to age 40. In Botswana, where the infection rate is more than one in three, his chances of surviving to age 40 are just 15 percent. The rate of infection has yet to peak, but already projections show that life expectancy at birth will be halved over the next 10 to 12 years in Zimbabwe and Botswana, from 67 years down to 33 years—solely as a result of the AIDS epidemic.

The World Bank estimates that instead of expanding, the economies of some African countries will shrink by up to 25 percent as AIDS tightens its grip on the continent. AIDS strikes at the most economically active sector of the population—people in their 20s and 30s. The deaths of highly skilled workers, engineers, miners, civil servants, nurses, and doctors weaken a nation's infrastructure. Equally as

serious, 860,000 primary school children in sub-Saharan Africa lost at least one teacher to AIDS during 1999. In South Africa the Natal education board expects two-thirds of its teachers to die of AIDS in the next five years. It has instructed the University of Natal to increase its teacher training output from 400 to 2,000 per year—a challenging proposition under any circumstances.

AIDS confronts humanity with the worst catastrophe since the plague wiped out one-third of Europe's population in the 14th century. The progressive destruction of the immune system by the human immunodeficiency virus (HIV) that leads to AIDS (acquired immunodeficiency syndrome) is slow, insidious, and irresistible. Death from AIDS-related diseases occurs within 16 years in 98 percent of cases. Very few infected individuals have demonstrated permanent natural resistance to the virus.

The AIDS virus is a devilishly successful organism, supremely well adapted to perpetuating its kind. It has a long incubation period, and thus its victims are liable to spread the disease widely before they are even aware of being ill. Furthermore, the virus mutates very rapidly, and its ability to evade host resistance amazes even scientists at the forefront of AIDS research. Already several types and subtypes of the virus have been identified, and the potential for more mutations is alarming, particularly in specifically African forms of the virus. The DNA of HIV samples taken from 10 women attending one clinic in Botswana, for example, showed significantly more variation than is evident in a collection of 500 samples taken from all over the world during the last 25 years.

The question of where the virus originated and exactly how it was transmitted to people is debated, but the evidence points persuasively to the conclusion that it evolved originally in West African populations of monkeys and chimpanzees and found its way into the human population via forest people who killed, handled, and ate these animals from time to time. The virus probably spread through the human populations of West and central Africa and killed many people over the years, but since they were seen to die from common diseases (that the virus had rendered them unable to fight off), AIDS was not identified as a specific disease until it had spread to gay men in Los Angeles who were affluent enough for the similarities of their deaths to attract attention. By then the virus had spread widely in Africa and abroad.

The United States alone spends about two billion dollars on AIDS research each year, and that is just a fraction of the total sum spent worldwide. The main thrusts of research have been to understand the properties of the virus and to find ways of preventing and treating the disease. The prospects for finding a cure are slight. Success has so far been limited to the development of drug therapies that slow down the physical deterioration that AIDS causes. But these cost from $10,000 to $20,000 per year for each patient and must be maintained for years—if not for life.

Expensive treatments for the disease are of little relevance to Africa. Few health budgets spend more than even $10 U.S. per person yearly (Tanzania, for example, spends just $2.71). A vaccine that staved off HIV infection would be more to the point. But developing such a vaccine is not an attractive proposition for Western pharmaceutical companies. Their research is driven by the search for billion-dollar markets, not the development of products needed in the developing world, where people have no money. Virtually no attention has been given to producing a vaccine to stave off the AIDS epidemic that looms so ominously over Africa.

Women bear the brunt of the AIDS epidemic in sub-Saharan Africa. Fifty-five percent of all infected adults are women, and in the sexually active age groups the proportion is even higher. Among adolescent girls, for example, the rates of infection are four times that of boys in the same age group. Among people in their early 20s, the rates are three times higher. Overall, HIV infection tends to peak in

women around age 25, whereas among men the peak comes 10 to 15 years later.

The reasons for these differences are various. As in many cultures, there is peer pressure among both boys and girls to have sex, but girls tend to have sex for the first time at an earlier age, and often with much older and promiscuous men who are likely to be infected—with sugar daddies, for example, who promise them money to pay school fees, or even with male school teachers who make a habit of coercing vulnerable girls into having sex with them. Some men believe that having sex with a virgin cures AIDS and will pay large sums for the privilege.

Being subordinate in African society increases women's risk of becoming infected. Laws that treat women as dependent minors or deny them the right to inherit land force many to trade sex for food and

most countries have no social security or pension schemes and where the instability of national currencies makes even personal savings pointless, there has never been a greater need for children. But they must be healthy children, free of AIDS. Although it is going to be a long haul, there are signs that Africa is moving in that direction—led by women.

Female education and empowerment are the key. Already, studies in AIDS-ridden African countries have shown that fewer girls with high school educations get HIV. This is easy to understand. When confronted by a man looking for sex, a girl who has not gone to school, who is illiterate and accustomed to carrying out orders at home, has neither the experience nor the confidence to say no. But the more highly educated a girl is, the less likely she is to indulge in unprotected sex.

THERE IS A glimmer of hope here, lit by the resolute determination and good sense of women who have always been the strength of African society. While the men seek jobs that will pay for the manufactured necessities of life, many African households depend upon the women to produce food that will nourish the family and children at home. Even today, 80 percent of the population of Uganda, for instance, lives directly off the land. Even those who have jobs in the cities and towns are likely also to have some land in the country with a stand of bananas. Having a few coffee trees can provide a useful supplementary income. Fishing the lakes was an important source of protein only at

other basic needs. Also, the virus moves more readily from male to female. Customs such as dry sex, polygamy, wife inheritance, and the widespread condoning of male promiscuity all add to the vulnerability of women. Most tragic of all is the fact that for many African women, the primary reason for having sex in the first place is not physical pleasure or to gratify a partner, but simply to have children. This makes nonsense of the condom—that most widely publicized and heavily funded item in the developed world's contribution to the battle against AIDS in Africa.

In rural and subsistence societies in Africa and elsewhere, large families have long since been the foundation of a secure old age. It was always assumed that children would take care of their aging parents, and the more children there were to share the burden, the better things would be. In Africa today, where

Introduced to Lake Victoria along with the Nile perch, the smaller tilapia has become important to the local economy. With collapse threatening the Nile perch industry, local communities are pressing for management of the lake's remaining fish resources and a fairer distribution of its benefits.

FOLLOWING PAGES: **The sun sets behind the rounded volcanic peaks of the Virunga Mountains at Lake Edward, Uganda.**

the local market level until the 1980s, when international and local developments opened a new world for the fishermen of Lake Victoria.

Beginning in the 1950s and 1960s, the worldwide consumer demand for fish has been steadily rising, causing what might be called the industrialization of the fishing industry. By the 1990s almost all the world's largest marine fisheries, and most of its freshwater ones too, had been overfished.

Still the demand for fish continued to grow, promoted by the rising incomes of people in the industrialized nations and their declining enthusiasm for meat. The world price for table fish rose steadily. Meanwhile, improvements in refrigerated transport were bringing down the cost of getting the catch from the fishery to the consumer. Before long

rising market prices and falling supply costs combined to make it profitable for entrepreneurs to begin flying planeloads of Nile perch from Lake Victoria to Tel Aviv, London, Frankfurt, and Paris. The first frozen fillets of Nile perch were exported from Kenya in 1987, and soon no fewer than ten factories were exporting the fish. The volumes were low initially, but by the mid-1990s frozen fillets of Nile perch were being exported from the Lake Victoria fishery at a rate of more than 44,000 tons per year, worth 130 million U.S. dollars. Local trade probably accounted for at least another 5,500 tons.

Quite apart from the export dollars gained, the Nile perch fishery provides a source of livelihood for over 30 million people in Kenya, Uganda, and Tanzania— boatbuilders, fishermen and their crews, transporters,

Among the cichlids of the Great Lakes, some species go to extremes to raise their young. *Tyrannochromis macrostoma* females take their eggs into their mouth after the male has fertilized them, releasing the young only when they are large enough to feed themselves.

processing staff, and fishmongers. The total value of the fishery could be as high as one billion U.S. dollars, according to one estimate. And what lies in the future? Exploiting the fishery's enormous potential in a sustainable manner will depend upon how successfully it is managed, and there are already some doubts about that. The basic problem is that the Nile perch is not indigenous to Lake Victoria. It was introduced in the 1950s and has subsequently wrought havoc with the ecology of the lake.

My visit to Ukara occurred at the time of the new moon, and each evening the lake sparkled with dozens of lights. Fishermen. Maneke laughed at my suggestion that they were helping to rid the lake of its intruder, the Nile perch. No, he explained, they were after *dagaa*, a tiny fish that swarmed to the lights on moonless nights and could be netted by the ton. The catches were so large, he claimed, that some canoes came ashore to unload two or three times during the night. The story seemed improbable, but I was obliged to revise my opinion next day, when the island tour brought us to the fishermen's beach. Maneke had not exaggerated. An area the size of a railway platform was strewn with these silvery slices of protein, drying in the sun. The senior fishermen were either asleep on the sand or mending nets while their young assistants constantly raked through the fish and tossed forkfuls into the air to hasten drying. The previous night's catch was already bagged up and awaiting shipment to the mainland, where a good price was anticipated.

The market for dagaa had expanded enormously in the past few years, Maneke explained, probably because the fish was so much easier to handle and the lake seemed to be full of it at the moment. Why? Mr. Maneke shrugged. Because Lake Victoria is a wonderful place, he suggested.

LAKE VICTORIA IS the largest lake in Africa and the second largest freshwater lake in the world (after Lake Superior). With a surface area of 26,828 square miles, it is only a little smaller than Ireland. The waters of the lake are shared by three countries— Tanzania, Uganda, and Kenya—and with a total length of 2,130 miles the shoreline is nearly as long as Africa is broad at the Equator. But statistics alone cannot give any true sense of the lake's formidable presence. It is better to think of an ocean—even though the lake lies at the very heart of a continent at an altitude of 3,700 feet above sea level. No tide, admittedly, but there are waves slapping on a rocky shore and a horizon where the water meets the sky in an unbroken line, curving with the circumference of the Earth. Massive granite outcrops rise as offshore islands and also form cliffs around the shore. Papyrus is rooted in the water at their feet. Pied kingfishers wait to dive from overhanging branches. Storks, kites, and cormorants constantly quarter the offshore waters of the bay, and swifts flash through the clouds of lake flies that are at times so dense along the shore that it seems you must hold your breath to avoid inhaling them.

The lake has sounds, gulfs, and channels of a size that would not disgrace a continental coastline, and hundreds of islands, some uninhabited, others populated by thousands of people, many of whom rarely visit the mainland. Nonetheless, the lake's expanses of open water are vast. Trawlers wishing to fish in the center of the lake from the Tanzanian port of Mwanza must reckon on a sailing time of close to 18 hours. And the open water is a dangerous place to be when the high winds and driving rain of a tropical squall sweep across the lake, whipping the choppy waters up into waves taller than a man and with not much more distance between them. Once I spied a capsized canoe, found drifting, the brilliantly patterned hull glistening like fresh paint, nets and floats entangled with the sodden sail. There can have been little hope

Brightly colored cichlids are popular aquarium fish. Most are raised in captivity, but breeders will pay good money for genetically pure wild stock. Rare wild species can fetch hundreds of dollars a pair. Supplying live and undamaged specimen cichlids has become a lucrative though challenging occupation for some of Lake Malawi's fishermen.

for the crew. Even the large modern ships that transport goods and passengers from port to port around the lake do not risk taking a shortcut across open water. They hug the coastline instead, which means that the sailing time from Mwanza to Musoma, for example, is nine hours, and a full circumnavigation of the lake, calling at the major ports of Tanzania, Uganda, and Kenya takes days.

Lake Victoria is a young lake, geologically speaking. It is located in a basin that was formed 400,000 years ago, when a fractured block of the Earth's crust tilted along the line of the Great Rift Valley, raising its western edge into a range of hills that broke the path of rivers flowing westward until that time. The rivers backed up—the Kagera even reversed its course—drowning the lattice of river valleys that had crossed the plateau, and eventually filling the basin to form the lake we now know. The basin is shallow—more a saucer than a basin—and Lake Victoria is nowhere more than 270 feet deep. Lake Tanganyika, by comparison, is 4,823 feet deep, filling a deep, steep-sided cleft in the Rift Valley floor. The shallowness of Lake Victoria and its very large surface area in relation to depth have made the lake highly susceptible to climate changes.

Since the rivers flowing into Lake Victoria are not very long, their volume is limited, amounting to no more than 13 inches per year, which represents only about one-fifth of the water the lake receives every year. The remainder, 49 inches, falls as rain, and since evaporation takes some 51 inches from the lake each year, and another 11 inches flows off into the Nile, any prolonged decrease in annual rainfall would rapidly deplete the volume of water in the lake. Indeed, cores taken from the deepest parts of the lake bed during the 1990s contained the roots and pollen of terrestrial plants at distinct levels, showing that the lake has dried out completely three times since its formation. These occurred at intervals of 100,000 years and appear to be linked to well-defined cycles of climatic change known as the Milankovitch cycles. Dating of the cores indicates that the most recent dry spell began around 17,300 years ago as the last major ice age locked a large fraction of the Earth's water in the polar ice caps, chilling the oceans and drying out the continents. The lake remained dry for several thousand years before climatic conditions improved and the lake began to fill again about 14,700 years ago.

That a body of water slightly smaller than Ireland should dry out and then fill again over such a short period of time (in geological terms) is startling. But people at least could adapt, or simply move away. Not so the fish. If the lake bed was dry for even a year or two—never mind millennia—no fish could have survived to repopulate the returning waters. Furthermore, without a lake there could have been no lake-derived moisture to make the clouds that are the source of most of the region's rainfall, and without rain there could not have been even residual ponds in which fish found refuge through the long drought.

Yet modern Lake Victoria has been home to more than 400 species of fish, most of which are not found anywhere else on Earth. The majority of these endemic fish species are cichlids (the family of tropical freshwater fish whose most colorful representatives are often seen flashing among the water plants of an aquarium). They share a common ancestry with fish elsewhere in the region, and some of those ancestors must have arrived at Lake Victoria as it began to fill again, 14,700 years ago, but their descendents can only have evolved into so many distinct species since that time. If this is true, the Lake Victoria cichlids are the fastest evolving large group of vertebrate species ever known.

THE BASIC SKELETAL structure of fish is very adaptable. They can evolve to become distinct species in a relatively short space of time. Cichlids, in particular, have skull and body proportions that are easily altered. In addition, they are the only freshwater fish with two sets of jaws: one in the mouth, with which they can suck, scrape, or bite off morsels of food; and another in the throat that enables them to crush or cut up the morsels before they are ingested. Both sets of jaws are highly adaptable—even able to change form within the lifetime of a single fish. Researchers have found that cichlids fed one kind of diet rather than another soon begin to look very different.

Reproductive strategies are another feature that has given the cichlids an evolutionary edge. The cichlids are caring parents. While most fish produce a superabundance of eggs and leave their fate mostly to chance, the cichlids lay few eggs and look after them very carefully. They make nests, which they guard and fan with fins and tail to maintain a flow of fresh water over the eggs. Many are mouth brooders, hatching the eggs in their mouths and releasing the young only when they are large enough to fend for themselves. Some cichlid mouths are large enough to accommodate up to 1,000 eggs, but most rear far fewer.

Nest guarding, egg turning and cleaning, and mouth brooding ensure the survival of a very high proportion of young fish and enable the cichlids to breed all year-round. Under the right conditions, the lake's original cichlids increase rapidly. A mere handful of species exploded into hundreds as the cichlids moved into the many ecological niches in Victoria and the other Great Lakes. For this reason they became one of the world's prime sites for the study of the roles of ecology and behavior in evolution.

Nowhere is this more true than in Lake Tanganyika. Its surface area is only half that of Lake Victoria, but it holds seven times the amount of water. Indeed, one percent of all the fresh water in the world is in Lake Tanganyika. It holds so much water because it is 4,823 feet deep (the second deepest lake in the world, after Lake Baikal at 5,715 feet). Lake Tanganyika is older than Lake Victoria and is known to be even richer in fish life, even though ichthyologists have explored only about 10 percent of its shoreline. One researcher found over 7,000 fish in a single square 21 yards by 21 yards, belonging to 38 different species—most of them cichlids.

From above there is not much to be seen where waves are breaking over a rocky shore, but an underwater view reveals that the brown and green (with blue spots) *Eretmodus* cichlids are right in among the waves, nipping algae from the rocks with their chisel-like teeth. The turbulent water actually pushes their specifically configured bodies onto the rock surfaces rather than sweeping them off. Cheek by jowl, the identically shaped *Tanganicodus* cichlids are also being tossed about by the waves, yet they ignore the algae. Instead they use their pointed heads, sharp snouts, and long fine teeth to pluck insect larvae from the rock crevices. In calmer waters, tiny *Lamprologus* females with eggs and young have taken up residence in old snail shells. The yellow, green, or brown males are too large to enter the refuge. So they steal the shells—sometimes with females inside—from one another, and posture and preen around their harems, like stags with their does.

Though body shape and behavior are often the distinguishing features of a cichlid population, color is the most striking aspect of their diversity. Coloring probably began with the need to escape hungry birds, reptiles, and larger fish—requiring

Water hyacinth is a runaway ornamental plant from South America that infests the shoreline of Lake Victoria.

most of them to adopt some form of camouflage for a large part of their lives. Females are often (but not always) drabber than males. Those that frequent open waters tend to be silver, like their marine counterparts. Shoaling species have prominent lines, spots, or bars, which probably serve as stop-go and orientation signals, naturalists suggest. Many, like chameleons, can change color at will and very quickly—as if at the flick of a switch. A shoal of inconspicuous fish suddenly bursts into a parade of color or, like the transvestite fish (*Pseudotropheus auratus*), turns from male to female coloration in a flash. Sibling populations enlist coloration to their service to inhibit interbreeding. It has been noted, for instance, that the patterns of closely related species frequently differ the most.

Lake Tanganyika has 33 genera of endemic cichlids, compared with just 4 in Lake Victoria. Here the process of evolutionary adaptation has been going on for so long that its fish even mimic other types of fish life. Among the Lake Tanganyika cichlids, for instance, are species resembling the tuna, snapper, and grouper of the ocean—much smaller, of course, but following similar lifestyles. The forms and variety of oceanlike life led early biologists to believe that the lake must have been connected to the sea at some stage.

The Lake Tanganyika cichlids have evolved ways of exploiting every kind of food source in every available location. There are bottom feeders and surface feeders, plankton eaters and algae eaters; some that live on fish eggs, some that eat fish, and some that must crack open a mussel or break into a snail shell for their meals. There is even a species with grotesquely swollen lips that does nothing but suck mayfly larvae from their burrows. But the most amazing feeding specialization of all is that of the *Perissodus* cichlids, whose diet consists only of fish scales taken from living fish. The scale eaters approach their victims from behind, stealthily, then suddenly dart in to rasp a mouthful of scales from their sides. The scales are stacked inside the throat, like pages in a book, to be broken up by the second set of jaws and ingested as packets of protein.

Seven species of scale eaters live in Lake Tanganyika, and one of them, *Perissodus microlepis,* occurs in two distinct forms: one with the head and jaws curved to the right and the other with the head and jaws curved to the left. These fish not only feed on scales, they also feed off only one side of the fish they take their meals from. The left-handed fish scrape scales from the right side of their victims, and the right-handed dine from the left side. Researchers believe this unusual asymmetry in body form within the same species evolved because a twisted head allows the fish to grasp scales more efficiently. The victims survive, it has been noted, though they soon become very wary. Indeed, with attackers specifically designed to scrape scales from either side of their bodies, they can never relax.

IF THE CICHLIDS have made Lake Tanganyika a unique laboratory for the study of natural selection and the evolution of species, then the rate at which cichlid species have been exterminated from Lake Victoria makes that lake an illuminating example of how quickly a natural wonder can be destroyed when people become involved. Most of the lake's cichlids have been brought to the point of extinction in less than half a century. Fifty years ago the cichlids made up more than 99 percent of Lake Victoria's fish biomass; today they account for less than one percent. Many cichlid species are

already extinct, and many more are so reduced in numbers that their chances of recovery are minimal. Scientists summarize the cause of this mass extinction with the acronym HIPPO: Habitat destruction, Introduced species, Pollution, Population growth, and Overexploitation. Together these factors have transformed Lake Victoria from a natural wonder into one of the most profoundly disrupted ecosystems ever observed.

The introduction of the predatory Nile perch in the 1950s, with its voracious appetite for other fish, has been the major force of destruction, but the problems can be traced back as far as the 1920s. That's when large forested areas of the lake's catchment were cleared for tea, coffee, sugar, and cotton plantations. Agriculture increased the amounts of soil, fertilizer, and pesticide residues being washed into the lake. The spread of human settlement around the shores added to the pollution. In 1989 came the water hyacinth, *Eichhornia crassipes,* an ornamental plant from South America that found its way into the lake along the Kagera River from Rwanda and Burundi. Fed to excess by nutrients flowing into the lake from intensified human activities around the shore, the tamed water hyacinth of the ornamental pond ran wild. In a mere 20 years it virtually encircled the 2,130-mile shoreline with an almost impenetrable 100-foot-wide mat of densely packed floating leaves and roots. Concerted attempts by local communities to clear the weed from the lake by hand have been futile. Weevils introduced from South America, where they are the water hyacinth's natural predator, have hardly touched the weed in Lake Victoria. As the search for a solution to the water hyacinth problem continues, some among the despairing authorities have wistfully suggested that the notorious defoliant Agent Orange might be the answer.

Meanwhile, the Nile perch and another introduced species that people find tasty, the Nile tilapia, were steadily munching their way through the lake's indigenous fish population. The Nile tilapia grows up to 7 pounds, but the Nile perch can weigh over 400 pounds, and cichlids feature prominently in its diet. By the mid-1980s the Nile perch had virtually taken over the lake, the cichlid population had fallen by a factor of 10,000, and the perch were beginning to make a meal of the introduced tilapia as well. Even more disastrously, many of the cichlids that the perch had wiped out were algae eaters. With them gone, algae blooms reached unprecedented levels. Uneaten algae, dead and decaying, sucked oxygen from the water as it accumulated on the lake bed. The depths of the already shallow lake are now so devoid of oxygen that scientists fear much of Lake Victoria is no longer capable of sustaining oxygen-dependent life. Furthermore, winds and currents carry these deoxygenated waters into the lake's shallow gulfs and bays, where they kill huge numbers of fish.

But the news from Lake Victoria is not all bad. Certainly the millions of people who feed their families either directly or indirectly from the lake have had a more positive view of events around the lake during the past half century. The human ecosystem has flourished as a result of changes in the lake. And even within the lake itself there have been positive developments. The tiny (about 2- to 3-inch long) *Rastrineobola argentea*, for instance, has flourished. *Rastrineobola* feeds on microscopic zooplankton, and as a small surface-feeding fish of the open lake waters, it is probably the only native fish that has not been seriously affected by the Nile perch. Indeed, the removal of some competing species has probably been to its advantage.

Unlike the cichlids, *Rastrineobola* grows fast, reproduces prolifically, and has a short natural life span. Such fast turnover rates make it exceptionally resilient to predation—whether by Nile perch or by fishermen. Dagaa, as the fish is known locally, congregates in dense shoals, especially on moonlit nights. Caught from canoes with cast nets or from the shore with seine nets, it was always a popular catch. Sun-dried, dagaa keeps well and, apart from feeding the family directly, can be sold at market. With its explosive growth following the introduction of the Nile perch, dagaa became a major fishery item. Larger boats joined in, working at night with pressure lamps to attract the fish. On a good night, boats returned to the jetty two or three times to unload their catch.

A day of good sunshine and fresh winds is enough to dry the fish completely, after which it is packed in large sacks for sale to dealers. At one Tanzanian landing point, 330 tons of dagaa are handled every month. Tanzanian railways alone carried 3,300 tons from the lake in 1989. From Lake Victoria the dried fish is sold throughout East Africa—even making its way to the markets of Tanga, on the Indian Ocean coast. In Kenya and Uganda, an increasing proportion of the dagaa catch is turned into a fish-meal animal feed, some of which is fed to tilapia in commercial fish farms.

By the mid-1990s, the dagaa fishery was second only to Nile perch in economic importance on Lake Victoria. With Nile tilapia, the lake was essentially a three-species fishery. Their combined catches total an estimated 550,000 tons per year, and some fear that the lake cannot sustain such a huge outtake. On the other hand, Lake Victoria may have yet more surprises in store. It has been found, for instance, that the 13 species of mud-feeding cichlids wiped out by the Nile perch soon after it was introduced to the lake have been replaced by massive populations of a single species of freshwater prawn. Nile perch are now growing to the size of small goats on freshwater prawns.

It would be interesting to know what Maneke thinks of these developments, though I can already predict his response: a shrug of the shoulders, a smile, and the comment "Lake Victoria is a wonderful place."

Charles Tinkewimenu has a problem. The fishing in Lake Victoria is not what it used to be. Catches have fallen, and there are more fishermen than ever on the lake. Ten years ago he sold three cows to buy a canoe and the nets he needed to get started as a fisherman, leaving his wife to manage their successful farm. A contract to supply the international animal feed industry enabled Charles to buy more canoes and hire more men. Business boomed. But not anymore.

Lake Victoria is nearly the size of Ireland, but not as permanent as it looks. The lake bed was grassland 15,000 years ago, when the last major ice age locked much of the Earth's water in the ice caps. As the lake basin refilled, it became a hothouse of evolution for fish. Four hundred species evolved. For centuries, the fishing on the lake was good. And it was even better when fishermen began catching the Nile perch introduced in the 1950s. Then the balance shifted. Having eaten many of the lake's fish species to extinction, the Nile perch itself was in trouble.

But Charles is an enterprising man. He plowed his fishing profits back into the farm, and the farm flourished. Now he will use farming profits to move into a new and growing business—tourism. He is buying a large motor launch that will ferry tourists to the chimpanzee sanctuary that has been opened on Ngamba Island.

Charles Tinkewimenu was born and brought up on a farm. He had not seen Lake Victoria until he visited it as a student, and did not think of working there until he heard of huge profits being made from fishing. "My first time on a boat was very scary, even though I was 30 years old," he admits. "But I had to be strong. I was determined to make a living from fish." Soon he owned several canoes and had crews working for him.

The introduced Nile perch has wiped out Lake Victoria's traditional fishing. Charles relies on the dagaa catch to meet his contract with an international animal feed company.

On cloudy and moonless nights, lanterns lashed to bamboo floats (above) attract shoals of a fish known locally as dagaa. The fishermen put out a number of lanterns, lay a net around each one, then haul in the catch (left).

Dagaa are small but occur in such huge numbers that fishermen sometimes fill the canoe several times in the course of a night.

Though dagaa are small, the catch puts a heavy strain on the light, fine-mesh net. The nets must be checked every day (right). Dried tilapia, another lake fish (below), supplies the local market.

Charles operates from a tiny island shared with 650 other fishermen.
Competition is fierce. "There are fewer and fewer fish," says Charles.
"It's threatening my livelihood. It's time to think of something new."
And Charles, ever the entrepreneur, has spotted an opening in the
tourist industry. "I need to buy a new boat," he says, "with strong
engines and all the other things necessary for tourists."

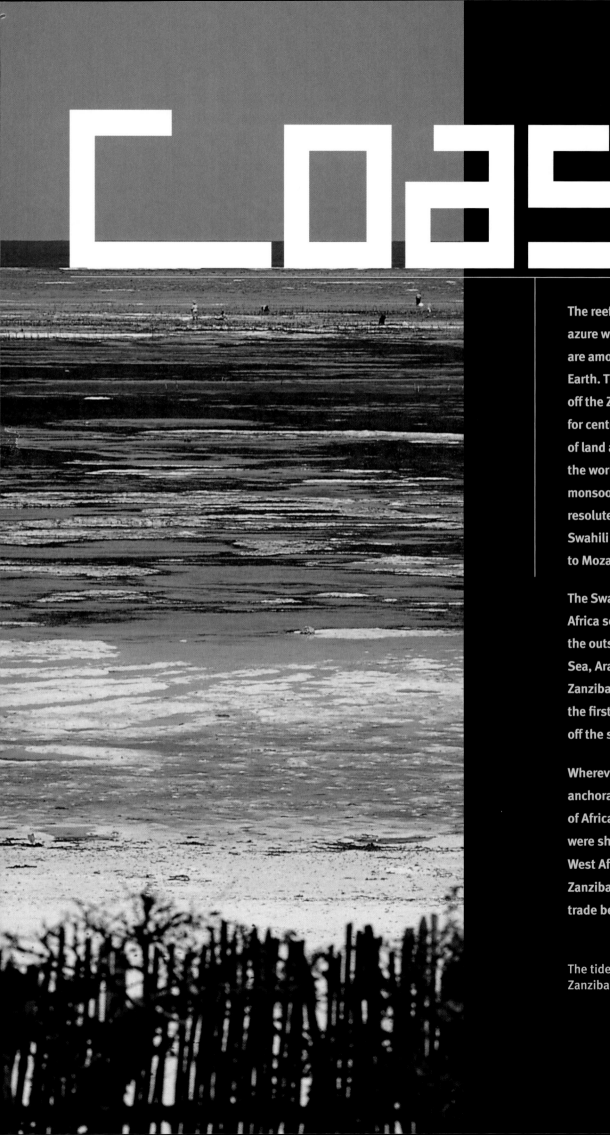

COaS

The reef
azure w
are amo
Earth. T
off the Z
for cent
of land a
the wor
monsoo
resolute
Swahili
to Moza

The Swa
Africa se
the outs
Sea, Ara
Zanziba
the first
off the s

Wherev
anchora
of Africa
were sh
West Af
Zanziba
trade be

The tide
Zanziba

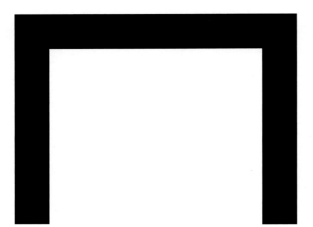ot so long ago, when it was still possible to travel in Sierra Leone with reasonable safety, I took the *pampa* that sailed twice a week across Yawri Bay from Tombo to Shenge. Distance 25 miles, journey time three hours. The pampa is an 59-foot open boat locally built of rough-hewn boards. It leaked. And with a 40-horsepower outboard engine driving it into a moderate swell and onshore breeze, it also took water over the bow and starboard gunwale.

The pampa occasionally flushed a flying fish from the cloudy waters of the shallow bay, but there was little to see by the time we were an hour from Tombo. I could see the bulk of the Freetown peninsula to the north, but to the south and east the coast was low and gray, like the first wash of a watercolor—an image so insubstantial that it might be a cloud bank.

The coasts of Africa are generally low-lying. Rugged cliffs are rare, and few shores have a backdrop of high mountains. Long sandy beaches predominate. Over long distances the coastline is unbroken by any large inlets, and of its major rivers only the Congo has an open estuary. The rest are either blocked by sandbars or reach the ocean via the twist-ing channels of a delta. Africa's largely impenetrable coastline helped to deter foreign invaders, while the paucity of protected natural harbors and navigable rivers hindered the development of the coast and its hinterland. Nonetheless, there were a few places where ships could anchor safely, and most of these were at some time or another used by vessels engaged in one of the most evil activities that humanity has ever devised—the African slave trade. Sir John Hawkins anchored in Yawri Bay in 1562, taking on board the cargo that would constitute the first shipment of slaves to be transported across the Atlantic to America.

PREVIOUS PAGES: **The culture of East Africa's Swahili coast is a vibrant mixture of Africa and exotic influence.** ABOVE: **At sunrise and low tide, fishermen from Bwejuu pole their boat across the shallow waters of the lagoon. The fishing is best off the reef, which lies a good distance offshore, but catches are faltering.**

Toward evening, as the sight of coconut palms and huts confirmed that Shenge was near, a flotilla of outrigger canoes sailed into view. Twenty-seven of them, on a fast reach across the onshore wind, spritsail rigged, each sail a random homemade patchwork of flamboyant cloth. All colors of the rainbow were there, as they might be in Montego Bay when vacationing windsurfers are out in force, catching the evening breeze. But the men from Shenge were going out for the night, catching their livelihood in the deep blue water that lies five miles offshore. Their course took the canoes close to Plantain Island, where slave traders coming after Sir John Hawkins had built a pen in which to hold their merchandise.

Ben Caulker showed me around Plantain Island the next day. A teacher whose family had lived in Shenge for generations, Ben had plans for making a tourist venue of the region, tasteful and low-key, he explained, where visitors could absorb the natural beauty, cultural heritage, and history of Shenge and Plantain Island. Villagers had been encouraged to

contribute to the fund he had set up; the government and foreign agencies had been approached. Tourists would of course visit the slave pen, which still stands at the northern end of the island—a square of stout stone walls, open to the skies. A path hewn through the boulders leads down to a jetty, pointing west, where the sun sets and ships disappear into the ocean.

T**HE SHIPPING OF** slaves across the Atlantic from the shores of West Africa is deeply etched into the conscience of the world. Less well-known is the trade from ports on the East African coast, which began earlier, went on longer, and at times equaled the Atlantic trade in its volume and depravity. Zanzibar was a center for the marketing and shipment of slaves to Arabia and across the Indian Ocean for more than a thousand years—a history that stands in stark contrast to its modern role as an exotic spice-island paradise for tourists.

The canoes with colorful sails scudding across the Zanzibar lagoons evoked memories of the Yawri Bay flotilla. Known as *ngalaus* in the coastal Swahili language, their crews have brought fish from the offshore waters for centuries, just as have the fishermen of Shenge. But nowadays the Zanzibar canoes are more often filled with tourists, variously attired in sun hats, T-shirts, swimsuits, flippers, snorkel, and mask. Escaping the heat, the tourists are sailing out for a glimpse of life on the coral reefs that line the offshore rim of the lagoon, where the waters change abruptly from the pale turquoise of the shallows to the dark ultramarine of the deep ocean.

The tourists go out at low tide. Floating on the surface, they have a privileged bird's-eye view of the fantastic world that lies just beneath them. Tropical coral reefs are the richest environments on Earth. A single reef may support as many as 3,000 different species of sea creatures. Shoals of small bright blue damselfish

The octopus can change color faster than a chameleon. It has eyesight and other senses to rival ours. It pumps blue blood, is jet powered, and can emit smoke screens of ink. It is also a very popular food on the Swahili coast.

flash through the branches of the antler coral, like flocks of birds in the rain forest, darting into the tangle of fronds at the slightest sign of danger. Butterfly fish move more sedately, each of their many species distinguished by a different pattern of brilliantly colored spots, dots, patches, and stripes. Like the vividly colored butterflies of the rain forest, each can recognize its own kind at a distance. The reef can be noisy too, with the sound of fish crunching coral, clicking triggerfish, and an evening chorus of squirrelfish.

The surface of the reef is packed with sponges, sea urchins, brittle stars, and sea fans. Sea anemones adorn the coral branches, their fronds waving with the current, like the exotic flowers on the branches of a rain forest tree. Sea lilies, bristle worms, and shell-less mollusks are constantly on the move, clambering among the corals. Moray eels lurk in small caverns, waiting to make a meal of any unfortunate that wanders within range. Along the edges of the reef drift the parrot fish, bedecked in stripes of green and blue and improbable shades of pink. With the sharp beaklike mouth to which they owe their name, the parrot fish nip off pieces of coral to extract the living polyps within.

Coral polyps are tiny creatures belonging to a group known as the Anthozoa—the "flower animals." With a flurry of tentacles extending from their cylindrical bodies, they do look like a vase of flowers. But the benign floral appearance is deceptive. These are carnivorous animals with deadly stingers on their waving tentacles, which are constantly taking a meal of microscopic prey from the passing currents. Coral polyps take calcium carbonate from the sea and build delicate protective chambers for themselves from which their tentacles can be extended and retracted at will. Each new generation of polyps builds directly upon the chambers of previous generations.

Reef-building corals grow best in waters less than 100 feet deep, and new reefs cannot form below 160 feet, where there is not enough sunlight to fuel their life processes. Even so, over time some reefs may become hundreds of feet deep. Their steadily increasing weight depresses the seabed on which they were founded, so that the surface is always underwater. But whatever depth of coral, only the surface of the reef is alive—like a thin skin covering layer upon layer of empty limestone chambers. Though lifeless, these abandoned properties continue to serve the colony by giving it a solid foundation.

The coral reef is often called the tropical rain forest of the sea. Both systems support a great diversity of life-forms that have evolved to fit every available niche. Although it would seem that no two environments could differ more than a forest and a reef, they are fundamentally very similar. Both depend upon profuse sunlight and oxygen. The living surface of the coral is bathed in sunlight, like the leaves in the canopy of the rain forest, while the waves breaking over the reefs and surging through the coral heads saturate the water with oxygen, like a wind blowing through the treetops. In addition, the dead coral that supports the living surface of the reef serves much the same function as the inert wood of the trees that hold the rain forest canopy aloft.

But of course, since all life began in the oceans, the reefs are considerably older than the rain forest. The earliest known fossils related to modern rain forest flora date back a mere 65 million years. An abundance of marine fossil evidence clearly shows that reefs with corals, sea urchins, sponges, and mollusks, all closely related to species found on the reefs today, were well established in the oceans by 200 million years ago. Ever since that time, there have always been places in the tropical oceans where polyps could continue building their castles of coral.

Superlatives crop up quite frequently in even the

Issa is building a house for himself in Bwejuu. The walls are made of rough coral blocks hewn from a nearby quarry. Much of the Swahili coast is fringed with low coral cliffs formed in the distant past when sea levels were much higher than today. Coral is the preferred building material, better suited to the climate (and cheaper) than brick or concrete.

most serious academic accounts of the tropical reefs. Their creation is one of the most remarkable achievements of the living world. Between 12,000 and 8,000 years ago, when sea levels were rising at a rate of about 32 feet per thousand years, the tiny polyps and their kind were laying down ten billion tons of calcium carbonate per year. Even today, with sea levels stable, they are adding 2.7 tons of material to the reefs each year. And while the polyps are piling up their tiny limestone dormitories, the growth rate of the reef's plants and symbiotic animals is greater than in any other ecosystem. Fully one-third of all the world's bony fish—8,000 species in all—as well as numerous less mobile creatures are constantly feeding. The density of fish alone is ten times greater than the densities attained in corresponding temperate coastal ecosystems. It is roughly equivalent to keeping a flock of 40 sheep permanently on one acre of grassland.

For many years it was believed that the life of a coral reef represented a point of equilibrium, or natural balance. The greatest possible diversity of organisms filled every available niche with the greatest possible numbers and collectively recycled energy through the system with the greatest possible efficiency. Equilibrium denoted stability, it was thought, and stability was the climax state toward which every natural system progressed and would maintain unless disrupted by external influences. Subsequent investigations have shown, however, that natural balance is a misnomer, equilibrium an impossibility, and stability a fantasy. Coral reefs, in particular, are dynamic and highly unstable ecosystems in which self-replacement and recovery from disturbances are normal and actually contribute to the diversity on the reef.

This is because coral reef communities have evolved in conditions that are subject to unpredictable and radical change. With hurricanes, storms, sea levels, and water temperature changes to contend with, coral reefs have to be adaptable. They are not as fragile as was previously thought, although the manner and speed of their recovery may vary a great deal. Complex reef systems may take 20 to 50 years to recover from a calamitous event, while a smaller, simpler reef may require only a few years. Currently, the resilience of coral reefs is being tested by the consequences of the 1998 El Niño, which raised ocean temperatures around the world, seriously damaging many reefs. Just how quickly they can recover remains to be seen.

In global terms, 1998 was the warmest year since the start of temperature recordings some 150 years ago, and 1990 to 1999 was the warmest decade. In addition, the El Niño of 1998 was the strongest ever recorded. All of these factors conspired to produce very high water temperatures in many parts of the oceans, particularly in the tropical Indian Ocean, where temperatures rose 5°F to 9°F above normal. High temperatures kill off the microscopic algae that live in a symbiotic relationship with the coral polyps, leaving the white lime skeleton of the corals visible through the transparent tissue of the polyps and giving the formation a bleached appearance. If normal conditions are reestablished within a few weeks, algae repopulate the coral, which then continues to grow normally. If not, the coral formation dies.

The 1998 El Niño led to massive bleaching and subsequent coral death throughout the tropics. On some Australian reefs, 70 to 100 percent of the shallow corals were bleached, and 80 percent died. Its effect on Indian Ocean reefs was particularly severe, with bleaching and mortality of up to 90 percent in many shallow areas and of 50 percent even where reefs were 65 feet beneath the surface. On the

The meticulous carving and bold brass work on traditional doors typifies the blend of African and Arabian influences that is found in Zanzibar's oldest quarter—Stone Town.

East African coast, virtually all Kenya's shallow reefs were bleached, and at least half of them died—as did Kenya's deepwater reefs. In the coral gardens of Tanzania's Mafia Marine Park, which was rated the best coral reef on the coast, between 80 and 100 percent of the coral died. Zanzibar was less badly affected, with between a quarter and a half of its reefs bleached and perhaps 40 percent mortality.

Coral reefs have been wiped out many times before in the past, and they have always recovered. If the 1998 El Niño was a rare event, then the affected reefs could recover within 25 to 50 years. People whose livelihoods depend upon the reef will be severely affected, but the reef itself will remain intact, breaking the force of ocean storms and currents and thus continuing to protect the coastline. But if the 1998 bleaching and mortality were mainly the result of global climate change and this change is continuing, there is much greater cause for concern. The events of 1998 will probably recur, in which case the coral reefs will never recover. The shoals of beautiful fish will disappear, and tourists will no longer sail out in ngalaus to see them. Most worrying of all, the threat of coastal erosion could become acute as the ocean steadily gnaws away the reefs that, while they were alive, had been building up the coastline year by year.

Thus the coral reefs of the Indian Ocean in particular have acquired the status of a global alarm system. The 1998 bleaching could be the first widespread early warning of the serious changes that global warming could inflict on sensitive environments.

THE SWAHILI FISHERMEN whose livelihood these days may depend more upon ferrying tourists to the reef than catching fish represent the eastern limit of the Bantu migration that began 5,000 years ago. After consolidating their numbers in the Great Lakes region, the Bantu farmers moved across the dry savannas to the coast—one of the most favored environments on Earth. Warm currents and easterly winds prevail along East Africa's equatorial coast. As the warm, wet sea air meets the land, it rises, cools, and sheds moisture, which in turn sustains vegetation of extraordinary diversity. Over 3,000 species of plants are found here, 500 of which grow nowhere else. One reason for this abundance is that this local climatic pattern has probably existed with little variation for more than 30 million years because its source, the Indian Ocean, has been a warm tropical sea throughout that time. Climatic stability is rare in Africa, and in this case it is limited to a narrow strip of coastal land that extends for just a few hundred miles south of the Equator. The environment was eminently suited to the needs of farmers.

The coastal settlers were of course blessed with the bounty of the sea as well as the land. Boats and inshore fishing are integral to Swahili culture. In addition, the sea brought the benefit and the tragedy of overseas influence. Ports along the shores of present-day Kenya and Tanzania were being visited by vessels from Arabia, India, and even China during the first centuries A.D., and a handbook of trade routes and ports on the Red Sea, the Gulf of Aden, the Arabian Sea, and the Indian Ocean compiled by an Egyptian-born Roman merchant sometime between A.D. 40 and 70 actually mentions an East African port by name—Rhapta, which is believed to have been situated near modern-day Dar es Salaam. Evidence of East Africa's trading links with foreign parts abounds. Parts of the Swahili coast are littered with sherds of early Chinese ceramics. Iranian pottery dating back to the fifth century has been excavated from sites lying 30 miles inland. Silver coins were in use at Shanga on the Lamu Archipel-

ago by the ninth century and probably were minted there. Coins from Sicily dated A.D. 1000 give an indication of how far afield the Swahili trade connections had reached by that time.

Wind and current brought the traders of China, the Red Sea, and India to the Swahili coast. Monsoon winds blow constantly along the East African coast, and they change direction with the seasons. As the Earth's orbit around the sun brings summer and winter alternately, so also it drags the pocket of weather swirling around the tropics north and south of the Equator, causing the winds circulating around the Indian Ocean to change direction. Along the East African coast the monsoon winds blow steadily from the northeast during the northern winter, then swing around 180 degrees to blow from the southwest during the northern summer. The winds are constant, and their speed of 9 to 18 miles per hour is enhanced by the fact that the currents that sweep along the East African coast change direction too. On the southwest monsoon, for instance, the Somali Current alone could carry even a rowboat northward at velocities of up to eight miles per hour.

The northeast monsoon, laden with moisture from the Indian Ocean, brings the long rains to East Africa between March and May. For centuries it also brought foreign merchants to trade with their counterparts on the Swahili coast. Lateen-rigged Roman vessels sailed here from Egypt's Red Sea coast in the first centuries A.D., as did Arabian, Persian, and Indian dhows. Chinese documents from the 12th century show that Chinese mariners were familiar with the towns of the Swahili coast by that date. They also knew of snow-capped Kilimanjaro 165 miles inland, as well as Lake Victoria and the Mountains of the Moon nearly 700 miles from the coast—and this was 500 years before anyone in Europe had more than the vaguest idea of Africa's hinterland. Chinese connections with Africa were so far advanced that in October 1415, a giraffe arrived in Peking. It came from Malindi, on the Swahili coast, and the emperor himself received the animal at the gate of the inner palace, while prostrate court offi-

cials congratulated their sovereign on the arrival of such a wondrous beast. An exquisite painting on silk from the period depicts the scene, showing the giraffe, with halter and lead rope, standing calmly beside its diminutive Chinese handler.

After Aksum in the highlands of Ethiopia, the Swahili coast was the first region of sub-Saharan Africa to establish trading links with foreign lands. The Swahili people established trading centers and built houses of coral limestone at Lamu, Malindi, Tanga, Shanga, Zanzibar, Kilwa, and numerous other places along the coast. They exchanged African produce for foreign goods and developed a distinctive urban society and culture in the process. The most enduring foreign import was the Muslim faith, as shown by a small mosque built at Shanga in the eighth century. But although the Swahili clearly embraced the world of Islam and foreign trade, there is ample evidence that the contacts reinforced rather than swamped the Swahili culture. Indeed, the history of the Swahili demonstrates the resilience of an indigenous system. At the coast, they took on the world and grew stronger. Their language, for instance, was enriched by the adoption of Arabic words and idioms for which there was no Swahili equivalent, but it remained a distinctly Bantu language and eventually became the lingua franca of people from the coast to the Congo Basin. Today, Swahili is probably the most widely spoken language in Africa south of the Sahara.

The demand for doors and chests carved in the traditional Zanzibar style is high, both for the local market and for tourists. The beautiful hardwoods come from the African mainland.

FOLLOWING PAGES: **A trading vessel makes for harbor on the Swahili coast. The triangular lateen sail is perfectly suited to the monsoon winds of the Indian Ocean, enabling vessels to sail closer to the wind than the square-rigged ships of the European tradition.**

The extent of Islamic influence in Swahili culture has inspired considerable debate as to which predominates. Was the Swahili coast merely the edge of the Islamic world, or was it the center of a significant African world? Increasingly, the evidence, both archaeological and documentary, indicates that the latter was the case. The architectural style of buildings on the Swahili coast was largely indigenous. Grand buildings, such as the 14th-century palace and commercial center of Husuni Kubwa south of Dar es Salaam—with its court, pavilion, bathing pool, domed and vaulted roofs, and Arabic inscriptions—bear signs of external influence. So too do the stone buildings at other centers. But further investigations have shown that stone buildings were just one aspect of the coastal settlements, part of a larger complex in which most buildings were made of wood, mud, and thatch. At Kilwa, for instance, the urban site covers about 70 acres but has only a scattering of stone buildings. Many of the nearly 200 sites that have been excavated along the coast are similar. Clearly, stone buildings were an integral part of an overall settlement pattern, not the major feature of trading cities that foreign merchants has established along the coast.

"Kilwa is one of the most beautiful and well-constructed towns in the world," the traveler and scholar Ibn Battutah wrote following his visit to the Swahili coast in 1331. Vasco da Gama must have thought the Swahili culture no less impressive when he dropped anchor in the harbor of Moçambique on March 2, 1498. Large dhows were anchored in the harbor, owned and manned by Arabs and far better equipped than the Portuguese caravels. Vasco da Gama was greeted by Swahili merchants dressed in rich linens and cottons with silk borders embroidered in gold. The Portuguese were impoverished by comparison, and a dignitary who visited the ships dismissed with contempt the hats, corals, and sundry items he was offered as gifts and demanded better—of which the Portuguese had none. In Mombasa, where da Gama

anchored a month later, a sheep and great quantities of oranges, lemons, and sugarcane were sent out to the ships as a token of peace, but da Gama could offer only a string of coral beads by way of return.

Vasco da Gama returned to the Swahili coast five years later, and an account of the voyage includes a description of Kilwa at what must have been the height of Swahili prosperity:

The city is large and is of good buildings of stone and mortar with terraces, and the houses have much wood works. The city comes down to the shore, and is entirely surrounded by a wall and towers, within which there may be 12,000 inhabitants. The country all around is very luxuriant with many trees and gardens and all sorts of vegetables, citrons, lemons, and the best sweet oranges that were ever seen, sugar canes, figs, pomegranates, and a great abundance of flocks, especially sheep, which have fat in the tail, which is almost the size of the body, and very savoury. The streets of the city are very narrow...and in the port there were many ships.

The Portuguese ships were better stocked on da Gama's second voyage, not so much with items to repay the generosity of their hosts on the Swahili coast as with the means of appropriating the prosperity they had glimpsed. The ships were heavily armed. Da Gama sailed into the harbors of the Swahili towns demanding submission to the rule of Portugal and the payment of large annual tributes. Towns that refused were attacked, their possessions seized, and protestors killed. Zanzibar was the first to be taken (in 1503). Malindi formed an alliance with the Portuguese, which hastened the fall of Mombasa in 1505; Kilwa was taken in the same year, as were several other towns. The Swahili towns were incapable of repelling a determined attack from ships armed with cannon, and their long-standing rivalry as trading centers worked against joining in a common defense.

The Portuguese justified their actions as battles in

the Christian war against Islam—a stage in the process of linking up with Prester John, the Christian king of Ethiopia—but there was a powerful mercenary motive too. A base on the Indian Ocean gave them access to the spice trade that otherwise reached Europe only via the Islamic Middle East. Also, as ever, there were rumors of gold in the Swahili hinterland. The Portuguese built forts at Mombasa, Kilwa, Moçambique, and Sofala. Their king was ecstatic when a commander reported that Sofala alone was capable of adding 4,000 tons of gold a year into the royal coffers. As it turned out, a mere 5.7 pounds was shipped from Sofala in the 15 months from the founding of the station in 1506, and exports were equally meager throughout the period for which records exist—up to 1513.

During the 16th century the Portuguese built an empire that included not only the territories on the Swahili coast but also places around the world, from South America to the Spice Islands of the Far East. But the cost of running the empire far exceeded the returns, imposing a drain on manpower and resources that a small, largely agrarian nation with a population of a million could not sustain. The empire collapsed. The Swahili forts were abandoned—the symbols of an overreaching ambition that had made very little impression on the region. No foreigners could reside on the coast for any length of time without Swahili consent and active assistance. They controlled access to the resources of the coast and, being traders, they were always ready to make a deal—how better to stave off the invaders?

Iron tools and luxury goods such as rich fabrics, china, and glass are likely to have been the main goods the Swahili imported. The items they offered in exchange were many, much more general, and plentiful. Food production on the Swahili coast was extensive. Fat-tailed sheep, goats, cattle, and chickens were raised, honeybees were kept in specially constructed hives, and plenty of fish was always being caught on the reef.

The modern supermarket has made shopping such a regimented ordeal that a visit to Zanzibar's central market is an exotic event. Yet the market is nothing special in the local context—merely the place where people go to buy their meat or fish, their vegetables, fruit, and other provisions. Ignore the plastic goods and blaring radios, and the market scene is timeless. The sailors who came ashore from Vasco da Gama's ships would have recognized virtually everything that is on sale today—and even perhaps looked for items that are no longer available. Apart from the commonly known vegetables and fruit, Swahili farmers supplied the market with millet, sorghum, taro, pomegranates, figs, and sugarcane. And their harvests were such that by the 19th century they were producing significant quantities of sorghum, sesame, and maize (and probably rice as well) specifically for export to the dry lands of Arabia. This trade had a long history, since contemporary Arab records show that the Red Sea port of Aden was importing rice from Kilwa even before the arrival of the Portuguese in 1498.

As significant as trading food was, though, the export trade of the coast was developed on the basis of other East African resources. The Swahili established trading links with the interior as well as abroad. Ivory was already a valued item of trade in the first century A.D. and was still important in the 19th century. Rhinoceros horn was in continuous demand too, both in Arabia as a scabbard and in the Far East, where it was ground up and used as an aphrodisiac. Gold and copper came from the hinterland of Sofala in the south. Frankincense and myrrh and tortoiseshell (actually the shell of sea turtles) came from the Horn of Africa in the north. Hides, beeswax, hippopotamus teeth, coconuts, shells, and orchilla (a vegetable dye) came from var-

FOLLOWING PAGES: Since its introduction to Zanzibar in 1989, seaweed farming has grown to an industry that employs 50,000 islanders and exports 2,200 to 3,300 tons dry weight annually.

ious parts of the coast. No less important was timber, especially mangrove poles for the building industry at Oman, Siraf, Basra, and other towns of Arabia and the Persian Gulf where no trees grew.

Many of these resources were important for local use as well, and some were important items of trade with the interior. Timber was especially important for local house construction and shipbuilding. Coral reefs left high and dry by the retreating oceans in past millennia likewise were important, both in the form of dressed stone and as lime for mortar and plaster. Salt was produced on the coast for local consumption and trade. Seashells were used too, either as raw material for beads or, in the case of cowries, for both decoration and as a form of currency. Palm trees supplied many things besides coconuts, such as the material for making ropes and mats and for caulking ships. Cloth was woven from cotton grown locally, and there was even some silk production. Thus there was a wide and varied base of production on the Swahili coast, available for local use, for the export trade, and for trade with the interior. It was particularly important to keep up production of goods for trade with the interior, for it was from that direction that the Swahili obtained their most valuable export commodities: ivory and slaves.

A 19th-century illustration depicts slaves marching to the Swahili coast. Zanzibar was a major center of the slave trade.

IN 1795 THE Scottish explorer Mungo Park traveled with a slave merchant from the western corner of present-day Niger via the Gambia River Valley to the Atlantic coast. The merchant had little more than a dozen slaves, the last of a much larger contingent captured north of the Niger River. Some had been sold to Tuareg nomads, and some had been sold at markets en route. The remainder were destined for shipment to America. Progress to the coast was painfully slow. The slaves were fettered in pairs, Park reports, the left leg of one chained to the right leg of another. They were also tied together in groups of four, with a strong rope of twisted thongs around their necks. As they walked, each man supported the weight of his fetters and chain with a length of string. At night, an additional pair of fetters was put on their hands, and sometimes a light chain was passed around their necks.

But despite the agonies of capture and the march, Park found that it was the end of the journey that the slaves feared most. They simply did not believe they would be shipped across the ocean to cultivate the land in another country, he reports. Instead, they believed "that the whites purchased Negroes for the purpose of devouring them, or of selling them to others that they may be devoured hereafter, [which] naturally makes the slaves contemplate a journey toward the coast with great terror."

The export of slaves from East Africa to Arabia, India, and the Indian Ocean islands was never as large as the Atlantic trade was from West Africa, but it began sooner and went on longer. So its effects gnawed just as deeply into the social fabric of the people it touched. Few parts of Africa were untouched by the slave trade during the centuries of its existence. The trans–Saharan trade was in operation by A.D. 650 at the latest, the Red Sea and East African coast by A.D. 800, and the Atlantic trade in the early 1400s. The export trade was internationally banned in the

1800s, but shipments continued throughout the 19th century. Best estimates put the total number of people sold out of Africa between 650 and 1900 at 21.4 million.

Some scholars believe that the impact of the slave trade, though horrific in its totality, was spread so thinly through the centuries and across Africa that its impact on society must have been slight. Others contend that the trade transformed human relations within the continent. I agree with the latter argument. Unlike the willing migration of millions from Europe to the United States, the effects of the slave trade's forced migration of millions from Africa were pernicious, were unrelenting, and went on for more than 1,000 years. The tragedy of the enslaved was compounded by the turmoil and fear of those who had seen them go. During the 1700s, for instance, a scattered community of 1,000 people living in the distant interior probably had between six and ten of their neighbors and kin abducted every year. Every small settlement was touched, some more than once, and as the slaving frontier advanced, it became almost inevitable that everyone would lose a close relative or friend.

Since disease and other natural causes probably accounted for the deaths of some 50 people per 1,000 each year, the enslavement of another 6 per 1,000 may not seem excessive. But enslavement was an ever present threat, a fear at the back of the mind, inducing a lingering fatalism in society as it passed from generation to generation.

Apart from its social effects, the slave trade also had a disastrous effect on the economic development of Africa. It imposed a massive cost in terms of people lost. Africa paid the bill, and in some respects is paying still. The shipping of 9 million slaves across the Atlantic between 1700 and 1850, for instance, actually required the capture of an estimated 21 million Africans, of whom 7 million were taken into domestic slavery and another 12 million died within a year of capture. Owing to the slave trade, the population of most of sub-Saharan Africa did not increase at all

in the hundred years between 1750 and 1850. How large would the population have been if it had not paid the cost of the slave trade? Assuming a growth rate of just 5 per 1,000 (0.5 percent) per year, there would have been close to 100 million people in sub-Saharan Africa in 1850, double the actual figure of about 50 million.

As if the human misery, social disruption, and stagnant population growth wrought by the slave trade were not enough, Africa's economic development was also severely affected. The slave trade shackled the continent to the commercial and political ambitions of Europe, creating an economic system that diverted resources from inland locales toward the coast, where their exchange for European goods represented a net loss to Africa. Some aspects of the trade actually multiplied European returns, to Africa's detriment. Distilled spirits, for instance, introduced new levels of drinking to the continent, and rum, a by-product of the Caribbean sugar plantations for which Africa had supplied the labor, was particularly profitable. Textiles constituted at least 50 percent of African imports. This huge market helped to stimulate the growth of the textile industry in Europe while inhibiting production in Africa. Similarly, the African market for metal goods contributed to the development of mass-production methods in Europe, whose low unit costs eliminated any incentive for developing such enterprises in Africa. Even the export of beeswax had a detrimental effect, since gatherers flushed out the bees with fire and responded to demands for more wax by seeking more nests to destroy rather than by adopting intensive and less wasteful methods, such as putting out reusable hives.

But the item of trade that did the most to keep the slave trade going was firearms. Africans were always keen to acquire guns. They quickly became a dominant feature of the slave trade, as demonstrated by shipping manifests giving the prices at which they were sold. In 1682, for instance, two guns were

Dhows from India, Arabia, and the Red Sea have been sailing to Zanzibar and the Swahili coast on the northeast monsoon and returning on the southwest monsoon for centuries. They brought in luxury goods and took away ivory, slaves, and spices. Today they carry beer, timber, and hardware—even cement.

traded for one male slave. By 1718, they were so common that up to 32 guns were exchanged for one slave. In 1704, the director of Dutch slaving operations on the Gold Coast reported that he could fill six ships full of slaves within four months if supplied with enough guns and powder. "The natives nowadays no longer occupy themselves with the search for gold," he wrote, "but rather make war on each other to furnish slaves." In 1721, a British trader put guns and gunpowder at the top of his list of goods that "everywhere are called for." Another who was buying slaves on the Gold Coast between 1772 and 1780 repeatedly advised that "guns were an absolute drug on the market."

In total, British traders alone shipped an average of 338,000 guns per year to West Africa between 1750 and 1807, along with an average of nearly 400 tons of gunpowder and 90 tons of lead shot. Estimates put the total of guns traded at not less than 20 million. The import of firearms into Africa fueled the slave trade and significantly influenced the economic development of the continent thereafter. There was no turning back from the barrel of a gun.

THE ABOLITION OF the slave trade began in the first decades of the 19th century. Yet while abolition first slowed, then finally halted the export of slaves, inside Africa it merely shifted enslavement from one area of economic activity to another. By the 19th century, the passage of 300 years had created a brutally efficient system of acquiring slaves and delivering them to the coast that could not be easily stopped. Without a market, the merchandise clogged the system, constituting not only a loss of

revenue but also a drain on resources—slaves had to be fed. The first response to abolition was therefore the most obvious. Slaves were set to work producing food in greater quantities than ever before. Ben Caulker told me that his antecedents had established a very profitable salt industry on the shores of Yawri Bay in the early 19th century. The slaves who previously were destined to be shipped across the Atlantic from Plantain Island were now set to work on the salt pans. The system was self-perpetuating: Salt produced by slaves was carried inland by slaves, where it was exchanged for more slaves, who in turn were employed on the salt pans as well as on plantations producing crops to feed slaves.

Meanwhile, the former slave-trading nations declared that the outlawed slave trade should be replaced by what was optimistically described as the "legitimate trade." Self-servingly, this trade consisted primarily of supplying Europe with raw materials and commodities that were expensive or unobtainable elsewhere, such as palm oil, ivory, hardwoods, rubber, beeswax, and gum arabic. African entrepreneurs also were encouraged to grow introduced crops such as groundnuts, sugar, cocoa, tea, cloves, and cinnamon for European markets, as well as coffee and coconuts.

All these activities were labor-intensive, and slaves who previously had been shipped abroad were put to work on the land. In this way the slave trade became an essential part of Africa's economy. The use of slaves in Africa became more common than ever before, and enslavement actually increased. Many more people were enslaved in Africa during the 19th century than when the Atlantic trade was at its height during the 17th century. Abolition hit the Asante especially hard. The slave population around Kumasi became so large that it aroused fears of revolt. By 1820, when British diplomatic missions made it clear that the slave trade would not be resumed, the Asante rulers adopted a policy of dispersing the slave population throughout the country, particularly to areas where gold was mined and kola harvested. Small-scale producers were given tax breaks in order to buy slaves.

In the forested and Sahelian regions of West Africa, there were nearly 70 major concentrations of slaves during the 19th century. In 1900, slaves constituted between 30 and 50 percent of all people living in French West Africa. The number of slaves in the Sokoto region of what is now northern Nigeria, for instance, was at least 2.5 million out of a total population of 10 million. Sokoto was probably the second largest slave society ever known. Only the United States, with 3.9 million slaves in 1860, had more slaves than Sokoto in 1900. East of Lake Chad, through the Sudan, along the Nile Valley, and in the highlands of Ethiopia—everywhere, the trend was the same.

Along the coast of East Africa where the Portuguese had only briefly interrupted Swahili-Arab trade, slavery kept the wheels of commerce turning. By the early 1800s, an average of 5,000 slaves per year had been shipped to Arabia, Persia, and India for nearly 1,200 years. Islam condoned slavery, and Swahili merchants did not regard abolition of the Atlantic slave trade as any reason to give up their own lucrative trade. The number of slaves shipped from the Swahili coast rose during the 19th century to an average of over 7,000 per year. At the same time, Arabs established plantations of cloves and cinnamon on Zanzibar and its smaller sister island, Pemba. These proved to be the East African equivalent of the Asante gold mines. They had no less intense demand for labor, and increasing numbers of slaves were being used on the plantations.

By the 1830s, the slave population of Zanzibar and Pemba was well over 100,000, and it remained that high for the rest of the century. Previously, the islands had been self-sufficient in food, but the spice plantations meant there was less land available for food crops and more mouths to feed. Production moved to the mainland. Rice in particular was grown along 70 miles of coastline directly opposite the spice islands, as well as at suitable locations from Somalia in the north to Mozambique in the south. Slaves provided the labor throughout. Indeed, as many slaves were used on the coast during the 19th century as were shipped abroad—not least because mortality rates were extremely high. On the Zanzibar plantations, between 15 and 20 percent of the slaves died each year and had to be replaced.

Z ANZIBAR'S SPICE TRADE began with a command from Sa'id ibn Sultan ordering farmers to plant two clove trees for every coconut on their holdings or risk having their land confiscated. That was in the 1820s. Within a few decades there were three and a half million clove trees on the Zanzibar and Pemba islands. Many of them are there still—grown gnarled and tangled but still producing a crop every five months. Joshua has 12 trees on his patch of the terraced hills above Chake Chake on Pemba, none dating back to the sultan's command, but no less demanding in the amount of labor and attention they require.

The clove tree is an evergreen that can grow up to 50 feet high, with glossy green foliage dense enough to encourage the idea that it would make a good hedge. The clove itself is the unopened bud of a waxy white flower growing in clusters on the tree's canopy of long thin branches. Picking them in the sultry heat is akin to slave labor, though Joshua's three children were inclined to regard the task as a holiday, for their school closes during the picking season so that everyone is available to help bring in the harvest before the buds open. The children scrambled through the branches unaided, while their parents used ropes and ladders to snap off the clusters of buds. Baskets were filled, and the cloves were laid out to dry in the sun, which could take up to a week. Any and every flat surface was covered with cloves. They were spread out on mats in front of houses, on concrete yards and roadsides, even on the local football field. As the cloves dried, the islands were bathed in their fragrant bittersweet scent.

The largest plantations on Zanzibar were owned by the ruling families of Oman, on the Arabian Sea. They had steadily intensified Arab involvement with the Swahili coast following the final expulsion of the Portuguese in 1698. Trade had grown during the 18th century as increasing numbers of slaves were shipped first to French sugar plantations on the Indian Ocean islands, then to the Americas, and finally to Madagascar. Ivory, another item of trade, combined well with slaving, because the one could be used to transport the other to the coast. The main import was cloth, because of its falling prices due to industrialization. Firearms were also important, with imports reaching nearly 100,000 a year during the 1880s.

With so much prosperity, the Omanis converted their trading influence into real authority. They took control of Kilwa in 1785, made Zanzibar their center of administration in 1800, placed governors in coastal ports during the 1820s and 1830s, and moved their capital from Oman to Zanzibar in 1840. There was Swahili resistance to the Arab takeover, but the Omanis were primarily interested in Zanzibar. They exercised minimal control on the coast and virtually none on the hinterland. This was the state of affairs when European determination to end the slave trade began to focus on the Swahili coast—and Zanzibar in particular.

British naval vessels began to intercept and seize Arab slave shipments in 1869, but years of diplomatic negotiation and pressure (with substantial financial inducements) were needed before the sultan of Zanzibar banned public slave markets in 1873 and formally abolished slavery in 1897. But it was a tricky business,

for the economy of Zanzibar was by then absolutely dependent on slave labor. To ensure that they kept on working, the new legislation obliged most of the slaves it freed to remain on the plantations as labor tenants—a move that sowed the seed of revolution that finally erupted on Zanzibar in 1964.

Meanwhile, the adjacent coast and its hinterland, Tanganyika, became first a German colony and then British after the First World War. Of all the nations that broke Africa into European colonies during the late 19th century, Germany was the most determined to make the colonies pay off. Germany's colonial

A stevedore works in Zanzibar docks, where the import and export of goods is heavily reliant on manual labor. The island was self-supporting in food until the early 1800s, when clove plantations were established on land previously reserved for food crops.

Some of the German achievements are to be commended. Each of the colonies achieved a miniature *Wirtschaftswunder* (economic miracle) during the last decade of German rule, when roads and railways and pioneering health, education, and agricultural services began to offer their African populations the promise of future prosperity. In German East Africa the decision to make Swahili the national language was to have a far-reaching and beneficial political effect. But some of the methods used to achieve their aims were less admirable. Forced labor in the cotton fields established to provide Germany with a reliable source of raw cotton provoked a rebellion in 1905, for instance. The German response was violent and uncompromising. At least 75,000 were killed in the crushing of the rebellion, and a further 200,000 to 225,000 died in the ensuing famine.

Defeat in the First World War brought an end to German ambitions in Africa, but not before the fighting between European armies in East Africa had exposed more than 50,000 African troops and over a million porters and laborers to appalling death rates from disease and exhaustion. More than 100,000 died, while throughout the continent more than 2.5 million Africans were involved with war work of some kind—a war from which Africa had nothing to gain.

Tanganyika became an independent country in 1961, led by the charismatic Julius Nyerere. His Tanganyika African National Union won strong support throughout the country. Alone among Africa's newly independent states, the Tanganyika government did not adopt the language of the former colonial masters for its administration. Instead it made Swahili the national language, thus unifying a score or more ethnic groups, each with its own language, under a single linguistic umbrella.

empire was the most short-lived in Africa (barely 30 years), yet it generated more official reports, statistics, and technical publications than any other part of colonial Africa, some so thorough that it is possible to trace the precise value, year by year, of even the horns and hooves exported from each colony.

Meanwhile, on Tanganyika's wealthy offshore neighbor, grown rich on its domination of the world clove market, the independence movement was tainted. There were elections in June 1963, supposedly democratic. But a coalition of parties drawing support from the Arab and wealthy communities contrived to win. Parties representing African communities formed a highly dissatisfied opposition.

In December 1963, Zanzibar was accepted as a full member of the United Nations, but its existence as a sovereign state was short-lived. The African opposition staged an uprising in January 1964. It was a fearful bloodletting that left Arabs slaughtered in the streets, and the mainland government could not ignore it. In 1964 Tanganyika and Zanzibar became one nation—with Zanzibar holding the status of a semiautonomous region in the United Republic of Tanzania.

I N THE 1820s, when the Omani Sa'id ibn Sultan ordered farmers on Zanzibar to plant two clove trees for every coconut or risk having their land confiscated, he instigated one of the most spectacularly successful agricultural ventures in history. Until then, clove production had been a monopoly of the East Indies. By establishing plantations on Zanzibar, the Omanis took over much of the world market. By 1840, when the Omani capital was transferred to Zanzibar, the island was already producing 3,500 tons per year. Before long, Zanzibar accounted for three-quarters of the total world production.

By the 1920s, the island was exporting an average of 10,000 tons of cloves each year. Zanzibar's domination of the world clove market continued through to the early years of independence, but the island's increasing dependence on a single crop made its economy very vulnerable. Since the 1964 revolution, the clove production and marketing have been handled by a state-run monopoly whose inefficiency has only compounded the problems of competition and falling prices on the world market. Indonesia was once a major customer but now grows ten times more than Zanzibar. From a peak of nearly $10,000 per ton in the early 1980s, the price fell to under $900 per ton in the late 1990s. Most of Zanzibar's crop is produced on small mixed-crop farms, typically with 10 to 50 clove trees, and many farmers leave the crop on the trees and apply their energies to more profitable activities.

Luckily, the decline of Zanzibar's clove industry coincided with the rise of its tourist industry. The number of tourists visiting the island increased more than four times between 1985 and 1996 and continues to rise—but not without bringing a new set of problems. Hotels, guesthouses, and other tourist facilities began springing up all over the place, many of them unplanned and in coastal areas that historically were relatively lightly populated.

Fishermen, long the main source of dietary protein for the island population, have been only too happy to give restaurateurs first choice from their catches, forcing up the price of fish on the local market and causing serious inroads into the stocks of some species on the reefs. Lobster, highlight of the gourmet tourist menu, was already being overfished by 1998. Other species are also declining to numbers at which they cannot maintain viable populations.

These very serious issues are unlikely to impinge much upon the pleasures of the determined tourists as they splurge on an extravagant lobster dinner. Ironically, the development they are most likely to notice is one that is simultaneously good for Zanzibar and bad for tourism—seaweed farming. Increasingly, the long beaches of white coral sand and sparkling turquoise waters are being outfitted with closely spaced wooden posts and nylon ropes. On these, cuttings of commercially valuable seaweed are attached and grown. Zanzibar's tourist operators complain that the island's pristine beaches are being spoiled and its lagoons rendered unsuitable for water sports. Nonetheless, seaweed farming has become a popular cottage industry.

Certain species of seaweed belonging to the genus *Eucheuma* contain high levels of carrageen, a polysaccharide (a form of sugar) that is in high demand today in the food industry as a thickener and emulsifier. Coastal peoples have been using carrageen as a food supplement for centuries, but only in the last 30 years have the Zanzibar islanders been growing it on a commercial scale. First brought from the Philippines in 1989, seaweed farming has grown to an industry that now harvests over 2,200 tons every month. The growth of the plant is unequaled. Within two to four weeks, small pieces of seaweed stem tied to ropes strung between mangrove poles grow tenfold and are ready for harvesting. The wet weed is laid out to dry on plaited palm fronds, then packed in sacks for sale to the United States and Europe.

With such incentives, and requirements limited to an expanse of clean water, plenty of sunshine, and high, strong tides to flush fresh water constantly over the growing stems, it is hardly surprising that seaweed farming has grown on Zanzibar almost as rapidly as does the plant itself. A 1995 survey found 10,000 people directly involved in seaweed production at not less than 19 locations, with another 40,000 people indirectly involved—and those figures have increased significantly since then. In some villages over 90 percent of adults were engaged in seaweed farming, with children also engaged as school hours permitted. The impact of these developments is social as well as economic. Seaweed farming is overwhelmingly a female activity (largely because the men did not take it seriously to begin with), and its success has given women a degree of financial independence that breaks the mold of gender relations in Zanzibar's devoutly Muslim society.

Whereas women previously were seldom seen selling or buying in the markets and had no control over the income their husbands gained from the crops they had grown, those in the seaweed business now sell their produce themselves, direct to the agents. They keep the income they earn and decide for themselves how it should be spent. Some are believed to have exercised their rights to divorce by paying back the bride wealth, and others have chosen to marry with the clear understanding that they are financially independent of their husbands.

THE SHORES THAT encircle Africa have been both a blessing and a curse to the continent. On the one hand, they offered people the benefit of access to the abundant resources of both land and sea. On the other, they exposed Africa to the exploitation of rapacious visitors. It was not just manpower that the slave trade shipped from Africa. The contribution that those missing millions would have made to the continent was lost with them. After abolition, the so-called legitimate trade, with its emphasis on the export of raw materials, created conditions that served Europe and America more than they served Africa. For more than 1,000 years the wealth of Africa was stolen away.

A thousand years of exploitation is not a legacy that is ever forgotten, but the wheel is turning. It will be some time before Ben Caulker and his fellow enthusiasts can use the quiet natural beauty of Shenge and the history of Plantain Island to their advantage, but the Zanzibar fishermen with their ngalaus full of tourists and the women harvesting seaweed are examples of humanity's irrepressible will to thrive. A generation of Africans has grown to adulthood in independent Africa. They are less inclined than their parents to blame Africa's woes on its colonial burden and more inclined to look for their future within the continent rather than beyond it. As they take the helm, Africa is poised to steer a new course, no longer bound by the legacy of its encircling shores.

issa Simai makes his living from the fish and the octopus he catches on Zanzibar's coral reefs. Every day he spends up to seven hours diving to depths of 65 feet, staying down for three minutes at a time. It is a punishing occupation, but he devotes his free time to an even more punishing activity—soccer. Issa plays for the Zanzibari Leopards, winners of the island's Southern Cup.

The coral reefs of the tropical seas are among the world's most productive environments—and one of the most useful from a human point of view. People have always been able to catch something to eat on the reef. In modern times the reefs are a tourist venue too, and Issa's catch supplies hotels and restaurants as well as the family kitchen. Right now, though, he and his teammates are diving overtime, catching the octopus and lobster that will pay for the Leopard's tournament trip to the mainland.

Zanzibar is the largest island on East Africa's Swahili coast. Monsoon winds blow steadily onto the coast from the northeast for half the year, then turn about to blow away from it for the other half. For 2,000 years, these powerful winds have carried trading dhows from and back to India, Persia, and Arabia. Since the seventh century, traders' influences have slowly fused with the existing African culture, and a new identity emerged: Swahili.

Issa Simai was born in Bwejuu, a small village on Zanzibar's eastern shore. The oldest of six children, he is the only one still living in Bwejuu. The others left for university and jobs in the city, but Issa decided to become a fisherman, like his father.

Issa was taught by his father, going farther out to sea each day until he was good enough to dive alone for octopus. "The sea is very frightening at first," Issa recalls. "It can take up to six months to get used to it."

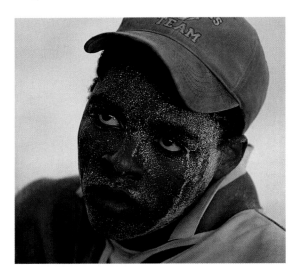

The Leopards are training for the biggest match of their careers. They have qualified for the national championships and will play a professional team in Tanzania's capital city— Dar es Salaam.

The British introduced soccer to Zanzibar in the 1930s, and the islanders
took to it with a passion. Issa is captain of the Zanzibari Leopards. When
he is not fishing, he is training with his teammates on a beach near
Bwejuu (above). Diving to save goals leaves goalkeeper Mrisho
Makama (left) with sand on his face by the end of a session.

Issa (left, with octopus) and his diving partner, Vuai (who is also the
Leopard's top goal scorer), are finding it hard to earn the money
they need for the trip to the mainland. Octopus is the catch that
is most in demand, but it is becoming difficult to find. Issa's father
boasts of regularly catching 50 a day when he was young, but Issa
is lucky to get 6.

A grove of coconut
palms (above)
shades Bwejuu
and also gives the
villagers an income
from the nuts.

n africa

Southern Africa is the continent's treasure house. Only the Earth's oldest rocks contain its most coveted substances—gold and diamonds. The precious minerals locked in rocks more than three billion years old have made South Africa a Croesus among nations, far richer than any other part of Africa. But such wealth was achieved only at an enormous cost to humanity.

For more than a century, Africans labored to produce the wealth—and were paid a pittance for their efforts. Laws hardened the prejudices of white settlers and immigrants, making second-class citizens of indigenous people.

With the fall of apartheid, South Africa has recovered its dignity. Free of the iniquities of white rule, Africa's industrial giant can at last contribute to the development of the continent, building hope for the future. The barriers apartheid erected across South Africa's physical and social landscapes are coming down.

"The fairest Cape we saw in the whole circumfrance of the earth."
Sir Francis Drake, 1580

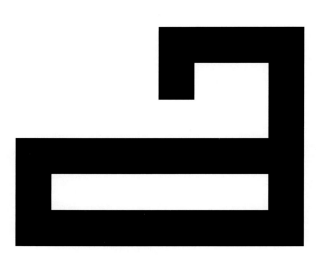

bout 30 percent of the world's population was living in sub-Saharan Africa in the year 1600. By 1800, its share of the world total had fallen to 20 percent, and by 1900 it had sunk to little more than 10 percent. A hundred years later, at the dawn of a new millennium, Africa's sub-Saharan population is still only 10 percent of the world total. The slave trade was principally to blame, as we have seen.

The slave trade has also had a deep psychological influence, imbuing global consciousness with the idea that Africans—and by extension, all blacks—are inferior.

Thomas Jefferson, for instance, knew enough about the human condition to anchor America's Declaration of Independence with the resounding phrase: "We hold these truths to be self-evident, that all men are created equal." Yet Jefferson owned slaves. He had been born and reared in a slave-based economy, and a lifelong association with slavery had led him to believe "that the blacks, whether originally a distinct race, or made distinct by time and circumstance, are inferior to the whites in the endowments of both body and mind." These sentiments, expressed or implicit, were widely shared and enduring. Racism has its roots here, encouraging people to believe that some uniquely African characteristic has rendered all blacks inherently inferior.

While abolition encouraged an enlightened few to hope that racism would disappear, the sad fact is that the newly developing sciences of the 19th century actually helped to perpetuate it. There is not a hint of racism in Charles Darwin's own work, but his theory of evolution introduced science to the idea that species evolve through time, "improving," generation by generation, as natural selection winnows out the weak and fosters the survival of the fittest. In lesser minds, this encouraged the belief of racist superiority.

PREVIOUS PAGES: **On a roadside at the edge of the Kalahari, passing tourists can buy beadwork and decorated ostrich eggshells from San Bushmen.** ABOVE: *Fynbos* **mosses and reeds flourish in a** *vlei* **in South Africa's Cederberg range.**

Ethnologists, for example, made comparative anatomical studies of groups of people around the world. They defined each in terms of what they described as its racial characteristics. Similarly, ethnographers recorded what they saw as the social and cultural distinctions of the races. From these studies, it was a short step to making qualitative assessments of how "evolved" each race was, from Stone Age to the civilized gentlemen who assembled in Victorian drawing rooms to look down upon the lesser races. The slaves may have been emancipated, but their descendants were still a long, long way from equality.

"Savagery was the formative period of the human race," a 19th-century book on ancient society informed its readers. "The inferiority of savage man...is...illustrated by the present conditions of tribes of savages in a low state of development, left in isolated sections of the earth as monuments of the past." It was pseudoscientific statements like this, as slavery was supplanted by segregation to maintain

authority over the so-called inferior races, that underwrite the modern history of southern Africa.

THE MODERN HISTORY of southern Africa effectively began on Wednesday, November 7, 1497, when Vasco da Gama's fleet of four ships anchored in a sheltered bay about 90 miles north of present-day Cape Town. Da Gama named the anchorage Sta. Ellena Bay (today it is St. Helena Bay). There was a Khoisan (Bushman) encampment near the shore, and da Gama's logbook provides the earliest surviving account of Europe's first contacts with the indigenous people of southern Africa:

The inhabitants of this country are tawny-coloured [the logbook reports]. Their food is confined to the flesh of seals, whales and gazelles and the roots of herbs. They are dressed in skins and wear sheaths over their virile members. They are armed with poles of olive wood to which a horn, browned in the fire, is attached. Their numerous dogs resemble those of Portugal, and bark like them...the climate is healthy and temperate, and produces good herbage.

From St. Helena Bay, da Gama sailed on, taking a wide sweep around the Cape of Good Hope and heading north to anchor in what is now Mossel Bay. Here too the Portuguese found the country inhabited by the Khoisan—"swarthy of appearance, like those of Sta. Ellena Bay," and the log records what must be one of the happiest encounters in the history of exploration:

On Saturday [2 December 1497] there arrived about 200 [Khoisan], large and small, bringing with them

Buffalo weavers live in colonies, nesting together in a huge mass of thorns and sticks, which they add to year by year until it may fill the canopy of a thorn tree. The birds enter the colony from below, each pair fashioning a domed nest lined with soft grasses.

about twelve cattle, oxen and cows, and four or five sheep; and when we saw them we went ashore at once. And they at once began to play on four or five flutes, and some of them played high and other played low, harmonising together very well...and they danced.... The Commander ordered the trumpets to be played, and we in the boats danced....When this festivity was ended we went ashore...and there we bartered a black ox for three bracelets. We dined off this on Sunday; and it was very fat, and the flesh was as savoury as that of Portugal.

As increasing numbers of voyagers anchored at the cape to reprovision during the 16th century, relations with the Khoisan remained reasonably good. By the early 17th century, however, the visitors were becoming less sympathetic and more inclined to regard the Khoisan as savages fit only to be exploited. Anchored in Table Bay in 1609, Cornelis van Purmerendt described them as:

... yellowish, ... very ugly, indeed horrible, with around their necks the guts of beasts plaited two or three times together, with the skin of a beast around their upper bodies but otherwise naked except that their male organs are covered with a little scrap of skin.... their houses stand twenty or more in a circle, like little kennels. They have an abundance of four-footed beasts such as oxen, also sheep with large fat tails: these they bartered with us for copper and iron. They are very thievish, and you must be well on your guard against them, lest you be cheated by them.

Van Purmerendt perceived the Khoisan to be cannibals, and his final comment on them is an ominous harbinger of the attitudes upon which southern Africa's centuries of oppression were to be founded: "In a word, it is a beast-like people."

The Cape of Good Hope lies as far south of the Equator as Greece is to the north of it. Early visitors from Europe were quick to note that its Mediterranean climate was ideally suited to growing crops that flourished in regions of warm summer sunshine and winter rain. Indeed, it was the *only* part of sub-Saharan Africa that was so well suited to European settlement. For this reason, the cape was devoid of Bantu farmers, whose millet and sorghum were adapted to the summer rainfall regimes of tropical Africa and therefore not suited to conditions in the cape. But the cape was not unpopulated. On the contrary, the region was home to an estimated 50,000 nomadic Khoisan pastoralists with substantial numbers of cattle and sheep. The overall population density of the Khoisan was very low, but then nomadic pastoralists are never spread evenly over the landscape. Seasonal migrations tend to crowd animals and people together in one place at a given time of year, leaving other regions empty. So early visitors who applauded the abundance of livestock in some places also wrote enthusiastically of the empty lands available for settlement in others.

In the European scheme of things, there was little room for the Khoisan, except as slaves working the land they had once roamed freely. In 1793, the settler population of the cape totaled 13,830, more than half of whom were children. Among them, these settlers owned 14,747 slaves, of whom over 9,000 were men. Slaves were the backbone of the colony's agricultural labor force and "cannot be dispensed with," the burghers protested as news of the abolition movement arrived from Europe. But, as elsewhere on the continent, the cape slaves were never a self-reproducing population. Mortality rates were high and more were needed constantly. More often than not, they came from the new lands over which the settlers claimed possession. As the settler frontier moved inland, Khoisan resistance hardened, sparking the Bushman Wars in which any Khoisan community was open to attack, the rebellious adults killed, and all others taken into slavery. The government told settlers to treat the Khoisan as vermin to be hunted

down and shot. Slaughter was widespread, even according to official records.

By the late 19th century, the Khoisan had been driven into regions that no settler would want to inhabit—the vast, waterless expanses of the Kalahari Desert. Forced to abandon their herding way of life, the Bushmen, as they became known, rediscovered the hunting and gathering skills of our ancestors. (The Kalahari is a desert only in its lack of permanent water.

Seasonal rains sustain abundant vegetation and game animals and fill local pans.) And of course this was how the ethnographers found them—and labeled them primitive hunter-gatherers—no longer the proud pastoralists who had sold beef and mutton to Vasco da Gama and other famished crews who had arrived at the cape over the centuries. No, they were savages, still living in the Stone Age.

The Bushmen now became objects of curiosity,

example of the steatopygia then said to be characteristic of her race, died in Europe and remains there still—her skeleton and genitalia preserved in the laboratory of a French museum.

Scientists looked upon the Kalahari Bushmen as little more than objects of study—to be treated with as much respect as they might grant a wild animal. The distinguished anatomist, Robert Broom, for example, thought nothing of burying dead Bushmen in his garden, to be exhumed for study when decomposition was complete. He is even said to have boiled their skulls clean on his kitchen stove. But as they delved more deeply into the life and ways of the Bushmen, more careful observers noted aspects of behavior that contradicted the image of primitive savagery. Their language, for instance, was extremely complex (and modern linguistic studies have confirmed that the Khoisan languages are phonetically the world's most complex). Their knowledge of the Kalahari environment was astoundingly comprehensive, and their technical skills were remarkably sophisticated. These were intelligent people, living in an environment requiring high degrees of skill and ingenuity. Furthermore, their social arrangements, kinship groups, and child raising were all far more sensitive and caring than would be expected of savages. They danced, sang, told jokes, and held deep beliefs about their world, its maker, and an afterlife that was peopled with their ancestors.

Also, they painted the walls of rock shelters that they frequented. These images of their world qualified as art by any definition of the term. The people

amusement, and wonder. Life casts were made for museum displays. In at least one instance, a body was skinned and stuffed by a skilled taxidermist. It was put on display in a Spanish museum of natural history and became a special attraction for generations of white schoolchildren. Live individuals were exhibited abroad too, in museums, in vaudeville shows, and on South African stands at world fairs. One woman, whose large buttocks were an extreme

The exaggerated size of the eland in this prehistoric rock painting as compared with the Bushman hunters indicates the importance of the eland to southern Africa's earliest inhabitants. The eland is a rich source of meat and fat, but also featured prominently in their ritual and beliefs.

FOLLOWING PAGES: **The Khomani were evicted from their corner of the Kalahari in the 1950s. Since the fall of apartheid, they have won back their rights to the land and are returning, though not to a fully traditional way of life.**

who made them were highly accomplished artists, with consummate skills and a unique interpretative vision. Working only with ocher-based pigments in red, maroon, orange, yellow, and brown, plus charcoal black and a thinned white clay, they juxtaposed form and color to create paintings that bring the beginnings of modern Western art to mind. A herd of eland, for instance, is painted in a Braque-like kaleidoscopic pattern of ocher, red-brown, and white, while nearby there are figures rendered in the simple fine detail that characterizes a Miró canvas. Such artistic skill put South Africa's rock art in a class apart from examples in other parts of the world.

There are over 30,000 rock art sites in South Africa, with well over a million images. Radiocarbon dating indicates that the oldest of the paintings were made 27,500 years ago, while some finely engraved stone slabs date from 10,200 to 40,000 years ago. The dating of South Africa's rock art is a recent and continuing science, but already it shows that artists were at work in Africa long before the practice began in other parts of the world. This information was not available to the first investigators of South Africa's rock art in the mid-1900s and they, schooled in the prejudices of 19th-century ethnology, leaped to the conclusion that art of this quality must have been produced by foreigners. It certainly could not be indigenous, they concluded, even though the Bushmen were known to have been making paintings less than 100 years before. The last-known Bushman artist was shot in the 19th century and found to have ten small horn pots of paint, each of a different color, hanging from a belt.

In a famous example of the prevailing political correctness, the principal figure at a site in Namibia was dubbed the "White Lady" by a distinguished expert on French rock art. He attributed the origin of the painting to artists from the Mediterranean, Crete, or Egypt. Furthermore, the figures depicted in the panel with the White Lady mostly belonged to European and Mediterranean races, he reported, and none

were Bushmen. Subsequent investigations have proved the expert wrong on virtually every count. Indeed, even the most cursory examination reveals that the White Lady is only superficially white and definitely not female. Professor Raymond Dart, whose discovery of the fossil *Australopithecus africanus* was the first suggestion that humanity had evolved from African origins, was similarly biased about African rock art. The headdresses shown in some paintings were identical to those worn in Babylonian times, he said, and therefore the artists must have come to South Africa by sea down the east coast centuries before the Portuguese arrived.

Even in the 1980s, one author claimed that South

The delicate tubular flowers of *Erica massonii,* one of many indigenous plants found in the South African fynbos, are covered with a film of adhesive sap. Like flies on flypaper, unwelcome visitors meet a sticky end. Only the hummingbird-like sunbirds can take nectar without getting stuck.

belief systems of the San people (as the Bushmen are now known).

With the collapse of apartheid, the 1994 election of a black government brought the repeal of laws that had denied the San descendants access to their lands. Katrina, Kaas, and Feke, for instance, are three sisters of the Khomani San, all in their 70s, who suffered the oppression of the former racist regimes. They say that in 1953, they were put on display in Johannesburg, much as freaks were shown at fairs around Europe in Victorian times. When they returned home, they found that their families had been evicted from their traditional lands and their father beaten to death by a policeman in the process. The Khomeni homeland had been given over to cattle ranching. Its former occupants were told to make a home for themselves in the shantytowns of Cape Town. For 40 years, they lived on the fringes of Cape Town's urban economy, spurned by the blacks, objects of curiosity to the whites. But the Khomani San never forgot, and in the late 1990s they won a landmark court judgment giving them full rights to the land they consider their own.

The Khomani San are going back, and Katrina, Kaas, and Feke are among the first to make a preparatory visit, accompanied by the PBS/NGS television crew. The sisters' reunion with the land is highly emotional. They immediately reestablish their territorial rights by digging up some of the food and medicinal roots and tubers that have not been harvested for decades. They chatter excitedly about the traditional ways, about the bounty of this seemingly impoverished land and how people can make a living here. They are happy now. They believe that when their time comes, they will die here—but not before they have passed their heritage on to the next generation, complete with title deeds.

Africa's rock art was painted and inspired by seaborne immigrants from India. A 1987 book on the subject written specifically for schoolchildren boldly stated,

The prehistoric European painters must have navigated their vessels along the rivers of the east coast of Africa in search of new hunting grounds. Whenever they came across caves they apparently practised their customs and rituals, thereby initiating the natives into such customs.

But in the 1990s, South Africa's apartheid regime collapsed. Objective science exposed the absurdity of the immigration theories. In some cases, the art is older than the sources it is supposed to derive from. Also the art closely portrays the subject matter and

Time moves on, and the women have adapted. They do not foresee a complete return to the old ways. They want an adequate supply of running water, sanitation, and electricity and expect to pay for these services by combining traditional San skills with ecotourism, which will consist primarily of conducting visitors on walkabouts. The Khomani San's lands lie alongside and within the Kalahari Gemsbok Park, which in April 1999 became part of a new and enlightened movement in conservation called the peace parks. Ten parks that cross national boundaries will open by 2003. The newly named Kgalagadi Transfrontier Park is the first, incorporating land from both South Africa and Botswana that will be extended to include land from Namibia.

The aim of these transnational peace parks is to encourage southern Africa's plains game to resume the migration routes along which they once roamed freely across the continent. The migrations will help to conserve the dwindling diversity of the surviving stock. The peace parks movement is also committed to engage local people in the planning and running of the parks—people like the Khomani San and their vanguard in the region: the sisters Katrina, Kaas, and Feke.

IT IS IN keeping with San society that women should have pioneered the return of the Khomani San to their homeland. The supremacy of the hunting male, braving the wilderness in search of meat for his dependent family, is very much a Western construct with not so much relevance in San society. Women are the breadwinners among the San, far more important in terms of the food they provide than the men. With the !Kung San people in northeastern Botswana in the early 1960s, researchers found that although men hunted and women gathered, no one had any doubt as to which made the greater contribution of food. When men went hunting, they came back empty-handed four times out of five, while the women always returned from a foraging trip with something to eat. Overall, women gatherers supplied 2.5 times more food than the hunting men.

While meat was much enjoyed by the !Kung San (and was nutritionally essential), plant food—nuts and roots, bulbs, leaves, fruits, and seeds—made up to 80 percent of their diet, most of it derived from 23 plants, although the women regularly gathered from a range of 85 as they became available through the seasons. One single item—the mongongo nut—supplied half of all the vegetable food eaten. This nut contains five times the calories and ten times the protein of the same amount of cooked rice or maize. The !Kung adults each ate about 7 ounces of mongongo nuts daily, which in nutritional terms was equal to 14 ounces of lean beef with 2.5 pounds of cooked rice. No wonder the !Kung San have declined invitations to grow food crops. "Why should we plant," they ask, "when there are so many mongongo nuts in the world?"

But in fact, it was probably ancestors of the present-day Khoisan-speaking peoples who left the world's earliest known evidence of people trying to grow food crops or, at the very least, to manage the natural vegetation so that it produced more of what they wanted to eat. In a cave near the mouth of the Klasies River on South Africa's Indian Ocean coast are the fossil remains of people who lived about 100,000 years ago. Archaeologists have also unearthed deposits of burned material that has been identified as the inedible residues of geophytes (underground plant foods such as tubers, roots, and corms). These deposits date from 70,000 years ago, and they could only have been brought into the cave by humans. The discovery indicates that people by then had already developed the practice of deliberately burning vegetation to promote growth—the very beginnings of agriculture.

The hunter-gatherers and protoagriculturalists who lived in the Klasies River mouth cave inhabited the most varied and densely packed area of vegetation on Earth—the *fynbos* (Afrikaans for "fine bush"). Though covering only 34,700 square miles of the southwestern cape, the fynbos region supports an astonishing 8,500 different plant species, and nearly 70 percent are found nowhere else in the world. By comparison, there are only 1,443 plant species in the entire British Isles, even though the total British land area is three and a half times greater than the fynbos. The captivating beauty of the fynbos, with its unique proteas, ericas, watsonias, gladiolas, and mesembryanthemums—to name but a few—has found its way into flower shops and garden centers around the world. In the botanical textbooks, it is a floral kingdom in its own right. The tiny Cape Floristic Kingdom or Fynbos Biome, though smaller than Portugal, is known scientifically as one of the world's six botanical kingdoms, on a par with the Boreal Kingdom, which covers almost the entire Northern Hemisphere.

The soils of the fynbos are generally sandy and coarse grits, derived from ancient sandstones, slates, and shales, and very low in nutrients or organic matter. It seems odd that so much plant life should grow on such poor soils, but the explanation lies with the compensations that a relatively stable climatic regime has brought to the region. A Mediterranean climate first developed in the cape three million years ago, when an atmospheric phenomenon known as the South Atlantic high pressure cell became fixed in relation to the landmass of southern Africa. And the cell has not moved since, not even during the ice ages. This meant that glaciers never scoured away its plant life. The region's vegetation did not have to start over from scratch, as occurred time and again in other parts of the world. It steadily built up extensive and diverse plant communities that are specifically adapted to flourish in the fynbos.

Africa is an ancient continent, and most of its soils are ancient too. Long ago they were leached of any mineral nutrients that the native rocks contained, and they cannot support the kinds of vegetation from which humus and thence an organic-rich soil might develop. Only where soils are derived from recently erupted volcanic rocks, rich in nutrients, as in Ethiopia, parts of East Africa, and the Great Lakes region, are the soils inherently fertile. But while soils derived from ancient rocks have made farming a challenging proposition for Africans, they have bequeathed other kinds of wealth to humanity—gold and diamonds, platinum, chromium, nickel, and other valuable metals. The oldest rocks contain the greatest wealth of valuable minerals, simply because the geochemical processes that produce them occur only in the portions of the Earth's mantle that lie underneath cratons—the great slabs of continental crust that in rare instances have remained intact for billions of years, as in Africa.

Diamonds are crystals of carbon, forming only at depths of 90 miles below the Earth's surface, where the overlying rock exerts immense pressure and temperatures are in the range of 1,800° F to 2,100° F. Most are more than three billion years old, sparkling with fire from the core of the Earth and brought to the surface with material from the mantle that has occasionally burst through the crust, like bubbles of steam rising through porridge. Alluvial deposits are the most common source of diamonds, but the stability of Africa has left the core of the continent and some of its diamond-bearing intrusions intact, especially on the Kaapvaal craton, which constitutes the largest single portion of the South African landmass. The Kaapvaal craton is one of only two places in the world (the other is Russia) where these intrusions have been located.

Gold also forms in the mantle beneath the cratons and is concentrated by superheated water under immense pressure, in which state the commonplace liquid dissolves substances normally considered insoluble, such as gold, and deposits them as veins of ore in the fissures of solidifying rocks. And again, as with diamonds, the Kaapvaal craton is also rich in gold. More than half of the gold ever produced in the world has come from its mines.

As if gold and diamonds were not wealth enough, geology has contrived even greater riches. Two billion years ago, volcanic spasms squeezed material from the mantle up through the crust and forced it to spread horizontally along planes of weakness in

the sedimentary layers above. The material solidi-fied, creating a subterranean island 250 miles long and up to 6 miles thick, all of one piece. Called the Bushveld Igneous Complex, this is a geological feature unmatched anywhere on Earth and the repository of unparalleled mineral wealth.

The complex is one of just 19 such features known from around the world. With its surface area of 25,480 square miles, bigger than Sri Lanka, it is twice as large as all the rest put together. Yet for all its size, its con-tent is even more remarkable.

As the mass of molten material cooled, the various

Lesotho has been supplying labor to South Africa's gold and diamond mines for over a century. Going to the mines is a rite of passage for Sotho men. Gum boots identify those who have just returned home.

to last 1,000 years at current mining rates. In 1995, the complex contributed over five billion U.S. dollars to the South African economy—5 percent of the country's gross national product, more than the combined GNP of Malawi and Tanzania, whose total population is more than that of South Africa.

In terms of the labor (mainly black) that has toiled to extract the wealth locked within and the contribution by which that wealth (mainly white) supported a political system, the complex has made a mark on the social landscape of South Africa as broad and deep as its impact on the physical landscape. Social and physical landscapes are thus linked, dynamically, though the landscape may appear to be no more than the indifferent stage on which people act out the drama of their lives.

THE FIRST HINT of South Africa's vast subterranean wealth was found in 1867 on the banks of the Vaal River, nearly 600 miles northeast of Cape Town, in a landscape more distinguished by poor soils, thorn trees, and a lack of rain than any evidence of riches. A Dutch settler, Schalk van Niekerk, was paying a visit to his neighbors, the Jacobs family, when he noticed their children playing with a collection of pretty stones they had found along the banks of the river. One stone in particular caught his eye. Though only the size of a hazelnut, it seemed heavier than it should be and looked different from any stone he had seen before. Suspecting it might be a gemstone, van Niekerk offered to buy it, but Mrs. Jacobs laughed at the idea of selling a stone. If it took his fancy, he could have it for nothing, she said.

The children's plaything was indeed a diamond. It was sold in Cape Town for £500—a fortune in those days—and within three years 5,000 prospectors were

minerals within it settled into layers, like a giant layer cake. Igneous rocks are often important sources of valuable minerals, and the Bushveld Igneous Complex is one of the world's great treasure houses. Its reserves of platinum, gold, chromium, copper, nickel, tin, fluorspar, vanadium, and iron ore are sufficient

staking their claims, digging, and sifting through the riverbank gravels, looking for their fortune.

There is no other commodity with such an irresistible fascination as diamonds. People will risk all for them. They will betray, cheat, lie, deceive and murder. They will forfeit honour, friendship and loyalty. They will suffer privations and danger. For diamonds make dreams a reality. They bring prestige and power. They open doors to presidents and kings. They magically transform poor men into millionaires. (Olga Levinson, Diamonds in the Desert)

Before long, prospectors located the mouth of the pipe that had brought the diamonds to the surface from deep in the Earth's crust—a patch of arid, scrubby farmland that today is known as Kimberley. Within a few years, miners had transformed the site into the biggest man-made hole the world has ever seen—985 feet across and 295 feet deep. The Kimberley magnates made millions and were poised to make yet more as they invested their profits from diamonds in the Transvaal goldfields, which were discovered in the late 1880s.

The Kimberley mine has yielded more diamonds than any other in the world. Even there, however, the concentration was little more than one part in three million. That makes finding diamonds like looking for a single glass bead about the size of a pea in a three-ton truckload of rock rubble. The material is dug from the mine, lifted to the surface, crushed, sieved, and then painstakingly picked over in the hope of finding the glittering prize. Large stones were found frequently enough to justify the tedious exercise, and even so, most of the diamonds were small.

Gold deposits are generally more concentrated than diamond deposits, but gold is less easily extracted from the rock. Thus both the diamond and gold reserves that brought South Africa such immense wealth depended upon cheap labor. From the beginnning, Africans near and far were enticed, cajoled, and coerced into working in the mines. They

Prominent lawyer Billy van der Merwe represented the Afrikaner's ascent to power in the realms of law, finance, and industry during the apartheid era. The Nationalist government came from the ranks of the 2.6 million Afrikaners who made up more than half of the country's white population.

had to work for a stipulated minimum number of months but might end up staying for years.

If the "dark satanic mill" is the abiding image of the industrial revolution in Britain, the pressures of capitalism on society in South Africa are symbolized by the mine—in particular by the mine compound, where miners were virtually imprisoned. The Kimberley mine had to rustle a workforce out of a precapitalist rural hinterland, but within a year of opening, almost every black society south of the Zambezi was represented in the diamond fields. By the early 1870s, a total of 50,000 migrants were working in the mines for varying periods each year.

Most of them traveled great distances to get there. Records for 1876, for example, show that 64 percent had come from over 500 miles away. For obvious reasons, they were also the workers who stayed the longest. By contrast, those who lived within 50 miles of Kimberley constituted less than one percent of the migrant workforce. Not only could they make more money at home, but they also knew that laboring in a mine was a very unpleasant occupation.

Before long, though, the migrant laborers began using the laws of supply and demand to their benefit. They refused to accept long-term contracts with any one employer, and with 5,000 claim holders competing for their services, they moved to whoever was offering the highest wages. Soon labor wages accounted for nearly 90 percent of the average miner's working costs. Black labor, a Kimberley newspaper proclaimed, was "the most expensive in the world."

During this period, migrant laborers sent good money home. Livestock were purchased to replenish depleted herds. Plows were bought to grow more crops. Among the Sotho, in particular, the adoption of the plow led to an expansion of both local agri-

culture and migrant labor. By 1875, three out of every four Sotho men sought work away from home each year—most of them making the 155-mile journey to the diamond fields. Meanwhile, their households each produced from 30 to 40 bags of grain, and the Sotho thus became major suppliers of grain, as well as labor, to Kimberley. In the four years before 1874, the Sotho acquired livestock and other property worth over one million pounds sterling from their dealings with the diamond fields.

But the mine owners' drive for profits could not allow the laborers' dominance of the Kimberley economy to continue. During the 1880s, as Cecil Rhodes moved steadily toward bringing all the claims being worked in the mine under the control of a single monopolistic company, De Beers Consolidated Company Limited, so too the mine managers sought to exercise greater control over the labor force, mainly by requiring laborers to live in company housing. Mine compounds providing barracks-type accommodation behind high corrugated-iron fences were constructed. By December 1880, 22,000 laborers were housed in compounds in the mine fields, and there were demands for more to be built so that employers might reduce wages to a "proper level." With labor shortages still a problem, De Beers took over some of Kimberley's custodial responsibilities. In 1884, the company built a prison and used its inmates as a source of free labor in return for paying the capital and running costs of the institution.

FOLLOWING PAGES: **The accommodation provided for South Africa's legions of domestic staff, cleaners, and caretakers is often primitive. In Johannesburg, some live in small shacks built on buildings in which they work.**

In 1891, the general manager of De Beers described the advantages of convict labor: "In the first place we have labour we can depend on and it is always to hand. The convicts cannot get away like ordinary labourers.... If the latter attempt to escape you cannot shoot them, whereas the sworn officials of the Gov-

ernment can shoot a convict if he attempts to escape."

Convicts working in the De Beers mine were better fed and clothed than the inmates of the city jail, but they worked even longer hours than prisoners on hard-labor sentences and were searched on entering and leaving the convict station. They went to their cells

Putswa Tekane has been working in the Carltonville gold mines near Johannesburg since 1980. He lives in a hostel at the mine and goes home to his family in Lesotho at infrequent intervals. A deeply religious man whose age and experience are highly respected, Putswa is a valuable source of advice for younger men.

De Beers abandoned the practice of using convict labor in 1932, although the gesture was largely academic, since by then the company's compounds themselves were little better than jails. Once a man entered the compound, he was denied all access to the outside world for the duration of his contract. He moved between the compound and the mine through enclosed passages, and the compounds were roofed over with fine wire netting to prevent stolen diamonds being thrown over the fences. He was paid a wage but obliged to buy food and supplies from the compound stores.

The Kimberley compounds provided a model for the Transvaal gold mines that came onstream in the 1890s, and together the diamond fields and the gold mines established a precedent for the management of labor throughout Africa. The fact that laborers were black and uneducated encouraged employers to treat them as a race apart, with none of the aptitudes and aspirations of whites and unlikely ever to change. Managers believed that there was no point in raising wages in line with productivity. It would lead to only a small rise in the workers' standard of living, they said, while "the main result would be that the natives would work for a shorter period."

The mines' influence on southern Africa and beyond has been pernicious—and profound. The majority of the workers were migrants, living away from home in all-male compounds segregated from surrounding communities. Farms, factories, government agencies, and even employers of domestic labor perpetuated the system. Every urban center was surrounded by locations, compounds, and hostels in which its essential labor was housed at a distance from whites. Of course, the same sort of economic segregation was to be found in Europe—no loom operator could afford to live next door to the mill owner—but equality in law and edu-

naked each night, where blankets were the only available covering, and at the end of his sentence each prisoner was confined to his cell for five days, with unwieldy leather gloves locked on his hands. This practice was designed to flush out any diamonds he might have swallowed in the hope of selling them once free.

cation could change that. In Africa, color applied an indelible stain to such economic segregation, condemning blacks to a subservient status.

Caves near the Klasies River on South Africa's wild Tsitsikamma coast have yielded evidence of early human behavior. Fossil remains and stone tools from the caves have convinced archaeologist Hilary Deacon that people sheltering here periodically between 60,000 and 120,000 years ago not only looked modern but were modern in their thinking and behavior.

SEGREGATION AND ECONOMIC exploitation were high among the evils that Africans hoped independence would redress. After all, many nations had a healthy economy and balance of payments at the end of the colonial period, helped by a postwar boom in commodity prices. In Kenya, for instance, the easing of colonial restrictions enabled African farmers to expand their planting of the world's best tea from 2,470 to 12,350 acres in total, with parallel increases in coffee production. Smallholder production of groundnuts in Senegal and cocoa in the Côte d'Ivoire and Ghana also increased, while some enterprises raised agricultural production to an industrial scale—for instance, in sugar, cotton, and fruit growing.

But mineral resources remained Africa's primary asset. Both the expansion of existing operations and new discoveries added to the continent's potential for economic growth. Copper continued to enrich Zambia. Gold maintained Ghana's buoyant economy. Diamonds enlarged the nest eggs of Botswana, Sierra Leone, and Liberia. Cobalt made the former Belgian Congo a privileged trading partner of the United States. The same was repeated all over the continent. Uranium in Niger, iron in Mauritania and Liberia, bauxite in Guinea and Ghana, titanium ore in Sierra Leone, phosphates in Togo, manganese and uranium in Gabon, and oil in the Congo, Gabon, Angola, Cameroon, and Nigeria—all began providing new sources of wealth.

The postwar boom enabled colonial governments to implement social and economic development plans, which brought noticeable improvements to the lives of most people. Per capita food production was adequate. People were poor, it is true, but by no means the world's poorest. Since all the former colonies had experienced more than ten years of continuous economic growth, the newly independent governments based their plans for the future on the assumption that the trend would continue. Real growth did occur. Between 1965 and 1980, sub-Saharan Africa's per capita gross domestic product grew at an average rate of 1.5 percent per year. But 1980 was an economic turning point, for thereafter sub-Saharan Africa's growth rate fell into steady decline.

By the year 2000, African countries filled all the bottom places in the world tables on health, life expectancy, education, economic status, political stability, and development potential. According to the World Bank, only 15 percent of Africans were living in "an environment considered minimally adequate for sustainable growth and development." At least 45 percent lived in poverty, one in three were chronically undernourished, two-thirds did not have access to clean water. One-third was constantly exposed to malaria. One-quarter suffered repeated bouts of amebic dysentery. One-fifth was at risk from schistosomiasis (bilharzia). The tsetse fly threatened 60 million Africans (and their cattle) with trypanosomiasis (sleeping sickness). Twenty-five million were infected with the AIDS virus. Eighteen million were infected with river blindness, of whom over 300,000 were already blind. Rural children were heavily infected with roundworm and hookworm. Chronic diarrhea and respiratory diseases were endemic; epidemics of cholera were commonplace; hepatitis and typhoid were rife. All this was exacerbated by the impact of recurrent flood and drought, famine, collapsing infrastructure, governmental mismanagement, and civil war. So much misery in the human cradleland of beautiful landscapes, majestic wild animals, and exotic ceremonies that visitors flock to see. What went wrong?

SOME BELIEVE THAT Africans are inherently incapable of sustaining viable states without outside help, that their problems are simply a consequence of genetic predisposition. Such views can be dismissed as racist and plain wrong. After all, there is tribalism in Bosnia and the Middle East, dictatorship in Iraq, and corruption almost everywhere. These are the failings of humanity in general, not Africans alone. On the other hand, attributing Africa's plight solely to the way it has been treated by the rest of the world is not totally correct either. Africa was not the world's only victim of external forces. Parts of Asia and Latin America also suffered at the hands of imperialists, but they have nonetheless managed to establish viable states and successful economies.

The difference perhaps is that while other countries recognized the importance of accountability, making their leaders answerable to the people, African society never paid much regard to this basic concept of democracy. In Africa, a leader was expected to show that he (rarely she) had escaped from ordinary life and was a "Big Man," powerful and rich enough to be a benefactor of the people whose support he sought. Leaders have been expected to use their position for personal gain, and though Africans

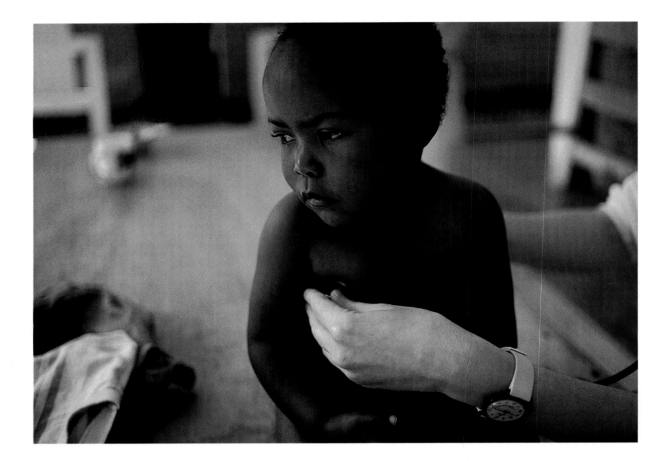

deplore the fact that Mobutu, Banda, Moi, Houphouet-Boigny, and the rest filched billions from the national coffers, their criticism is tempered with a fatalistic belief that this is what all leaders do.

The international financial institutions are the ones that complain the most when Uganda spends 30 million dollars on a presidential jet, yet the fact that President Mugabe could spend millions on state visits to 21 countries during Zimbabwe's 1999 year of crisis raises barely a ripple of concern at home. The tragedy is that the amounts stolen from Africa could have substantially reduced the continent's international debt burden. Virtually none of the loot was reinvested in Africa, where it might have done some good, but instead was invested in Europe and America or spent on conspicuous consumption. Not only presidents had privileged access to national wealth. The Côte d'Ivoire, for example, may be on the lower rungs of world health tables, but still had a middle

class wealthy enough to be the world's leading per capita consumers of champagne in 1995.

Corruption? That's a matter of perception," a professor of political science at the University of Sierra Leone remarked. "You could see it as an extension of the gift principle: The most successful deserves the most reward. Or what some might call the Robin Hood syndrome: Constituents send their representatives to parliament not to work on national issues for the national good but to grab as much as they can from the center, which they must bring back to be shared among the local people, each according to their status.

Fortitude and tolerance have been both a blessing and a blight for Africans. On the one hand, these qualities have enabled people to live in the most testing of environmental circumstances. But on the other, they induce a fatalistic acceptance of the status quo. "We have a tendency to confuse problems and situations," the foreign minister of Sierra Leone

Though sub-Saharan Africa has only 10 percent of the world's population, it has 71 percent of its HIV and AIDS cases. Seventeen million Africans have died of AIDS and 12 million children have been orphaned, many infected from their mother's womb. Average life expectancy in southern Africa is likely to plummet by 2010—from 64 years down to 37.

said shortly before his government was overthrown in 1992.

The electricity supply did not deteriorate to its present state overnight; it gradually got worse while we bought candles. There were holes in the roads—small ones to begin with—that gradually got bigger as we drove around them. The electricity supply and the roads should have been dealt with as soon as the problems became apparent. But we did nothing. Instead of dealing with the problems, we simply accepted them as situations that we should adapt to.

By the 1990s, many Africans were less willing to look upon the continent's plight this way. The men and women who had grown to maturity in independent Africa wanted the continent's problems to be confronted and solved. Furthermore, they were less inclined to blame Africa's woes upon the tyrannies of the past. The effects of the slave trade and colonialism would never be forgotten, but everyone knew that the continent's rampant corruption, political chicanery, poor government, and lack of accountability were problems that Africans themselves had created. Attitudes outside Africa had changed too. The end of the Cold War brought an end to unquestioning support for strategically important regimes, such as those in Ethiopia and Zaire. Loans from the World Bank and International Monetary Fund came with tough demands for economic reform, more accountability, democratization, and free elections.

The release of Nelson Mandela from jail on February 11, 1990, was a key moment in these developments. In 1964, he and other leaders of the African National Congress (ANC) had been found guilty of conspiracy to overthrow the South African govern-

ment and were sentenced to life in prison. If the apartheid government had expected that locking Mandela away would erase him from the political consciousness of South Africa, they could hardly have been more wrong. In fact, incarceration strengthened his influence. Other reputations waxed and waned as the ANC was rocked by internal quarrels and splits, but the name and stature of Nelson Mandela rose steadily over South Africa and the world. He became the leader, mighty through absence, a prisoner of conscience—silent but forever attached to the truths he had embraced.

Those truths were stated most memorably at his trial. Instead of following the customary procedure of testimony and cross-examination, Mandela had given a full and unambiguous statement of the ANC's political ideals and intentions. He spoke for four hours, concluding with the words:

During my lifetime I have dedicated myself to this struggle of the African people. I have fought against white domination, and I have fought against black domination. I have cherished the ideal of a democratic and free society in which all persons live together in harmony and with equal opportunities. It is an ideal which I hope to live for and to achieve. But if needs be, it is an ideal for which I am prepared to die.

Mandela and his codefendants had been charged under the Sabotage Act, which carried the death penalty. On June 11, 1964, the judge delivered a verdict of guilty on Mandela and nine others. Sentencing was reserved for the following day. "I was prepared for the death penalty," Mandela wrote in his autobiography. "We were all prepared, not because we were brave but because we were realistic."

A sentence of death would have made Nelson Mandela a martyr to the cause of African freedom. He was sentenced to life imprisonment instead. Still, he would emerge 27 years later, age 71, with the reputation of a saintly hero. Unbowed by the oppression of the white regime, untainted by the failures of African independence, steeled by years of study and contemplation, Nelson Mandela had precisely the qualities that the historic moment demanded. He was not a great speaker like Martin Luther King, nor did he have the artful shrewdness of someone like Mahatma Gandhi. Mandela simply radiated the unflinching, honest authority of an entirely good man. He was patient. His timing was flawless. He took command of his own captivity and delayed his release until his conditions had been met. Most important, he understood white fear and how to manipulate it. He knew that the government's fear of black majority rule could be transformed into fear of an even more terrifying prospect. Without reform, South Africa would collapse into chaos.

By the late 1980s, South Africa was facing bankruptcy. Apartheid had become a preposterous extravagance. Three parliamentary chambers, ten departments of education, health, and welfare (one for each "race" and homeland), plus huge military and state security budgets put an enormous load on the country's economy. Foreign sanctions and disinvestment increased the strain. Spiraling unemployment, poverty, and civil unrest heightened tension. The conclusion was becoming inescapable. Apartheid would have to go, and with it white rule. Once the government had recognized this bleak reality, its leaders saw clearly that only a negotiated settlement with Nelson Mandela and the ANC could hope to solve South Africa's mounting economic and social problems.

The negotiations were protracted and difficult, but Nelson Mandela never lost sight of the cherished ideal that he had been prepared to die for: a democratic and free society in which all persons live together in harmony and with equal opportunities.

South Africa's first elections under its new constitution were held in April 1994. The scenes at polling stations throughout the country, with millions of voters waiting patiently in lines that wove erratically through rural homesteads, townships, and suburban streets, was one of the most heartening events in modern history. It was the first time that many of the electors had voted, and the first time that an African election had received so much favorable attention from abroad. Never before had the international media reported so extensively on an item of good news from Africa. After so much war, drought, and catastrophe, the world stopped to look appreciatively at the face of Africa and Africans.

With a black majority government and Nelson Mandela as president, South Africa rejoined the mainstream of African history. The last vestige of white supremacy had been banished from the continent.

FEW LEADERS HAVE generated such universal affection and admiration as Nelson Mandela. Fewer still have relinquished power so soon after achieving it. He had spent more than 50 years fighting for black African rights in South Africa, but he stepped down as president after just 5 years. The constitution allows a president to stand for a second term. Mandela was 81 years old by the time of the elections in 1999. Still sprightly, he certainly would have been reelected, but unlike many African leaders, he had no wish to take the presidency to his grave. Besides, he had married again, and he wanted to spend more time with his grandchildren.

In 1999, Mandela's deputy, 57-year-old Thabo Mbeki, was elected president. Son of Govan Mbeki, an ANC leader convicted and imprisoned with Mandela, he also had devoted his life to the struggle for freedom. After being arrested in southern Rhodesia (now Zimbabwe) on suspicion of terrorist activity, Mbeki was granted political asylum in Tanzania before going to study at the University of Sussex, where he was awarded an M.A. in economics in 1966. For the next ten years he represented the ANC around the world before joining the organization's National Executive.

As the ANC's director of international affairs, Thabo Mbeki played a key role in the negotiations that led to the release of Nelson Mandela and the advent of black majority rule. With those tasks accomplished, Mbeki turned his attention to the economic and social problems confronting people in South Africa and throughout the continent. "The full meaning of liberation will not be realized until our people are freed both from oppression and from the dehumanizing legacy of deprivation.... I am my brother's keeper; I am my sister's keeper," he pledged in his inaugural speech.

Playing Young Turk to Mandela's elder statesman while deputy president, Thabo Mbeki had called for Africa to rediscover the strengths that made it the birthplace of humanity. He spoke of an African Renaissance stirring the soul of the continent as a prelude to mastering its political and economic problems. In the European context, the Renaissance refers to the 14th-century reawakening of interest in Greek and Roman art and culture. In Africa, Mbeki sought to reawaken the genius that inspired the giant obelisks at Aksum, the Egyptian pyramids, the labyrinthine stone walls of Great Zimbabwe, the Benin bronzes, San rock paintings, ancient Carthage, the universities at Alexandria, Fez, and Timbuktu, and the Zulu defeat of British forces at Isandhlwana in 1879.

In the new South Africa, carvings are priced to give craftsmen a good living wage. Large items may cost hundreds of dollars.

Mbeki drew attention to African achievements of the past, but his message was clearly addressed to the post-independence generation and its demand for solutions to the problems of contemporary Africa. He said:

The call for an African Renaissance is a call to rebellion. We must rebel against the tyrants and the dictators, those who seek to corrupt our societies and steal the wealth that belongs to the people. We must...conduct war against poverty, ignorance and the backwardness of the children. Surely, there must be politicians and business people, youth and women activists, trade unionists, religious leaders, artists and professionals from the Cape to Cairo, from Madagascar to Cape Verde, who are sufficiently enraged by Africa's condition in the world to want to join the mass crusade for Africa's renewal. It is to these that we say, without equivocation, that to be a true African is to be a rebel in the cause of the African Renaissance, whose success in the new century and millennium is one of the great historic challenges of our time.

Mbeki's call for an African Renaissance has won headlines around the world, heralding new leadership, more democracy, resurgent economies, and a significant new role for Africa on the world stage. Already the signs of renewal are evident throughout the continent. Twenty-five democratic elections were held during the 1990s. Dictatorships that once characterized African governments are shunned. Economic reforms have led to phenomenal growth, with more than half of African countries growing at 5 percent or more. A new wave of foreign investment is injecting hundreds of millions of dollars into African industry.

Though daunting problems remain, Africa has the energy, resources, and workforce to become the economic giant of the 21st century. But the prize is more than the wealth and well-being of people within the continent's encircling shores. Africa concerns us all. We hold everything in common—not least our destiny, now that the limits of global exploitation are understood. "The African Renaissance addresses not only the life of the peoples of Africa," says President Mbeki, "it extends the frontiers of human dignity."

When South Africa's reviled apartheid regime collapsed and democratic elections brought a black government to power in 1994 with Nelson Mandela as president, a new era of opportunity opened for the victims of racial segregation. But few were as bold as 26-year-old Xoliswa Vanda, who set her sights on becoming the first woman to manage one of South Africa's premier gold mines. Within years, she was the first black woman in the country to hold a blasting certificate and the only woman in a workforce of 5,000 men. Now, if she passes crucial exams, she will be on the company's fast track to management status.

South Africa is the richest nation in Africa, its wealth built upon the enormous reserves of precious minerals. The miners work nearly two miles underground, where heat from the Earth's core pushes the temperature to 104° F. Space at the work face is limited and the sound of pneumatic drills deafening. And even here, in one of the world's richest gold mines, the prize they seek is all but invisible. From every ton of ore sent to the surface, a matchhead-size piece of gold is extracted.

Xoliswa is in charge of the explosives used to blast the gold-bearing seam, which may be anything from 1.5 to 8 feet high. She decides where to place charges and how much explosive should be used, and she is legally responsible for the safety of everyone with her.

Xoliswa Vanda (left) is a pioneer—the first black woman to hold a blasting certificate in a South African gold mine. What's more, she's the only woman in a workforce of 5,000. The miners aren't accustomed to taking orders from a woman. But Xoliswa understands their culture very well, she says. "I know how to talk to the men and get them to do exactly what I want. What you mustn't do is take away the dignity of a person."

Xoliswa is in charge of the explosives. She decides where they are set and will detonate the charge. It is a demanding job that puts a heavy load of responsibility on her shoulders. "I am legally responsible for the safety of everyone who works here," she says.

Deep underground
in the Savuka Mine,
Xoliswa directs
operations as holes
are drilled for the
dynamite that
will blast out the
gold-bearing ore.
Conditions in the
shaft are cramped.
Temperatures soar
to 104° F, humidity
stands at 100 percent,
and the noise is
deafening.

With her friend Thabitha Machaba, an engineering student who hopes to join Xoliswa in the mining industry, Xoliswa (left, on the right) is out shopping at the Randburg waterfront (above) and at a top Johannesburg jeweler, Brown's (left), where she tries on a gold ring. "Well, hey, I've been working hard to get it out from underground, so to be able to wear gold is quite a matter of pride," she says. "I do think gold looks good on my skin. I love gold, which is also why I got into gold mining."

Chapter 1

Aiello, Leslie C., and Wheeler, Peter. 1995. The expensive-tissue hypothesis: The brain and the digestive system in human and primate evolution." *Curr. Anthrop.* 36(2):199-221.

Alexander, R. McNeill. 1992. Human locomotion, in: *Cambridge Encyclopedia of Human Evolution.* 1992. Cambridge: Cambridge University Press. 80-85.

Ambrose, Stanley H. 1984. The introduction of pastoral adaptations to the highlands of East Africa, in: Clark, J. D., and S. A. Brandt (eds.) 1984. *From Hunters to Farmers: The Causes and Consequences of Food Production in Africa.* Berkeley: University of California Press. 213-39.

Baker, B.H., Mohr, P.A. and Williams, L.A.J. 1972. *Geology of the Eastern Rift System of East Africa.* Boulder, Colo.

Briggs, J.C. 1987. *Biogeography and Plate Tectonics.* Amsterdam.

Brown, Eric W. 1988. *An Introduction to Solar Energy.* Feneric@ccs.neu.edu

Croze, Harvey, and John Reader. 2000. *Pyramids of Life.* London: Harvill. 11, 32.

Harrison, G.A., H. J. M.Tanner, D. R. Pilbeam, and P. T. Baker. 1992. *Human Biology.* Oxford: Oxford Science Publications. 452.

Houston, D.C. 1979. The adaptations of scavengers, in: Sinclair A.R.E., and M. Norton-Griffiths (eds.) 1979. Serengeti: *Dynamics of an Ecosystem.* Chicago and London: University of Chicago Press. 263-286.

Iliffe, John. 1995. *Africans: The History of a Continent.* Cambridge: Cambridge University Press. 112.

Leakey, M.D., and J. M. Harris (eds.) 1987. *Laetoli: a Pliocene Site in Northern Tanzania.* Oxford: Clarendon Press.

Lithgow-Bertelloni, Carolina, and Paul G. Silver. 1998. Dynamic topography, plate driving forces and the African superswell. *Nature* 395:269-272.

Lovejoy, C.O. 1981. The origin of man. *Science* 211:341-50.

Meadows, M.E. 1996. Biogeography, in: Adams, W.M., A.S. Goudie and A.R. Orme (eds.) 1996. *The Physical Geography of Africa.* Oxford: Oxford University Press. 161-172.

Muriuki, Godfrey. 1974. *A History of the Kikuyu.* Nairobi: Oxford University Press. 21-3, 45-7, 62-3.

Nance, R. Damian, Thomas R. Worsley, and Judith B. Moody. 1988. The supercontinent cycle. *Sci. Am.*, July, 44-51.

Nyamweru, Celia. 1996. The African Rift System, in: Adams, W.M., A.S. Goudie and A.R. Orme (eds.) 1996. *The Physical Geography of Africa.* Oxford: Oxford University Press. 18-33.

Pollitz, Fred F. 1999. From rifting to drifting. *Nature* 398:21-22.

Reader, John. 1999. *Africa: A Biography of the Continent.* New York: Vintage Books. 4, 686.

Ross, Philip E. 1991. Hard words. *Sci. Am.* 264(4): 71-79.

Rouhani, Shanin, and Steve Jones. 1992. Bottlenecks in human evolution, in: *Cambridge Encyclopedia of Human Evolution.* 1992. Cambridge: Cambridge University Press. 281-83.

Routledge, W.S. and K. 1910. *With a Prehistoric People: The Kikuyu of British East Africa.* London. 6.

Schaller, G.B., and G. R. Lowther. 1969. The relevance of carnivore behavior to the study of early hominids. *SW. J. Anthrop.* 25 (pt 4): 307-41.

Sinclair A.R.E., and Peter Arcese (eds.) 1995. *Serengeti II: Dynamics, Management, and Conservation of an Ecosystem.* Chicago and London: University of Chicago Press. 6.

Steudel, Karen L. 1994. Locomotor energetics and hominid evolution. *Evol. Anthrop.* 3 (pt 2): 42-47.

Summerfield, Michael A. 1996. Tectonics, geology, and long-term landscape development, in: Adams, W.M., A.S. Goudie, and A.R. Orme (eds.) 1996. *The Physical Geography of Africa.* Oxford: Oxford University Press. 1-17.

Tattersall, Ian. 2000. Once we were not alone. *Sci. Am.*, January, 38-44.

Van Hoven, W W. 1991. Mortality in kudu populations related to chemical defence in trees. *Revue Zoologique Africaine* 105:141-5.

Wheeler, P.E. 1984. The evolution of bipedalism and loss of functional body hair in hominids. *J. Hum. Evol.* 13:91-98.

Wheeler, P.E. 1992. The thermoregulatory advantages of large body size for hominids foraging in savannah environments. *J. Hum. Evol.* 23:351-62.

Wilson, A.C. et al. 1987. Mitochrondrial clans and the age of our common mother, in: Vogel, F. and K. Sperling (eds.) 1987. *Human genetics: Proc. 7th Int. Congr.* Berlin: Springer. 158-64.

Wright, Robert. 1991. Quest for the mother tongue. *Atlantic Monthly,* April, 39-68.

Chapter 2

Attenborough, David. 1984. *The Living Planet.* London: Collins.141.

Baier, Stephen, and Paul E. Lovejoy. 1977. The Tuareg of the central Sudan, in: Miers, Suzanne and Igor Kopytoff (eds.) 1977. *Slavery in Africa: Historical and Anthropological Perspectives.* Madison: University of Wisconsin Press. 400.

Beazley, C.R., and E. Prestage (trans. & eds.) 1896, 1899: Azurara, G.E. de. c.1450. The *Chronicle of the Discovery and Conquest of Guinea* [1441-48], 2 vols. Cambridge: Hakluyt Society, Ser. 2, vols. 95, 100.

Berger, A. 1988. Milankovitch and climate. *Rev. Geophys.* 26 (pt.4): 624-57

Bulliet, Richard B. 1975. *The Camel and the Wheel.* Cambridge, Mass.: Harvard University Press.

Butzer, Karl. 1976. *Early Hydraulic Civilization in Egypt: A Study in Cultural Ecology,* Chicago: University of Chicage Press. 83.

Caton-Thompson, G. 1934. The camel in dynastic Egypt. *Man* 34:21

Cloudsley-Thompson, J.L. (ed.) 1984. *Sahara Desert.* Oxford: Pergamon Press. 3.

Clutton-Brock, Juliet. 1993. The spread of domestic animals in Africa, in: Shaw, Thurstan, Paul Sinclair, Bassey Andah, and Alex Okpoko (eds.) 1993. *The Archaeology of Africa: Food, Metals and Towns.* London: Routledge, 66-67.

Curtin, P.D. 1984. *Cross-cultural Trade in World History.* Cambridge: Cambridge University Press. 21.

Curtin, P.D. 1969. *The Atlantic Slave Trade: A Census.* Madison: University of Wisconsin Press. 268, 287.

El-Baz, Farouk. 1998. Aeolian deposits and palaeo-rivers of the Eastern Sahara. *Sahara* 10:55-66.

Garrard, Timothy F. 1982. Myth and metrology: The early trans-Saharan gold trade. *J. Afr. Hist.* 23:443-61.

Gowlett, John. 1984. *Ascent to Civilization.* London: Collins. 181.

Haaland, Randi. 1992. Fish, pots and grain: Early and Mid-Holocene adaptations in the central Sudan. *Afr. Archaeol. Rev.* 10:43-64.

Heinzel, H., R. Fitter, and J. Parslow. *The Birds of Britain and Europe.* London: Collins.

Hopkins, A.G. 1973. *An Economic History of West Africa.* London: Longman. 82.

Iliffe, John. 1995. *Africans: The History of a Continent.* Cambridge: Cambridge University Press. 82, 130.

Imbrie, John. 1982. Astronomical theory of the Pleistocene Ice Ages: A brief historical review. *Icarus* 50:411.

Junge, C.E. 1979. The importance of mineral dust as an atmospheric constituent in the atmosphere, in: Morales, C. (ed.) *Saharan Dust.* New York. 49-60.

Kassas, M., and K. H. Batanouny. 1984. Plant ecology, in: Cloudsley-Thompson, J.L. (ed.) 1984. *Sahara Desert.* Oxford: Pergamon Press. 77-90.

Keenan, Jeremy. 1977. *The Tuareg.* London: Allen Lane. 5-6.

Keenan, Jeremy. 2000. The father's friend: Returning to the Tuareg as an elder. *Anthrop. Today* 16(4): 7-11

Lamprey, H.F. 1988. Report on the desert encroachment recconnaisance in Northern Sudan. (UNESCO/UNEP) [*Desertification Control Bull.* 17, 1.]

Lancaster, Nicholas. 1996. Desert Environments, in: Adams, W.M., A.S. Goudie, and A. R. Orme (eds.) 1996. *The Physical Geography of Africa.* Oxford: Oxford University Press. 211-237.

Levtzion, N., and J. F. P. Hopkins. 1981. *Corpus of Early Arabic Sources for West African History.* Cambridge: Cambridge University Press. 27-8.

Lhote, Henri. 1987. Oasis of art in the Sahara. *Nat. Geog.,* August, 181-191.

Lovejoy, Paul E.1986. *Salt of the Desert Sun: A History of Salt Production and Trade in Central Sudan.* Cambridge: Cambridge University Press. 40.

Markham, Clements R. (ed.) 1878. *John Hawkins: The Voyages.* Cambridge: Hakluyt Society, vol. 57: 5.

McCauley, John F., et al. 1986. Palaeodrainages of the Eastern Sahara: The Radar rivers revisited (SIR-A/B implications for a Mid-Tertiary Trans-African Drainage System), *IEEE Trans. Geosci. Remote Sens.* GE-24 (pt.4): 624-47.

McGinnies, W., B. Goldman, and P. Paylore. 1968. *Deserts of the World.* Tucson: University of Arizona Press.

Moreau, R.E. 1972. *The Palearctic-African Bird Migration Systems.* New York: Academic Press.

Multhauf, Robert P. 1978. *Neptune's Gift: A History of Common Salt.* Baltimore: Johns Hopkins University Press. 4.

Nachtigal, Gustav. *Sahara and Sudan,* vol. 2: *Bornu, Kanem, Ennedi.* Trans. A.G.B. and H.H. Fisher. 1980. New York: Holmes and Meier. 97.

Nickling W.G., and J. A. Gillies. 1993. Dust emissions and transport in Mali, West Africa. *Sedimentology* 40(5): 859-68.

Nicolaisen, J. 1963. *Ecology and Culture of the Pastoral Tuareg.* National Museum of Copenhagen. 7.

O'Connor, David. 1993. Urbanism in bronze age Egypt and northeast Africa, in: Shaw, Thurstan, Paul Sinclair, Bassey Andah, and Alex Okpoko (eds.) 1993. *The Archaeology of Africa: Food, Metals and Towns.* London: Routledge. 570-86.

Oliver, R. 1991. *The African Experience.* London: Weidenfeld and Nicholson.

Pettet, A. 1984. Migratory birds, in: Cloudsley-Thompson, J.L. (ed.) 1984. *Sahara Desert.* Oxford: Pergamon Press. 241-250.

Polis, Gary A. (ed.) 1991. *The Ecology of Desert Communities.* Tucson: University of Arizona Press. 1-25.

Pratt, D.J., and M. D. Gwynne. 1977. *Rangeland Management and Ecology in East Africa.* London: Hodder and Stoughton. 35-37.

Prospero, J.M., R. A. Glaccum, and R. T. Nees. 1981. Atmospheric transport of soil dust from Africa to South America. *Nature* 289:570-2.

Reader, John. 1999. *Africa: A Biography of the Continent.* New York: Vintage Books. 276.

Roset, J.P. 1987. Palaeoclimatic and cultural conditions of neolithic development in the early Holocene of northern Niger, in: Close, A.E. (ed.) 1987. *Prehistory of Arid North Africa.* Dallas: Southern Methodist University Press. 189-210.

Rowley-Conwy, Peter. 1988. The camel in the Nile valley. J. Egypt. *Archaeol.* 74:245-48.

Said, Rushdi. 1993. *The River Nile: Geology, Hydrology and Utilization.* Oxford: Pergamon Press. 55.

Said, Rushdi. 1997. The role of the desert in the rise and fall of Ancient Egypt. *Sahara* 9:20.

Saunders, A.C. de C.M. 1982. *A Social History of the Black Slaves and Freemen in Portugal 1441-1555.* Cambridge: Cambridge University Press. 59.

Shaw, Thurstan, Paul Sinclair, Bassey Andah, and Alex Okpoko (eds.) 1993. The Archaeology of *Africa: Food, Metals and Towns.* London: Routledge.

Smith, Andrew B. 1992. *Pastoralism in Africa: Origins and Development Ecology.* London: Hurst. 70.

Smith, G. 1984. Climate, in: Cloudsley-Thompson, J.L. (ed.) 1984. *Sahara Desert.* Oxford: Pergamon Press. 17-30.

Stemler, Ann. 1984. The transition from food collecting to food production in northern Africa, in: Clark, J.D., and S. A. Brandt (eds.) 1984, *From Hunters to Farmers: The Causes and Consequences of Food Production in Africa.* Berkeley: University of California Press. 127-31.

Sultan, Mohamed, et al. 1999. Monitoring the urbanization of the Nile Delta, Egypt. *Ambio* 28 (7): 628-31.

Swain, Ashok. 1997. Ethiopia, Sudan, and Egypt: the Nile River dispute. *J. Mod. Afr. Stu.* 35 (4): 675-694.

The Times Atlas 1985. London: Times Books. Map 81.

Theroux, Peter. 1997. The imperilled Nile Delta. *Nat. Geog.*, January, 8.

Tucker, C.J., H. E. Dregne, and W. W. Newcomb. 1991. Expansion and contraction of the Sahara Desert from 1980 to 1990. *Science* 253:299-301.

Tucker, Compton J., and Sharon E. Nicholson. 1999. Variations in the size of the Sahara Desert from 1980 to 1997. *Ambio* 28 (7): 587-591.

Vines, Gail. 1992. Winning streak for sheiks. *New Sci.* 136:22-25.

Wickens, G.E. 1984. Flora, in: Cloudsley-Thompson, J.L. (ed.) 1984. *Sahara Desert.* Oxford: Pergamon Press. 67-73.

Willert, Dieter J. von, et al. 1992. *Life Strategies of Succulents in Deserts.* Cambridge: Cambridge University Press. 30, 48-55.

World Resources Institute. *World Resources 1998-99: A Guide to the Global Environment.* Oxford: Oxford University Press.

Chapter 3

Akobundu, I.O. 1991. Weeds in human affairs in sub-Saharan Africa: Implications for sustainable food production. *Weed Technol.* 5:680-90.

Bailey, Robert C., and Thomas N. Headland. 1991. The tropical rain forest: Is it a productive environment for human foragers? *Hum Ecol.* 19 (2): 261-81.

Boyce, Nell. 2000. Blocking malaria. *New Sci.*, 8 July, 15.

Breasted, J.H. 1906-7. *Ancient Records of Egypt.* 5 vols. Chicago: University of Chicago Press. Paragraphs 333-36, 353.

Campbell, Bernard. 1983. *Human Ecology.* London: Heinemann. 30.

CLIMAP Project Members. 1976. The surface of the ice-age Earth. *Science* 191:1131-7.

Connah, Graham. 1987. *African Civilizations: Precolonial Cities and States in Tropical Africa: An Archaeological Perspective.* Cambridge: Cambridge University Press. 134-6.

Deacon, J. 1990. Changes in the archaeological record in South Africa at 18000 BP, in: Gamble, C.S., and O. Soffer (eds.) 1990. *The World at 18000 BP,* vol. 2: *Low Latitudes.* London: Unwin Hyman. 170-88.

Dobson, Andrew. 1993. People and disease, in: *Cambridge Encyclopedia of Human Evolution.* 1993. Cambridge: Cambridge University Press. 411-20.

Fairhead, James, and Melissa Leach. 1996. *Misreading the African Landscape.* Cambridge: Cambridge University Press.

Fairhead, James, and Melissa Leach. 1998. *Reframing Deforestation.* London: Routledge.

Flenley, John R. 1979. *The Equatorial Rain Forest: A Geological History.* London: Butterworth. 2.

Fuller, F. 1921 (1967). *A Vanished Dynasty: Ashanti.* London: Cass.

Gowlett, John. 1984. *Ascent to Civilization.* London: Collins.103.

Grainger, Alan. 1996. Forest environments, in: Adams, W.M., A. S. Goudie, and A. R. Orme (eds.) 1996. *The Physical Geography of Africa.* Oxford: Oxford University Press. 173-195.

Hamilton, Alan. 1976. Significance of patterns of distribution shown by forest plants and animals in tropical Africa for the reconstruction of Upper Pleistocene palaeoenvironments. *Palaeoecol. Afr.* 9:63-97.

Harlan, J.R. 1976. *Crops and Man.* Madison: University of Wisconsin Press. 71-2, 199-200.

Harrison, G.A., H. J. M.Tanner, D. R. Pilbeam, and P. T. Baker. 1992. *Human Biology.* Oxford: Oxford Science Publications. 233.

Hodgkin, T. 1975. *Nigerian Perspectives.* Oxford: Oxford University Press. 176.

Hopkins, A.G. 1973. *An Economic History of West Africa.* London: Longman. 46.

Iliffe, John. 1995. *Africans: The History of a Continent.* Cambridge: Cambridge University Press. 129, 144.

Kingdon, Jonathan. 1989. *Island Africa: The Evolution of Africa's Rare Animals and Plants.* London: Collins.109.

Livingstone, Frank B. 1958. Anthropological implications of sickle cell gene distribution in West Africa. Am. *Anthrop.* 60:533-62.

Mattingly, P.F. 983. The palaeogeography of mosquito-borne disease. *Biol. J. Linn. Soc.* 199:185-210.

Mayr, E., and R. J. O'Hara. 1986. The biogeographical evidence supporting the Pleistocene refuge hypothesis. *Evolution* 40:55-69.

Meadows, M.E. 1996. Biogeography, in: Adams, W.M., A.S. Goudie, and A.R. Orme (eds.) 1996. *The Physical Geography of Africa.* Oxford: Oxford University Press. 161-172.

Miracle, Marvin P. 1965. The introduction and spread of maize in Africa. *J. Afr. Hist.* 6:39-55, 43.

Mitchell, Peter, 1990, in: Gamble, C.S., and O. Soffer (eds.) 1990. *The World at 18000 BP, vol. 2: Low Latitudes.* London: Unwin Hyman. 195.

Myers, Norman. 1996. Biodiversity and biodepletion, in: Adams, W.M., A.S.Goudie, and A.R.Orme (eds.) 1996. *The Physical Geography of Africa.* Oxford: Oxford University Press. 356-366.

Ndoye, O., and D. Kaimowitz. 2000. Macro-economics, markets and the humid forests of Cameroon, 1967-1997. *Journal of Modern African Studies.* 38 (2): 225-253.

Nisbet, Euan. 1991. *Living Earth: A Short History of Life and Its Home.* London: Chapman and Hall. 164.

Pearce, Fred. 1997. Lost forests leave West Africa dry. *New Sci.,* 18 January, 15.

Pearce, Fred. 2000. Malariasphere. *New Sci,* 15 July, 32-35.

Phillips, Perrot. 1992. Banking on it. *Weekend Guardian,* 3 October.

Richards, P.W. 1993. Africa the "Odd Man Out", in: Meggers, B.J., E. S. Ayensu, and W. D. Duckworth (eds.) *Tropical Forest Ecosystems in Africa and South America: A Comparative Review.* Washington, D.C. 21-6.

Roberts, Neil. 1992. Climatic change in the past, in *Cambridge Encyclopedia of Human Evolution.* Cambridge: Cambridge University Press. 174-78.

Roth, H.L. 1903. *Great Benin: Its Customs, Art and Horrors.* Halifax: King.

Schebesta, P. 1933. *Among Congo Pigmies.* London: Hutchinson.

Tewolde, Berhan. 1992. Amani forest [Tanzania] study, cited in The Environmental Problems of *Northern Ethiopia.* Addis Ababa: Department of the Environment (Ethiopia). 2.

Van Zinderen Bakker, E.M. 1982. African palaeoenvironments 18,000 years before present. *Palaeoecol. Afr.* 15:79-99.

Vansina, Jan. 1990. *Paths in the Rainforest.* Madison: University of Wisconsin Press. 55.

Whitmore, T.C. 1998. *An Introduction to Tropical Rain Forests.* Oxford: Oxford University Press. 31.

Wilks, I. (ed.) 1993. *Forests of Gold: Essays on the Akan and the Kingdom of Asante.* Athens: Ohio University Press.

Wilks, I. 1975. *Asante in the Nineteenth Century: The Structure and Evolution of a Political Order.* Cambridge: Cambridge University Press.

World Health Organization. 2001.Malaria statistics from WHO Fact Sheet No 94, October 1998, at: http://www.who.int/int-fs/en/Fact094.html

World Resources Institute. 1998. *World Resources 1998-1999: A Guide to the Global Environment.* Oxford: Oxford University Press. 295.

Chapter 4

Baker, B.H., P. A. Mohr, and L. A. J. Williams. 1972. *Geology of the Eastern Rift System of Africa.* Boulder, Colo.

Barker, Brian J. 1989. *Dias and Da Gama: The Portuguese Discovery of the Cape Sea-route.* Cape Town: Struik.

Brandt, Steven A. 1984. New perspectives on the origins of food production in Ethiopia, in: Clark, J.D., and S. A. Brandt (eds.) 1984. *From Hunters to Farmers: The Causes and Consequences of Food Production in Africa.* Berkeley: University of California Press. 174-90.

Butzer, Karl W. 1981. Rise and fall of Axum, Ethiopia: a geo-archaeological interpretation. *Am. Antiq.,* 46 (3): 471-95.

Buxton, B.R. 1970. *The Abyssinians.* London: Thames and Hudson.

Casson, Lionel. 1989. *The Periplus Maris Erythraei.* Lawrenceville, NJ: Princeton University Press.

Connah, Graham. 1987. *African Civilizations: Precolonial Cities and States in Tropical Africa: An Archaeological Perspective.* Cambridge: Cambridge University Press,

Contenson, H. de. 1981. Pre-Aksumite culture, vol. I, in: UNESCO, 1981-93. *General History of Africa.* 8 vols. London: Heinemann. 341-61.

Crawford, O.G.S. 1958. *Ethiopian Itineraries, c1400-1524.* Cambridge: Hakluyt Society series 2, 109: 5, 13-20, 212-15.

De Waal, Alex. 1997. *Famine Crimes, Politics and the Disaster Relief Industry in Africa.* African Rights. Bloomington: Indiana University Press. 107, 109, 117, 125.

Demissew, S. 1988. The floristic composition of the Menagesha State Forest and the need to conserve such forests in Ethiopia. *Mount. Res. Devel.* 8: 243-247.

Ermias, Bekele. 1986. Landuse planning and towards its policy in Ethiopia. *SINET Ethiop. J. Sci.* 9 (suppl.), 81-94.

Eshetu, Zewdu, and Peter Hgberg. 2000. Reconstruction of forest site history in Ethiopian highlands based on 13C natural abundance in soils. *Ambio* 29:83-9.

Fattovich, Rudolfo. 1990. Remarks on the Pre-Axumite period in northern Ethiopia. *J. Ethiop. Stud.* 23: 1-34.

Jones, Glyn. 1988. Endemic crop plants of Ethiopia: I. T'ef (Eragrostis tef). *Walia* 11:37-43.

Kingdon, Jonathan. 1989. *Island Africa: The Evolution of Africa's Rare Animals and Plants.* London: Collins. 149-50, 153-5, 158-9, 162, 164, 166.

Kobish(ch)anov, Y.M. 1981. Aksum: political system, economics and culture, first to fourth century, vol. 2, in: UNESCO, 1981-93, *General History of Africa.* 8 vols. London: Heinemann. 381-400.

Kobishchanov, Y.M. (trans. L.T. Kapitanoff) 1979. *Axum.* (ed. J.W. Michels). London: Pennsylvania State University Press. 104-5, 175, 265.

Korn, David A. 1986. *Ethiopia, the United States and the Soviet Union.* London: Croom Helm.

Lefort, René. 1983. (trans. A.M. Bennett). *Ethiopia: An Heretical Revolution?* London: Zed Press.

Munro-Hay, Stuart. 1991. *An African Civilisation: The Aksumite Kingdom of Northern Ethiopia.* Edinburgh: Edinburgh University Press.

Phillipson, D.W. 1994. Aksum: the ancient capital of Christian Ethiopia. (unpub. summary MS).

Pohjonen, V., and T. Pukkala. 1990. *Eucalyptus globulus* in Ethiopian forestry. *For. Ecol. Mgmt.* 36:19-31.

Rodgers, A. 1992. Ethiopia, in: Sayer, J.A., C. S.Harcourt, and N. M. Collins (eds.) 1992. The *Conservation Atlas of Tropical Forests: Africa.* New York: IUCN. 148-160.

Sauer, C.O. 1952. *Agricultural Origins and Dispersals.* New York Geographical Society.

Seaman, John, and Julius Holt. 1975. The Ethiopian famine of 1973-4. I. Wollo Province. *Proceedings of the Nutritional Society* 34:114A.

Simoons, F.J. 1965. Some questions on the economic prehistory of Ethiopia. *J. Afr. Hist.* 6:1-13.

Summerfield, M.A. 1996. Tectonics, geology and long-term landscape development, in: Adams, W.M., A. S. Goudie, and A. R. Orme (eds.) 1996. *The Physical Geography of Africa.* Oxford: Oxford University Press. 1-17.

Tamrat, Tadesse. 1972. *Church and State in Ethiopia.* Oxford: Clarendon Press. 254, 256-7, 266.

Taylor, David. 1996. Mountains, in: Adams, W.M., A. S. Goudie, and A. R. Orme (eds.) 1996. *The Physical Geography of Africa.* Oxford: Oxford University Press. 287-306.

Turnbull et al. 1988. Volume production in intensely managed eucalypt plantations. *Appita* 41:447-450.

Williams, J.E., and I. H. Booker (eds.) 1997. *Eucalypt ecology.* Cambridge: Cambridge University Press.

Yalden, D.W. 1983. The extent of the high ground in Ethiopia compared to the rest of Africa. *SINET, Ethiop. J. Sci.* 6(1): 35-38.

Chapter 5

Classon, A.T. 1980. The animal remains from Tell es Sinn compared with those from Bouqras. *Anatolica* 7:35-52.

Clutton-Brock, Juliet. 1992. Domestication of animals, in: *Cambridge Encyclopedia of Human Evolution.* 1992. Cambridge: Cambridge University Press. 380-85.

Clutton-Brock, Juliet. 1993, The spread of domestic animals in Africa, in: Shaw, Thurstan, Paul Sinclair, Bassey Andah, and Alex Opoko (eds.) 1993. *The Archaeology of Africa: Food, Metals, and Towns.* London: Routledge. 61-70.

Cook, G.C., and S. K. Kajubi. 1966. Tribal incidence of lactase deficiency in Uganda. *The Lancet,* 2 April, 725-30.

Ellis, William E. 1987. Africa's Sahel: The stricken land. *Nat. Geog.,* August, 140-179.

Gerster, Georg. 1986. Tsetse, fly of the deadly sleep. *Nat. Geog.,* December, 814-833.

Giblin, James. 1990. Trypanosomiasis control in African history: an evaded issue. *J. Afr. Hist.* 31:59-80.

Grigson, C. 1980. Size and sex: evidence for domestication of cattle in the Near East, in: Milles, A., D. Williams, and N. Gardner (eds.) *The Beginnings of Agriculture.* Oxford: British Archaeological Reports (Int. Ser. 496). 77-109.

Johnson, R.C., R. E. Cole, and F. M. Ahern. 1981. Genetic interpretation of racial and ethnic differences in lactose absorption and tolerance: a review. *Hum. Biol.* 53:1-13.

Kay, R.N.B. 1997. Responses of African livestock and wild herbivores to drought. *J. Arid Environments.* 37 (4): 683-694.

Kretchmer, Norman. 1972. Lactose and lactase. *Sci. Am.* 227 (4): 70-80.

Leak, S.G.A. 1999. *Tsetse Biology and Ecology.* Oxford: CABI Publishing. 87, 277, 304, 355, 357.

Lowe-McConnell, R.H. 1984., The biology of the river systems with particular reference to the fishes, in: Grove, A.T. (ed.) 1984. *The Niger and Its Neighbours.* Rotterdam: Balkema, 101-40.

MacFarlane, W.V. et al. 1971. Hierarchy of water and energy turnover of desert mammals. *Nature* 234:483-4.

McCracken, Robert D. 1971. Lactose deficiency: an example of dietary evolution. *Curr. Anthrop.* 12:479-519.

McIntosh, R.J. and S.K. 1984. Early Iron Age economy in the inland Niger Delta (Mali), in: Clark, J.D., and S. A. Brandt (eds.) 1984. *From Hunters to Farmers: The Causes and Consequences of Food Production in Africa.* Berkeley: University of California Press. 158-172.

McIntosh, R.J. 1992. Historical view of the semiarid tropics. Paper presented at the 1992 Carter Lecture Series, Center for African Studies, University of Florida. (MS), 33.

McIntosh, S.K. and R.J. 1993. Cities without citadels: Understanding urban origins along the middle Niger, in: Shaw, Thurstan, Paul Sinclair, Bassey Andah, and Alex Opoko (eds.) 1993. *The Archaeology of Africa: Food, Metals, and Towns.* London: Routledge. 621-41.

McIntosh, S.K. and R.J. 1980. Prehistorical investigations in the region of Jenne, Mali. *Brit. Archaeol. Reps.* Oxford. 308, 333, 335, 337.

McNaughton, S.J. 1979. Grazing as an optimization process: grassungulate relationships in the Serengeti. *Am. Nat.* 113: 691-703.

Meadows, Michael E. 1996. Biogeography, in: Adams, W.M., A. S. Goudie, and A.R. Orme (eds.) 1996. *The Physical Geography of Africa.* Oxford: Oxford University Press. 161-172.

Nash, T. A. M. 1969. *Africa's Bane.* London: Collins.

Pearce, Fred. 2000. Inventing Africa. *New Sci.,* 12 August, 30-33.

Riesman, Paul. 1984. The Fulani in a development context, in: Scott, Earl (ed.) 1984. *Life Before the Drought.* Boston: Allen & Unwin. 171-191.

Schmidt-Neilsen, K. 1964. *Desert Animals.* Oxford: Oxford University Press. 79-80.

Simoons, F.J. 1973. The determinants of dairying and milk use in the Old World: Ecological, physiological and cultural. *Ecol. Food Nutr.* 2:83-90.

Smith, Andrew B. 1992. *Pastoralism in Africa: Origins and Development Ecology.* London: Hurst. 63.

Spencer, Paul. 1968. *The Samburu: A Study in Gerontocracy in a Nomadic Tribe.* London: Routledge and Kegan Paul.

Sterile sex conquers sleeping sickness. 1997. *New Sci.* 156:12.

Waller, Richard D. 1990. Tsetse fly in western Narok, Kenya. *J. Afr. Hist.* 31: 81-101.

Wendorf, Fred D., and Romuald Schild. 1995. Are the early Holocene cattle in the eastern Sahara domestic or wild? *Evol. Anthrop.* 3(4): 118-28.

Wendorf, Fred, and Romuald Schild. 1984. The emergence of food production in the Egyptian Sahara in: Clark, J.D., and S. A. Brandt (eds.) 1984. *From Hunters to Farmers: The Causes and Consequences of Food Production in Africa.* Berkeley: University of California Press. 93-101.

World Resources Institute. 1998. *World Resources 1998-99: A Guide to the Global Environment.* Oxford: Oxford University Press. 244, 276.

Zimmer, Carl. 1998. A sleeping storm. *Discover,* August, 86-94 .

Chapter 6

Adams, William M. 1996. Lakes, in: Adams, W.M., A. S. Goudie, and A. R. Orme (eds.) 1996. *The Physical Geography of Africa.* Oxford: Oxford University Press. 122-33.

African Rights. 1995. *Rwanda: Death, despair and defiance.* London: Africa Rights. 16, 100, 176.

Argyle, W.J. 1971. A critique of one rural-urban dichotomy. Unpublished MS, quoted in: De Haas, Mary. 1987. *Natal/KwaZulu: Present Realities, Future Hopes.* Durban: Centre for Adult Education, University of Natal. 23.

Balihuta, Arsene M. 1999. Education provision and outcome in Uganda: 1895-1997. *Uganda Journal* 45 (August): 27-38.

Berger, A. 1988. Milankovitch and climate. *Rev. Geophys.* 26 (pt 4): 624-57.

Croze, Harvey, and John Reader. 2000. *Pyramids of Life.* London: Harvill Press. 185.

Cohen, Jon. 2000. The hunt for the origin of AIDS. *Atlantic Monthly,* October, 88-104.

Cotton, Ann. 2000. Sex and education. *The Guardian,* 7 July, 22.

De Langhe, E., R. Swennen, and D. Vuysteke. 1996. Plantain in the early Bantu world, in: Sutton, J.E.G. (ed.) 1996. The growth of farming communities in Africa from the equator southwards. *Azania.* (Nairobi: British Institute in East Africa.) 29-30:147-60.

De Waal, Alex. 1994. Genocide in Rwanda. *Anthrop. Today.* 10(3): 1-2.

Essex, Myron. 1999. The new AIDS epidemic. *Harvard Magazine,* Sept-Oct 1999, and pers. com. Rockefeller Study & Conference Center, Bellagio, 6 Nov. 2000.

Fryer, G. 1997. Biological implications of a Late Pleistocene desiccation of Lake Victoria. *Hydrobiologia* 354:177-182.

Gibbon, Peter. 1997. *Of saviours and punks: The political economy of the Nile perch marketing chain in Tanzania.* CDR Working Paper 97.3. Copenhagen: Centre for Development Research.

Harris, Craig K., David S. Wiley, and Douglas C. Wilson. 1995. Socio-economic impacts of introduced species in the Lake Victoria fisheries, in: Pitcher, Tony J. and Paul J. B. Hart (eds.) 1995. *The Impact of Species Changes in African Lakes.* London: Chapman and Hall. 215-242.

Iliffe, John. 1979. *A Modern History of Tanganyika.* Cambridge: Cambridge University Press. 322-24.

Imbrie, John. 1982. Astronomical theory of the Pleistocene Ice Ages. *Icarus* 50:411.

International Food Policy Research Institute (IFPRI). 1991. *Facts and Figures: International Agricultural Research.* New York: Rockefeller Foundation. 31.

Johnson, Thomas C. et al. 1996. Late Pleistocene desiccation of Lake Victoria and rapid evolution of cichlid fishes. *Science* 273:1091-93.

Johnson, Thomas C., Kerry Kelts, and Eric Odada. 2000. The Holocene history of Lake Victoria. *Ambio* 29, No. 1: 2-11.

Kasoki, A.B.K. 1999. Regional inequality in Uganda could lead to social conflict. *The Uganda Journal* 45 (August): 1-38.

Kingdon, Jonathan. 1989. *Island Africa: The Evolution of Africa's Rare Animals and Plants.* Princeton: Princeton University Press. 218, 220, 226-9.

Louis, W.R. 1963. *Ruanda-Urundi 1884-1919.* Oxford: Clarendon Press. Chapter 11.

Lowe-McConnell R.H. 1987. *Ecological Studies in Tropical Fish Communities.* Cambridge: Cambridge University Press. 3, 76, 89.

Morris, Mike (Head of Development Studies, University of Natal). Pers. com. Rockefeller Study & Conference Center, Bellagio, 25 Sept. 2000.

Ochumba, Peter B.O. 1995. Limnological changes in Lake Victoria since the Nile perch introduction, in: Pitcher, Tony J., and Paul J. B. Hart (eds.) 1995. *The Impact of Species Changes in African Lakes*. London: Chapman and Hall. 181-214.

Oliver, Roland. 1991. *The African Experience*. London: Weidenfeld and Nicholson. 145.

Prunier, Gerard. 1995. *The Rwanda Crisis 1959-1994: History of a Genocide*. London: Hurst. 49, 213-29, 262-63, 164-65.

Reynolds, J. Eric, Dominique F. Gréboval, and Piero Mannini. 1995. Thirty years on: The development of the Nile perch fishery in Lake Victoria, in: Pitcher, Tony J., and Paul J. B. Hart (eds.) 1995. *The Impact of Species Changes in African Lakes*. London: Chapman and Hall. 181-214.

Roberts, Andrew D. (ed.) 1990. *The Colonial Moment in Africa*. Cambridge: Cambridge University Press. 24-76.

Stiassny, Melanie L. J., and Alex Meyer. 1999. Cichlids of the Rift lakes. *Sci. Am.*, February, 44-49.

Sutton, John E.G. 1990. *A Thousand Years of East Africa*. Nairobi: British Institute in East Africa.

Sutton, John E.G. 1993. The antecedents of the interlacustrine kingdoms. *J. Afr. Hist.* 34: 33-64.

Vail, Leroy (ed.) 1989. *The Creation of Tribalism in Southern Africa*. London: James Currey. 7.

World Resources Institute. 1998. *World Resources 1998-99: A Guide to the Global Environment*. Oxford: Oxford University Press. 244, 299.

Wrigley, Christopher. 1989. Bananas in Buganda. *Azania* 24:64-70.

Chapter 7

Attenborough, David. 1984. *The Living Planet*. London: Collins. 277-82.

Axelson, Eric. 1949/1969. *South-east Africa 1488-1530*. New York: Kraus (1969). 47, 108-111.

Bakari, Razack, and Jessica Andersson. 1998. Economic liberalization and its effect on the exploitation of crustaceans in Tanzania. *Ambio* 27, no. 8: 761-62.

Casson, Lionel. 1989. *The Periplus Maris Erythraei*. Lawrenceville, NJ: Princeton University Press.

Connah, Graham. 1987. *African Civilizations: Precolonial Cities and States in Tropical Africa: An Archaeological Perspective*. Cambridge: Cambridge University Press. Chapter 7.

Connell, J. 1978. Diversity in tropical rainforests and coral reefs. *Science* 199:1302-1310.

Crowder, M. 1985. The First World War and its consequences, in: UNESCO, 1985 *General History of Africa*, vol. 7. London: Heinemann. 283-311.

Eltis, David. 1990. The volume, age/sex ratios, and African impact of the slave trade: some refinements of Paul Lovejoy's review of the literature. *J. Afr. Hist.* 31: 485-92.

Eltis, David. 1987. *Economic Growth and the Ending of the Transatlantic Slave Trade*. New York: Oxford University Press.

Freeman-Grenville, G.S.P. 1975. *The East African Coast: Select Documents from the First to the Nineteenth Century*. 2nd edition. London: Collings.

Gann, L.H.. 1975. Economic development in Germany's African empire, 1884-1914, in: Duigan, P., and L. H. Gann (eds.) 1975. *Colonialism in Africa*, vol. 4: *The Economics of Colonialism*. Cambridge: Cambridge University Press. 213-55.

Hodges, G.W.T. 1978. African manpower statistics for the British forces in East Africa. *J. Afr. Hist.* 19:101-16.

Iliffe, John. 1979. *A Modern History of Tanganyika*. Cambridge: Cambridge University Press. 200.

Iliffe, John. 1995. *Africans: The History of a Continent*. Cambridge: Cambridge University Press. 135, 181.

Inikori, J.E. 1977. The import of firearms into West Africa 1705-1807: a quantitative analysis. *J. Afr. Hist.* 28:339-68.

Johannes, R.E. 1975. Pollution and degradation of coral reef communities, in: Ferguson-Wood, E.J., and R. E. Johannes (eds.) *Tropical Marine Pollution*. Amsterdam: Elsevier. 13-50.

Johnstone, Ron W., Christopher A. Muhando, and Julian Francis. 1998. The status of the coral reefs of Zanzibar: one example of a regional predicament. *Ambio* 27, no. 8: 700-707.

Kingdon, Jonathan. 1989. *Island Africa: The Evolution of Africa's Rare Animals and Plants*. Princeton: Princeton University Press. 129.

Lovejoy, Paul E. 1989. The impact of the Atlantic slave trade on Africa: a review of the literature. *J. Afr. Hist.* 30:365-94.

Lovejoy, Paul. 1983. *Transformations in Slavery: A History of Slavery in Africa*. Cambridge: Cambridge University Press. 19, 25, 60, 106, 150-1,163, 167, 172, 184-5, 203, 224, 283-7.

Lowe-McConnell, R.H. 1987. *Ecological Studies in Tropical Fish Communities*. Cambridge: Cambridge University Press. 180.

Manning, Patrick. 1990. *Slavery and African Life: Occidental, Oriental and African Slave Trades*. Cambridge: Cambridge University Press.

Metcalf, George. 1987. A microcosm of why African sold slaves: Akan consumption patterns in the 1770s. *J. Afr. Hist.* 28:377-94.

Miller, J.C. 1988. *Way of Death: Merchant Capitalism and the Angolan Slave Trade 1730-1830*. Madison: University of Wisconsin Press. 113-14, 153-55.

Omar, Nasib S. 1997. *Zanzibar Clove Industry*. Zanzibar State Trading Corporation website.

Orme, Antony R. 1996. Coastal environments, in: Adams, W.M., A. S. Goudie, and A. R. Orme (eds.) 1996. *The Physical Geography of Africa*. Oxford: Oxford University Press. 238-66.

Reader, John. 1999. *Africa: A Biography of the Continent*. New York: Vintage. 437.

Richard, W.A. 1980. The import of firearms into West Africa in the eighteenth century. *J. Afr. Hist.* 2:143-59.

Snow, Philip. 1988. *The Star Raft: China's Encounter with Africa*. London: Weidenfeld and Nicolson. 1, 15, and plate 1 opposite 138.

Sorokin, Yuri I. 1995. *Coral Reef Ecology*. Berlin: Springer. 9, 17, 25, 45, 215-16, 225.

Sutton, J.E.G. (ed.) 1996. The growth of farming communities in Africa from the Equator southwards. *Azania* (Nairobi: British Institute in East Africa) 29-30: 227-262.

Wilkinson, Clive et al. 1999. Ecological and socioeconomic impacts of 1998 coral mortality in the Indian Ocean: an ENSO impact and warning of future change? *Ambio* 28, no. 2: 188-196.

World Resources Institute. 1998. *World Resources 1998-99: A Guide to the Global Environment*. Oxford: Oxford University Press. 244.

Zanzibar's seaweed farming. 1995. *Ambio* 24 (December), no. 7-8.

Chapter 8

Africa: The heart of the matter. 2000. *The Economist*, 13 May. 24.

Allen, Harriet D. 1996. Mediterranean environments, in: Adams, W.M., A. S. Goudie, and A. R. Orme (eds.) 1996. *The Physical Geography of Africa*. Oxford: Oxford University Press. 307-25.

Bangura, Palo. 1991. Interview on 7 October 1991, Fourah Bay College, Freetown..

Boyd, F.R., and J. J. Gurney. 1986. Diamonds and the African lithosphere. *Science* 232:472-77.

Cocks, L.M.R. (ed.) 1981. *The Evolving Earth*. Cambridge: Cambridge University Press: 44-45.

Cowling , R.M., P. M. Holmes, and A. G. Rebello. 1992. Concepts and patterns of endemism in the Cape Floristic Region, in: Cowling, R.M. (ed.) 1992. *The Ecology of the Fynbos*. Oxford: Oxford University Press.

Deacon, H.J., 1989, Late Pleistocene palaeoecology and archaeology in the Southern Cape,

South Africa, in: Mellars, Paul, and Chris Stringer (eds.) 1989. *The Human Revolution: Behavioural and Biological Perspectives on the Origins of Modern Humans*. Edinburgh: Edinburgh University Press. 547-64.

Deacon, Janette. 1999. South African rock art. *Evol. Anthrop.* 8 (2): 48-63.

Denny, Charlotte. 2000. Uganda losing its lustre as star pupil. *The Guardian*, 21 July. 14.

Dumbuya, Ahmed R. 1991. Voice of America interview, 5 October 1991, Freetown, Sierra Leone.

Elphick Richard, and H. Giliomee (eds.) 1989. *The Shaping of South African Society, 1652-1840*. Cape Town: Maskew Miller, Longman. 3, 27, 138.

Findlay, G. 1972. Dr. Robert Broom, F.R.S. Cape Town: Balkema. 50-1.

Geological Society of South Africa. *Some Superlatives of Geology in South Africa*. Johannesburg. 2.

Hunter, D.R., and P. J. Hamilton. 1978. The Bushveld complex, in: Tarling, D.H. (ed.) 1978. *Evolution of the Earth's Crust*. London: Academic Press. 109.

Iliffe, John. 1995. *Africans: The History of a Continent*. Cambridge: Cambridge University Press. 252-53, 266.

Jefferson, Thomas. 1782. *Notes on Virginia*, quoted in: West, Richard. 1970. *Back to Africa: A History of Sierra Leone and Liberia*. London: Jonathan Cape. 95.

Lee, R.B. 1969. Eating Christmas in the Kalahari. *Natural History*, 14-22 December, 60-63.

Lee, R.B. 1968. What hunters do for a living, or, how to make out on scarce resources, in: Lee, R.B., and I. Devore (eds.) 1968. *Man the Hunter*. Chicago: Aldine. 30-48.

Levinson, Olga. *Diamonds in the Desert*.

Mbeki, Thabo. 1998. The African Renaissance Statement, 13 August 1998. http://www.anc.org.za/ancdocs/history/1998/tmo813.htmmime.

Morgan, l. 1964. *Ancient Society*. New York: Kerr. Facsimile reprint of 1877 original, 8, 41-42, 506, quoted in: Wilmsen, Edwin N. 1989. *Land Filled with Flies*. Chicago: University of Chicago Press. 15, 21.

Nisbet, E.G. 1991. *Living Earth: A Short History of Life and Its Home*. London: Chapman and Hall. 61.

Plateau, J.-P. 1990-1. The food crisis in Africa, vol. II, in: Drèze, J. and A. Sen (eds.) 1990-1. *The Political Economy of Hunger*. 3 vols. Oxford. 281.

Robertson, Marion. 1974. *Diamond fever: South African Diamond History 1866-9 from Primary Sources*. Cape Town: Oxford University Press. 70.

Shillington, Kevin. 1989. *History of Africa*. London: Macmillan. 105.

Swarns, Rachel L. 2000. Gaborone Journal. *New York Times*, 6 October. A4.

Thompson, Leonard. 1990. *A History of South Africa*. New Haven: Yale University Press. 35-36.

Transparency International. 2000. Zimbabwe: the most travelled African leader. *Corruption Reports*, April 2000.

Traill, A. 1978. The languages of the Bushmen, in: Tobias, Philip V.T. (ed.) 1978. *The Bushmen: San Hunters and Herders of Southern Africa*. Cape Town: Human and Rousseau. 139.

Turrell, R.V. 1982. Kimberley: labour and compounds 1871-1888, in: Marks, Shula, and Richard Rathbone (eds.) 1982. *Industrialization and Social Change in South Africa: African Class Formation, Culture and Consciousness, 1870-1930*. New York: Longman. 45 -76.

Turrell, R.V. 1984. Kimberley's model compounds. *J. Afr. Hist.* 25:59-75.

Turrell, R.V. 1987., *Capital and Labour of the Kimberley Diamond Fields, 1871-1890*. Cambridge: Cambridge University Press. 5-6, 240 n.11.

Van der Horst, Sheila. 1942. *Native Labour in South Africa*. Johannesburg. 134, 192, 205.

Worger, William H. 1987. *South Africa's City of Diamonds: Mine Workers and Monopoly Capitalism in Kimberley, 1867-1895*. New Haven: Yale University Press. 20, 71-2, 75, 82-3, 112.

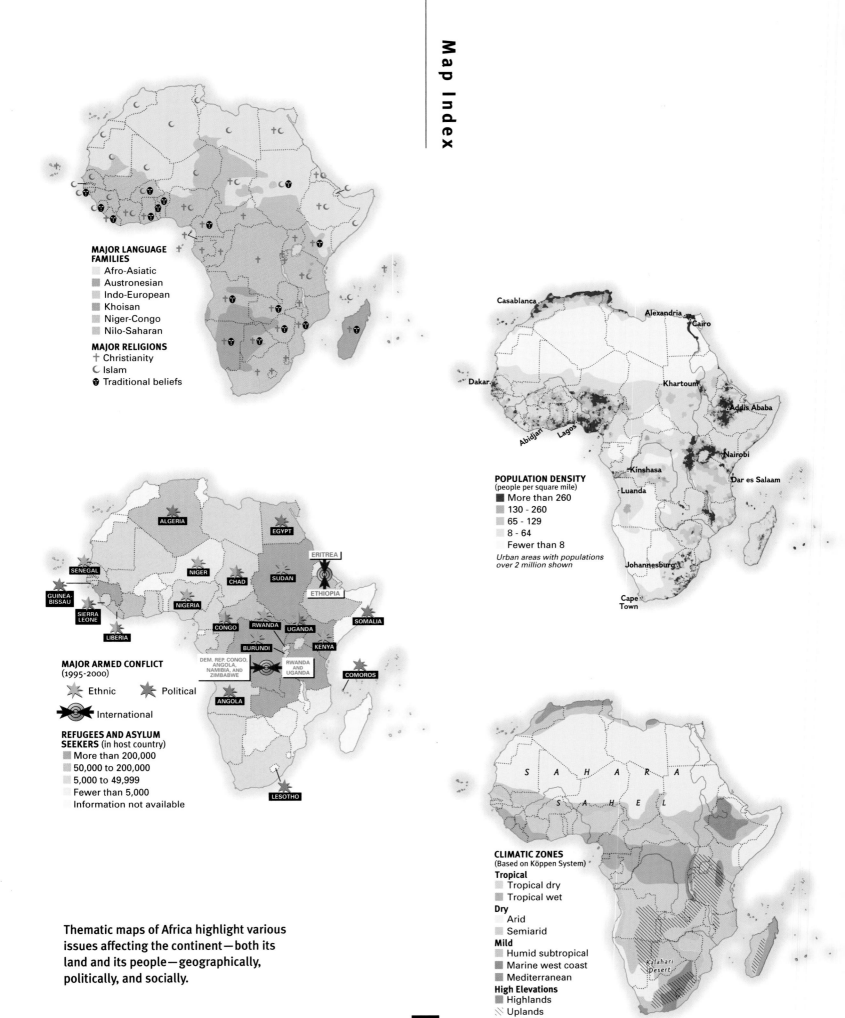

MAJOR LANGUAGE FAMILIES

Afro-Asiatic
Austronesian
Indo-European
Khoisan
Niger-Congo
Nilo-Saharan

MAJOR RELIGIONS

† Christianity
☾ Islam
♱ Traditional beliefs

POPULATION DENSITY
(people per square mile)

More than 260
130 - 260
65 - 129
8 - 64
Fewer than 8

Urban areas with populations over 2 million shown

MAJOR ARMED CONFLICT
(1995-2000)

✦ Ethnic   ✦ Political

☣ International

REFUGEES AND ASYLUM SEEKERS (in host country)

More than 200,000
50,000 to 200,000
5,000 to 49,999
Fewer than 5,000
Information not available

ALGERIA, EGYPT, SENEGAL, NIGER, CHAD, SUDAN, ERITREA, ETHIOPIA, GUINEA-BISSAU, SIERRA LEONE, LIBERIA, NIGERIA, CONGO, RWANDA, UGANDA, SOMALIA, BURUNDI, KENYA, DEM. REP. CONGO, ANGOLA, NAMIBIA, AND ZIMBABWE, RWANDA AND UGANDA, COMOROS, ANGOLA, LESOTHO

Casablanca, Alexandria, Cairo, Dakar, Khartoum, Addis Ababa, Abidjan, Lagos, Nairobi, Kinshasa, Dar es Salaam, Luanda, Johannesburg, Cape Town

CLIMATIC ZONES
(Based on Köppen System)

Tropical
Tropical dry
Tropical wet

Dry
Arid
Semiarid

Mild
Humid subtropical
Marine west coast
Mediterranean

High Elevations
Highlands
Uplands

SAHARA, SAHEL, Kalahari Desert

Thematic maps of Africa highlight various issues affecting the continent—both its land and its people—geographically, politically, and socially.

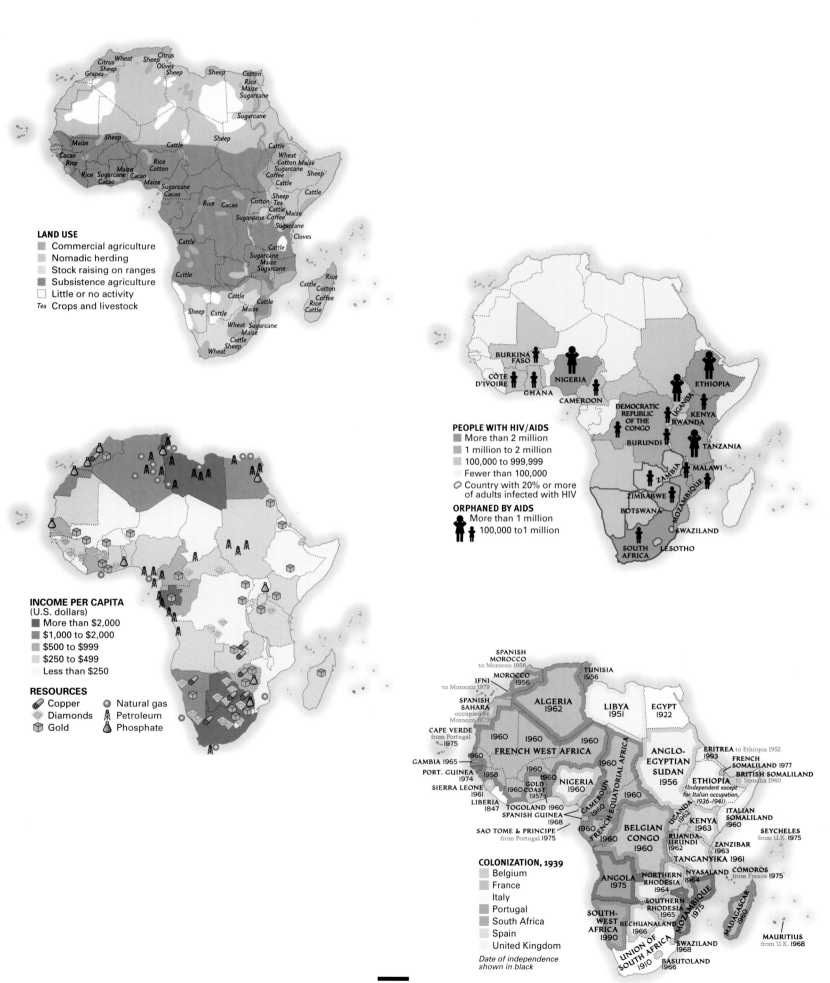

LAND USE
- Commercial agriculture
- Nomadic herding
- Stock raising on ranges
- Subsistence agriculture
- Little or no activity
- *Tea* Crops and livestock

INCOME PER CAPITA
(U.S. dollars)
- More than $2,000
- $1,000 to $2,000
- $500 to $999
- $250 to $499
- Less than $250

RESOURCES
- Copper
- Diamonds
- Gold
- Natural gas
- Petroleum
- Phosphate

PEOPLE WITH HIV/AIDS
- More than 2 million
- 1 million to 2 million
- 100,000 to 999,999
- Fewer than 100,000
- Country with 20% or more of adults infected with HIV

ORPHANED BY AIDS
- More than 1 million
- 100,000 to 1 million

COLONIZATION, 1939
- Belgium
- France
- Italy
- Portugal
- South Africa
- Spain
- United Kingdom

Date of independence shown in black

JOHN READER

FILM CREW WORKING IN CAMEROON

MICHAEL S. LEWIS

FILM CREW IN MALI

All images by Michael S. Lewis except the following:

p. 4-5, Hugh Sitton/STONE; p. 10-11, Robert Caputo, Aurora & Quanta Productions; p. 12-13, José Azel, Aurora & Quanta Productions; p. 15, Laurent Renaud/Saola/LIAISON AGENCY; p. 17, Wolfgang Kaehler; p. 18-19, Stuart Franklin; p. 20-21, Charles V. Angelo/Photo Researchers, Inc.; p. 23, Ernst Haas/STONE; p. 24-25, Wolfgang Kaehler; p. 26-27, Chris Johns, National Geographic Photographer; p. 28, Guido A. Rossi/IMAGE BANK; p. 34-35, Robert Caputo, Aurora & Quanta Productions; p. 48-49, Hugh Sitton/STONE; p. 50-51, Thierry Borredon/STONE; p. 56-57, Nigel Press/STONE; p. 62-63, John Chard/STONE; p. 69, Maggie Steber; p. 74-75, Theo Allofs/STONE; p. 88-89, JACANA/Photo Researchers, Inc.; p. 90-91, Michael Nichols; p. 93, Joe McDonald/OKAPIA/Photo Researchers, Inc.; p. 97, Michael Nichols; p. 105, James L. Stanfield; p. 106-107, CAROL BECKWITH and Angela Fisher; p. 122-123, Nevada Wier; p. 124-125, Eric Meola/IMAGE BANK; p. 135, R. Van Nostrand/Photo Researchers, Inc.; p. 150, Robert Caputo; p. 154, Steve Raymer; p. 162-163, José Azel, Aurora & Quanta Productions; p. 200-201, Frank & Helen Schreider/Photo Researchers, Inc.; p. 206, Robert Caputo, Aurora & Quanta Productions; p. 210-211, James A. Sugar; p. 217, The Granger Collection, New York; p. 222-223, Robert Caputo, Aurora & Quanta Productions; p. 224, p. 226-227, Bill Curtsinger; p. 240-241, Hodalic-Brecelj/Saola/LIAISON AGENCY; p. 244, Zena Holloway, www.zena.com; p. 252-253, Arne Hodalic/GLMR/LIAISON AGENCY; p. 258, The Granger Collection, New York; p. 264-265, Hodalic-Brecelj/Saola/LIAISON AGENCY; p. 274-275, Telegraph Colour Library/FPG; p. 279, Nigel J. Dennis/Photo Researchers, Inc.; p. 282-283, Holton Collection/Super Stock, Inc.; p. 286-287, Mark W. Moffett; p. 290-291, Pool Raid Gauloise/LIAISON AGENCY; p. 293, David Turnley; p. 294-295, D. Obertreis/Bilderberg/Aurora & Quanta Productions; p. 299, Kenneth Garrett; p. 300, Michael Coyne/Black Star; p. 303, Chris Johns, National Geographic Photographer; p. 318 (top), Jerry Bauer.

Metric Conversion Tables

CONVERSION TO METRIC MEASURES

WHEN YOU KNOW	MULTIPLY BY	TO FIND
LENGTH		
inches	2.54	centimeters
feet	0.30	meters
yards	0.91	meters
miles	1.61	kilometers
AREA		
square inches	6.45	square centimeters
square feet	0.09	square meters
square yards	0.84	square meters
square miles	2.59	square kilometers
acres	0.40	hectares
MASS		
ounces	28.35	grams
pounds	0.45	kilograms
short tons	0.91	metric tons
VOLUME		
cubic inches	16.39	milliliters
liquid ounces	29.57	milliliters
pints	0.47	liters
quarts	0.95	liters
gallons	3.79	liters
cubic feet	0.03	cubic meters
cubic yards	0.76	cubic meters
TEMPERATURE		
degrees Fahrenheit	5/9 after subtracting 32	degrees Celsius (centigrade)

NATIONAL GEOGRAPHIC
TELEVISION

NATURE

The AFRICA series is a co-production of National Geographic Television, Thirteen/WNET New York's NATURE series, Tigress Productions UK, and Magic Box Mediaworks.

First I want to thank the scientists, historians, commentators and interviewees for the information that forms the basis of my narrative. In other books I have acknowledged sources by citing individual references, but here the exigencies of publishing require that a comprehensive chapter by chapter bibliography should suffice. I trust it will, and hope the individuals concerned will understand that my appreciation of their contributions is not diminished in any way. I of course remain responsible for any misinterpretation.

The publication of my *AFRICA: A Biography of the Continent* in 1997/8 coincided most fortuitously with planning for the NGS/PBS series on Africa. As consultant to the series I also undertook to write this companion volume—all of which leaves me indebted to Jeremy Bradshaw and Andrew Jackson, Chris Weber, Fred Kaufmann, Jennifer Lawson and, not least, Kevin Mulroy. Pat Kavanagh and Rosemary Scoular scrutinized developments with their customary care and aplomb. My thanks to all.

The task of writing a first draft was eased considerably by an Ella Walker Fellowship from the Rockefeller Foundation. My thanks are due to the Foundation—to Lincoln Chen and Susan Garfield in New York, and most especially to Gianna Celli and the staff of the Villa Serbelloni in Bellagio.

In many ways, this book is an extension of *AFRICA: A Biography of the Continent*. It draws upon my research to 1995, and brings the subjects it touches up to date. But the structure is completely different. Where the Biography took an in-depth chronological approach, Africa examines the subject from a more directly environmental point of view. Thus the two books are complementary—neither replaces the other.

Andrew Franklin at Hamish Hamilton and Carol Janeway at Knopf nurtured *AFRICA: A Biography of the Continent* to publication. Now I am indebted to them again, but this is wholly National Geographic's book, and I have nothing but praise for the manner of its production. Kevin Mulroy has been a wonderful commissioning editor; Johnna Rizzo has been a first-class coordinator; Greta Arnold has been a most perceptive picture editor; John Paine has been an embarassingly good line editor, and Michael Lewis has illustrated the book beautifully.

But nothing gets built without a sound foundation, and on this score I am profoundly grateful to Brigitte and our daughter Alice for the love and constancy that make life—and work—a joy.

WITHDRAWN

No longer the property of the
Boston Public Library.
Sale of this material benefits the Library.

AFRICA
John Reader

Published by the National Geographic Society
John M. Fahey, Jr., *President and Chief Executive Officer*
Gilbert M. Grosvenor, *Chairman of the Board*
Nina D. Hoffman, *Executive Vice President*

Prepared by the Book Division
Kevin Mulroy, *Vice President and Editor-in-Chief*
Charles Kogod, *Illustrations Director*
Barbara A. Payne, *Editorial Director*
Marianne R. Koszorus, *Design Director*

Staff for this Book
Kevin Mulroy, *Editor*
John Paine, *Text Editor*
Greta Arnold, *Illustrations Editor*
Marty Ittner, *Art Director*
Johnna Rizzo, *Assistant Editor*
Anne Withers, *Researcher*
Carl Mehler, *Director of Maps*
Jerome N. Cookson, NG Maps, *Map Production*
Joseph F. Ochlak, *Map Research*
Melissa Farris, *Design Assistant*
Carol B. Lutyk, *Contributing Editor*
Gary Colbert, *Production Director*
Richard S. Wain, *Production Project Manager*
Cynthia Combs, *Illustrations Assistant*

Manufacturing and Quality Control
George V. White, *Director*
John T. Dunn, *Manager*
Phillip Schlosser, *Financial Analyst*

Copyright © 2001 National Geographic Society.
All rights reserved. Reproduction of the whole or any part
of the contents without permission is prohibited.

Library of Congress Cataloging-in-Publication Data
Reader, John.
Africa / John Reader ; photographs by Michael S. Lewis.
p. cm.
Companion volume to the 8 hour PBS series Africa.
Includes bibliographical references and index.
ISBN 0-7922-7681-7 -- ISBN 0-7922-6440-1 (deluxe)
1. Africa–Geography. 2. Africa—Pictorial works. I. Lewis, Michael, 1952
Feb. 5- II. Title.

DT6.7 .R43 2001 960--dc21 00-069555

The world's largest nonprofit scientific and educational organization, the National Geographic Society was founded in 1888 "for the increase and diffusion of geographic knowledge." Since then it has supported scientific exploration and spread information to its more than eight million members worldwide.

The National Geographic Society educates and inspires millions every day through magazines, books, television programs, videos, maps and atlases, research grants, the National Geographic Bee, teacher workshops, and innovative classroom materials.

The Society is supported through membership dues, charitable gifts, and income from the sale of its educational products.

Members receive NATIONAL GEOGRAPHIC magazine—the Society's official journal—discounts on Society products, and other benefits.

For more information about the National Geographic Society, its educational programs, publications, or ways to support its work, please call 1-800-NGS-LINE (647-5463), or write to the following address:

National Geographic Society
1145 17th Street N.W.
Washington, D.C. 20036-4688 U.S.A.

Visit the Society's Web site at
www.nationalgeographic.com.

Printed and bound by R.R. Donnelley & Sons. Willard, Ohio. Color separations by Quad Graphics, Martinsburg, West Virginia. Dust jacket printed by Miken Companies, Cheektowaga, New York.